The Prospect of Cities

Also by John Friedmann

Empowerment: The Politics of Alternative Development

Planning in the Public Domain: From Knowledge to Action

Life Space and Economic Space: Essays in Third World Planning

Territory and Function: The Evolution of Regional Planning

The Good Society: A Personal Account of Its Struggle with the World of Social Planning and a Dialectical Inquiry into the Roots of Radical Practice

Retracking America: A Reissue of the Classic Book on Transactive Planning

Regional Development Policy: A Case Study of Venezuela

The Prospect of Cities

John Friedmann

University of Minnesota Press
Minneapolis / London

Chapter 4 is a substantially revised and expanded version of "Local and Insurgent Citizenship," *Plurimondi* 2 (December 1999): 287–303. An earlier version of chapter 5 first appeared in *DISP* 136/137 (1999): 4–11; reprinted by permission of *DISP*—ETH Zurich. An earlier version of chapter 6 first appeared in *International Journal of Urban and Regional Research* 24.2 (2000): 460–72; copyright 2000 by the Urban Affairs Association and reprinted by permission. Figure 2.1 is reprinted by permission of Taylor & Francis, Ltd., P.O. Box 25, Abingdon, Oxfordshire, OX14 3UE.

Published by the University of Minnesota Press
111 Third Avenue South, Suite 290
Minneapolis, MN 55401-2520
http://www.upress.umn.edu

Library of Congress Cataloging-in-Publication Data

Friedmann, John.
    The prospect of cities / John Friedmann.
      p.   cm.
    Includes bibliographical references and index.
    ISBN 0-8166-3884-5 (HC/j : alk. paper)
    1. City planning.   2. Cities and towns.   I. Title.
    HT166 .F738 2002
    307.76—dc21

                        2001007065

Printed in the United States of America on acid-free paper
The University of Minnesota is an equal-opportunity educator and employer.

12 11 10 09 08 07 06 05 04 03 02   10 9 8 7 6 5 4 3 2 1

For Leonie, my partner in life and work

Contents

Acknowledgments

Chapters 1 through 6 were originally presented as lectures in the Department of Urban Studies and Planning at the Massachusetts Institute of Technology in October and November 1999. I am deeply grateful to Professor Bishwapriya Sanyal for inviting and encouraging me to prepare these lectures for publication.

I would also like to thank my good friend Professor Mike Douglass of the University of Hawai`i. Over the past thirty years, we have worked together on many occasions and it is largely thanks to him that I have acquired some knowledge and, more important, have deepened my understanding of the East Asia region and its spatial development. He may not know it, but his wry observations over the years underlie a number of the essays in this volume.

Introduction
Urban Futures as Ideology

The Great Vanishing Act

The city is dead. It vanished sometime during the twentieth century. As it grew in population and expanded horizontally, many attempted to rescue it, to revive it, to hold back urban sprawl, to recover a sense of urbanity and civic order. But the forces that led to its demise could not be held back, much less reversed. What remained were palimpsests and memories; the city had become a metaphor. I shall refer to these remains as "the urban."

The historical city had never, of course, conformed to a single type. Without attempting to trace their evolution from the proto-cities of Meso-America, the Middle East, and Asia, we do know that urban centers in Islamic countries, in precolonial West Africa, in Tang dynasty China, in medieval Europe, and in colonial America were very different from one another in the several dimensions that count: the architecture of built form, political-administrative structure, social relations, cultural meanings, and the economy. Still, because they were cities and thus by their relative density and physical form a specific form of human settlement, they stood out against the surrounding countryside and thrived chiefly through trade and manufactures. This, at least, is what they all had in common.

Academic discourse about cities picked up on this diversity. Lewis Mumford (1938) and Carl E. Schorske (1980) wrote about the culture of cities; Georg Simmel (1969) and Richard Sennett (1990) focused on social relations; Hannah Arendt (1958) wanted to resurrect the Greek *polis* in the political sense; Spiro Kostof (1992) lovingly collected images of "the city assembled"; and historians such as Fernand Braudel (1992) studied the city from the perspective of its economic relations. But like the smile of the Cheshire cat, the historic city gradually faded away, the urban rose in its place, and economic discourse became dominant. What we still sometimes refer to as city—and that now, in many parts of the world, can extend over hundreds and even thousands of square kilometers, housing many millions of people—is now seen almost exclusively from the standpoint of capital accumulation and of people making a living. The city has become, in the language of statisticians, an agglomeration without clear boundaries.

Along with this dramatic transformation, the perspective on the urban has gone global. When there were still cities, differences among them had seemed important, and their economy was merely one feature among others. But as the urban took hold of the imagination, these differences were increasingly ignored. Statisticians, economists, geographers, sociologists, and planners all converged on the urban problematic, some emphasizing poverty, others the impact of population growth on the natural environment, and still others how to articulate the various parts of vast urban agglomerations to one another through infrastructure. But, in the end, all of these topics came to be subsumed under a single master narrative: the intense competition among all urban centers for a share in global markets. As everyone knew, there would be winners as well as losers in this game.

Turn of the Century: What Urban Futures?

As the twentieth century drew to a close, the United Nations Centre for Human Settlements convened a world conference, usually referred to as Habitat II, in Istanbul that brought together international organizations, national governments, local authorities, the private sector, and nongovernmental organizations (NGOs) to confront, in the words of Boutros-Boutros Ghali, Secretary General of the United Nations, "common urban problems and address development tasks that must be undertaken in partnership" (Ghali 1996). This mega-event generated a great deal of interest and, in turn, spawned a number of international conferences to ponder the question of urban futures.

The first of these conferences, sponsored by the French government, was held in the medieval town of La Rochelle on the Atlantic coast under the somewhat helpless title "Cities in the 21st Century: Cities and Metropolises: Breaking or Bridging?" The question was whether the cities of the new century would break abruptly with known patterns or continue along a more familiar evolutionary trajectory. The following year, the University of California at Los Angeles sponsored a similar event with a focus on what the organizers called global city regions. And in July 2000, two more conferences took place. The first of these, convened by the German government in their new capital, Berlin, had been given the grand name "The Future of the City: URBAN 21," and was followed a few days later by a more modestly titled conference, "Urban Futures" (in the plural) under the joint sponsorship of the University of Witwatersrand and the Greater Johannesburg Metropolitan Council. The South African organizers posed the following questions:

> Will Johannesburg look more like Lagos or Kuala Lumpur in the twenty-first century? Will our lives resemble something from a Japanese manga movie? Will we be living in a gritty post-modern city like the one portrayed in *Bladerunner* or will the rough edges be smoothed off by the technocratic virtual reality of a *Matrix*-style universe? People's lives will be determined globally by an urban existence in the next millennium. The big, sprawling city is increasingly the focus of local and global concerns about the future possibilities of governance, management, peace, security, employment, municipal finance, equal opportunities and sustained development. (From the conference announcement, December 1999)

It was a set of questions suspended between fear and hope.

A German Ideology

The Berlin conference deserves a closer look because it reveals more clearly than any of the other conferences the ideological character of the hegemonic neoliberal paradigm being promoted as a basis for urban policies as well as some of the sources of resistance to it. In April 2000, I received an e-mail message addressed to myself and forty-four other urban scholars in Western Europe and North America who were widely known for their politically "progressive" views. The origin of this communication was a Berlin-based publication, *MieterEcho* (Renters' Echo), published by the NGO *MieterGemeinschaft* (Renters' Association). Attached to the e-mail was the executive summary and text of a draft paper that would eventually be presented at the Berlin conference as the outcome of the deliberations of the World Commission 21, headed by Sir Peter Hall. The draft had been prepared by empirica, a German think tank reputedly with close links to the Social Democratic Party. The forty-five recipients were invited to write a short comment on this draft. The staff at *MieterEcho* hoped to use the upcoming world conference "to force an international debate in which progressive and forward-looking people give their opinions."

The document itself had been prepared without consulting the NGO community, and URBAN 21 would be a strategic opportunity to make alternative voices heard in a global forum. In view of this, German and French urban social movements had decided to stage a "supplementary" parallel conference in Berlin, "Cities for All—Local Heroes 21—European Meeting of Urban Grassroots Organizations." Its aim was to provide a forum for the role of civil society in shaping urban futures. According to the official invitation, the forum would discuss three sets of questions with specific reference to the changes since Habitat II, when grassroots organizations had been very much more in evidence:

1. What strategies should be developed for a city without exclusion and discrimination and which offer equal access to all urban resources?

2. What strategies will best contribute to the realization and maintenance of rights to decent housing, self-determination, and a permanent, secure housing supply?

3. How can local civil society be reinforced? How can it contribute to a responsible local and global development of a city?

What follows is a summary of my commentary on the draft world report, *Reinventing the City: Urban Future 21* (empirica 2000), which I forwarded to *MieterEcho* in response to their request.[1] I also draw on two other responses to *MieterEcho,* which I received from Roger Keil (2000) and Neil Brenner (2000). My purpose here is to reveal the thinking behind what undoubtedly went forward as yet another example of a so-called global consensus about cities. After all, the main event in Berlin, as distinct from the self-identified grassroots organizations, had no qualms talking about urban future in the singular.

I should perhaps preface my comments by pointing out that the draft "world report" had a fatal flaw that rendered much of its substantive discussion irrelevant for practice: the world has thousands of cities, each with its distinctive history, political capacities, cultural practices, and regional and national setting. The drafting organization, empirica, must have been dimly aware that all cities can't be treated alike, because it managed to collapse the world's immense urban variety into just three broad categories that would become the basis for sketching its proposals:

- poor cities of hypergrowth
- middle-income cities undergoing rapid urban development
- mature aging cities

Boiled down to essentials according to this classification, the salient difference among cities is that some are poor and young, some are rich and old, and some are in-between—not, one might say, a very insightful typology. But, insightful or not, it did serve notice that, so far as this document was concerned, we would be working with a typology based primarily on economic criteria. All other differences were buried.

The draft report (empirica 2000) can be summarized in seven propositions, which I briefly address here.

1. Almost the whole world will coexist in a single global urban network, driven by worldwide competition.

Worldwide competition among city-regions is identified as the dynamo driving the emerging global system. We are not told for what prizes they are competing, whether for power, glory, or a share in the global marketplace. But whatever else they might be, the stakes are clearly economic. The "global urban network" is the equivalent here of Manuel Castells's abstract *space of flows,* which he imagines as consisting of three layers: (1) a circuit of electronic impulses that links up with (2) specific places—nodes and hubs—with well-defined characteristics and (3) a layer of dominant managerial elites that exercise the directional functions around which the space of flows is articulated (Castells 1996, 410–19). Projected throughout the world, this is a space of wealth and power. In the formulation of the draft world report, the urban is thus reduced to this one dimension, which subsumes all other forms of diversity under the logic of free markets.

2. All the people in all the cities of the world will share common aspirations.

What all people will want, assert the authors of the report, is nothing less than the good life enjoyed by the German middle class: "To own affordable homes, to find jobs that bring them decent incomes, to have access to clean air, water, modern sanitation and affordable health care, to send their children to good schools, to commute expeditiously to and from work, to live in a clean, green, safe, and culturally vibrant environment, to feel they are truly stakeholders in their own cities" (empirica 2000, 1). The chief problem with this homogenized image of aspirations is that it tells us nothing about relative priorities. Yet real politics, which the authors seem to ignore, is precisely about priorities that are both general and specific, for example, about whose priorities should be given the green light in this particular city at this time. For most of the world's population, life is a daily struggle of survival, a way of living by one's wits in the interstices of a social order not of their making. This majority has nothing in common with the preferred lifestyles of the German middle class.

Then why is this idea of common aspirations posited? Because the economic model that underlies the report is the "stages of growth" model of W. W. Rostow (1961) with its famous thesis of the "take-off" into self-sustaining cumulative economic growth that in a relatively short time will lead into the final stage (the end of history?) of high mass consumption. Originally billed as a "non-Communist manifesto," Rostow's view of economic history has become part of the natural order of market fundamentalism.

3. Good governance has to be the instrument for promoting the common goal of sustainable development.

With this proposition, the argument shifts subtly from the underlying if unspoken thesis of global capitalism—the thesis of self-sustaining cumulative economic growth—to the now more fashionable mantra of a "sustainable" development that acknowledges that economic growth is somehow embedded in the natural environment, and that, according to some Cassandras, there may even be some ultimate limits to growth. But the central goal of "sustainability" is here said to be primarily a *communal* goal, requiring no specific responses from global capital, while shifting major responsibility (but few resources) to local governments.

Ensuring that whatever growth takes place in the urban is environmentally sustainable is said to be a matter of "good governance." Indeed, good governance is set equal to sustainability. The report offers only pabulum as its understanding of what that might mean. Its authors, most likely schooled in the eternal verities of neoclassical economics, haven't the faintest idea of what "governance" entails, except that it is supposed to bring together "partners" from both the private sector and "civil society" (see proposition 4). Neil Brenner, a political scientist, comments on this part of the report:

> The contradictory sociopolitical and class interests that underpin any effort to govern a city only become evident when generic notions such as "work and wealth," "empowering the citizenry," and "stable ecosystems" are concretized with reference to particular socioeconomic conditions, political institutions, societal forces, and social movements. Once this is accomplished, it becomes readily obvious that massive trade-offs are involved in nearly all forms of urban policy, that the prioritization of some political goals necessarily entails the marginalization or suppression of others, and that the power to influence such processes is distributed quite unsymmetrically within contemporary cities. . . . Once such rudimentary aspects of urban political and economic life are taken into consideration, we can recognize Figure 1 [an abstract representation of good governance] as the expression of *pure ideology* in Ernst Bloch's classic sense of promoting "the premature harmonization of social contradictions within existing social relations." (Brenner 2000, 2)

4. What is needed to achieve sustainable urban development is decisive local political action in cooperation with civil society.

Civil society is said to be a new partner in good governance. But what exactly is civil society? And is it found throughout the world or only in some parts? And where it exists, is it prepared to cooperate with the local state? And on the basis of whose agenda?

As various authors have pointed out, autonomous civil society can have both a friendly and a vicious face: it can be a club of ikebana fanciers or a mafia of local snakeheads. Neither of these social groupings is particularly interested in cooperation with the state; they pursue their separate interests. Or perhaps the reference is rather to the alphabet soup of local NGOs, community-based organizations (CBOs), quasi nongovernmental organizations (QUANGOs), and so forth, which have been harnessed to deal with the soft issues of poverty, community development, and social dysfunctions in both rich and poor countries, some of them barely differentiated from their respective sponsors of state, international organizations, and organized religion. Always kept on a short leash, their fragmented, partial approach cannot go much beyond charity work. Fitful attempts at country or even regionwide coordination have failed. Moreover, in many countries, such as China, the concept of civil society is virtually unknown. And whence comes the idea of harmonious cooperation with the state, when the real, everyday politics of the disempowered sectors of the population is so often in opposition to it? Underlying this call for cooperation is the recent neoliberal discovery of that ancient human faculty governing social relations, "trust." In a variation on de Tocqueville (1966 [1848]), a good civil society is said to be a trusting society. Only when people trust their government and each other can "good governance" be achieved. With this in mind, a cooperative civil society is a manager's dream that enables him to avoid the inherently conflictual, painful nature of politics.

5. Urban economies will move from goods production to service delivery. This shift will allow cities to emancipate themselves from their traditional resource base and take their economic destiny into their own hands.

Here is a brave prediction: Urban economies in the global network will be shifting from manufacturing to the provision of services. This shift will emancipate cities from what is called their traditional resource base and, to echo a recent World Bank statement, put them in the driver's seat. So where, one might ask, will manufacturing be done in order to provide (per proposition 2) for the aspirations of "all the people"? Perhaps in distant countrysides where a plentiful supply of often female labor that economists call "surplus to rural production" can be exploited? Or is the prediction merely a pious wish that the old blue-collar industries, with their belching smokestacks and poisonous effluents, will somehow go away—it doesn't matter where to—so long as the population living in the new service cities can enjoy "clear water and blue skies"? If this is indeed the urban future, there is no evidence that it is happening, at least in the Asia Pacific, the most rapidly urbanizing and simultaneously industrializing global region.

But suppose that the prediction miraculously comes true. Would a shift to services really "emancipate" cities from their traditional resource base? The answer, quite plainly, is no. California's Silicon Valley is no more liberated from its traditional resource base than nearby Oakland with its blue-collar workers; it has merely created a new set of resources in a particular combination of very skilled and unskilled manpower. And neither place is even remotely "in charge" of its own fortunes. Nor did Germany's former coal and iron complex in the Ruhr Valley suddenly perk up when its backbone of heavy industries was displaced abroad. This doesn't mean that cities can't do anything for themselves; they most certainly can, and they must. But the claim that they will become "masters of their destiny" once their economies cease to be based on manufacturing is nothing more than ideological cant.

6. Twenty-first-century cities can draw on the experience of those that have successfully managed their development in the late twentieth century.

The report here evokes the current buzzphrase of *best practices,* which, along with *benchmarking,* is now part of the jargon of the competitive race that is the new urban Olympics. Poorly managed cities should learn from those that have become more globally "competitive." The executive summary mentions no specific model cities, but one imagines perhaps a Curitiba (the state capital of Paraná, Brazil), the city-state of Singapore with its "clean as a whistle" public image, or perhaps Bilbao ("Get a Guggenheim and live happily ever after!"). All have been much admired for their undoubtedly impressive achievements. And yet, I know of no instances anywhere in the world of a Curitiba II or Singapore II. The reason is not hard to find. There are thousands of cities, as I said earlier, and they are all different. Management techniques (if indeed they are techniques rather than styles or specific innovations, such as Curitiba's bus system, and always of course a particular politics) are not easily transplanted. This proposition, then, makes sense only if you accept the report's major premise, that all cities are fundamentally alike and are merely situated on different points along a trajectory from poor to rich, their relative position on this chart the only significant difference among them.

7. To be truly successful, cities of the twenty-first century will need greater autonomy. After a long era in which centralized government was the norm, a new balance of power has to be established.

This proposition is a call for a restructuring of the national state in the direction of the virtual city-states of the future. There has been a trend along these lines, and the report picks up on it, arguing for a more proactive policy on the part of the many cities throughout the world that are subject to national control, beginning with budgetary resources. But it is one thing to advocate this restructuring in the Federal German Republic, with its long tradition of municipal autonomy, and quite another to propose it as an appropriate model, for example, for France or Japan with their equally strong tradition of centralized administration. And as for countries that are barely able to staff the agencies of national government with competent bureaucrats let alone city governments— Mozambique or Bolivia, for example—urging greater local autonomy is not necessarily good advice. Moreover, state-local relations in many countries are already in a precarious balance, depending on which party or political faction is in power. Except for Colombia and Mexico, urban issues in Spanish Latin America tend to be concentrated in the capital cities and are consequently a major concern of central governments. Some of these countries, particularly in Central America, are already city-states in all but name, yet have not been able to replicate Singapore's march to prosperity. Elsewhere, the national government is so corrupt that to argue for a further devolution of powers would have catastrophic results. In short, there are no grand, across-the-board solutions to urban governance arrangements and the territorial division of powers.

According to Brenner (2000, 4), proposition 7 reveals the deeper political agenda of the report, which is to promote a new form of *national* political regime in which intense competition between municipalities for external investment capital is institutionalized. "In the USA," he writes,

> intense inter-municipal competition for corporate and property tax revenues—coupled with nimbyist suburban secessionist movements based upon the principle of "home rule"—have long been institutionalized and were actually intensified under Reagan's New Federalism. The Urban Future 21 World Report can thus be viewed as a manifesto in favor of new, highly polarized national political geographies in which all cities would be forced to rely chiefly upon their own socioeconomic assets in order to secure revenues through which to provide public services. . . . In this sense . . . the agenda of good governance is premised upon a distinctively geographical ontology of inside vs. outside: cooperation, solidarity, and democracy may be permitted *within* an urban territory; but beyond it, a logic of market anarchy, profit maximization and cut-throat interspatial competition is to reign supreme and unchallenged.

These, then, are the main features of the new ideology so far as the future of city-regions is concerned. It is not empty talk. The strategic plan for the Hong Kong Special Administrative Region, for example, corresponds point for point with the Berlin agenda (Friedmann 2000). It is a plan made by a business-oriented government for a city that they regard as little more than a platform for the world's busiest export economy. The social and environmental costs of this approach are all but ignored in both plan and practice.

Unfortunately, the economism of the Berlin conference left the advocates of an alternative, "grassroots" approach to merely bark on the margins of the main event. Some say more than three thousand people attended the Berlin conference, while the parallel people's forum attracted a mere two hundred. *MieterEcho* was prohibited from distributing its broadsheets (as well as a rather impressive *Reader*) outside the conference hall (MieterEcho 2000). And the final resolution of the activists from civil society (!) was a statement of weakness rather than strength, containing little more than a plea for channeling more resources to social projects.

One may well ask, then, whether the neoliberal project has the only going vision for humanity at this time. The third sector, as some call the world of voluntary agencies, with its focus on poverty and its fervent hopes for community, is too myopic to come up with an alternative global project. David Harvey (2000) has recently elaborated on what he calls dialectical utopianism, and this, I believe, is more on the mark. He involves us in a complex exercise of reflection that is at once critical and forward-looking, passionate and practical, spatial as well as temporal, normative but attentive to process. Like Harvey's, the essays in this volume are an attempt to go beyond mere nay-saying and critique. Each starts with analytical questions and then moves forward to proposals that, in various ways, run counter to the dominant paradigm. But unlike Harvey's, they do not contemplate a radical break with the present system. Whether we like it or not, global capital has an astounding capacity for reconfiguring itself. It is likely to be around for some considerable time, and what changes will actually occur in due course as the multiple contradictions of the global order/disorder work themselves out, only historians of the future will be able to tell. But I live now, and I am willing to deal with questions piecemeal rather than holistically, embrace the dialectics of both/and, and accept pragmatic solutions based on negotiation and compromise. Mine is a utopia of the possible that lies somewhere between Leonie Sandercock's "a thousand tiny empowerments"(1999) and David Harvey's utopian project provocatively couched in the language of either/or (2000), yet reaches out to both.

The Essays

The following chapters address a variety of issues that have a direct bearing on urban futures. The title chapter takes a broad sweep over the terrain of urbanization as we complete the transition to a fully urbanized world. Three assumptions guide me in this exploration of the future of cities: first, that the global integration of markets will continue; second, that the urban transition will draw nearly to completion by the mid–twenty-first century; and third, that city-mediated relations will become increasingly prominent and transnational. Distinguishing among three meanings of urbanization—demographic, economic, and sociocultural—I argue that new forms of urbanization will not only further diminish subsistence farming as a way of life, but create cities that are structured as regions, incorporating vast areas that are needed to sustain urban life even when they appear to be open landscapes of fields, forests, lakes, and mountains. The skein of the urban will thus extend over close to the entire world. After reviewing the evidence for a class of cities I call world cities that articulate the global economy in geographic space, I shift attention to the many world peripheries that remain on the margins of these global centers. I introduce a typology of peripheral areas that emphasizes the entropic forces at work, as they deepen poverty, increase violence, and deny a flourishing democratic life. But the world we live in is indivisible. It is a small planet, and we cannot afford to turn our backs on these regions, many of which are sinking into anarchy at a horrific human cost.

The second chapter, "City Marketing and Quasi City-States: Two Models of Urban Development," is essentially an argument about city-regional development that favors endogenous over exogenous approaches. The city marketing approach in favor today is being promoted by market fundamentalists who, on one hand, claim that cities can export their way to prosperity and, on the other hand, look on cities as sites for global investment. Under the second model, the city together with its ambient region is regarded as a collective actor having substantial autonomy—hence, the tag, quasi city-state—aiming at a sustainable development through investment in its own resource complexes: human, social, cultural, intellectual, environmental, and so on. Neo-liberal economists tend to regard endogenous development as an aberration, confusing it with self-sufficiency and withdrawal from the world economy. But city-regions can reach out to one another in ways that temper intercity competition with collaboration in joint initiatives. The chapter closes with a brief account of Eurocities, a network of some sixty important cities, as an example that may hold lessons for the rest of the world, particularly in the newly urbanizing regions of East Asia.

"Transnational Migration: Spaces of Incorporation" (chapter 3) opens a window on an increasingly important dynamic of the global urban system. Transnational migrants are people who work in one country but whose lives are lived "at a distance" in another. In the major nodes of the system they may constitute more than 30 percent of the population. Three case studies help to clarify the meaning of the concept: (1) the multistranded social relations connecting the cities of Monterrey in northern Mexico and Houston in southern Texas and that have over time evolved as a hybrid subculture in language, customs, food, and music on both sides of the border; (2) the political/religious associations of Turkish families who live and work in Germany but whose political loyalties and enthusiasms remain "at home" in Anatolia; and (3) Chinese businesspeople and professionals whose work takes them across the Pacific, whose families are scattered among several countries, who may travel on two or more passports, and who have been tagged by the popular media in Taipei as "trapeze artists."

The second part of the chapter looks at the question of migrants' incorporation into the culture of their host city. Despite its considerable importance, this is an understudied aspect of the sociology of migration. Using Pierre Bourdieu's related concepts of habitus and field, we follow an imaginary journey of Algerian Kabyle workers and their families to Frankfurt. Their concentration in a working-class district of Germany's finance capital leads to conflict with their German blue-collar neighbors who, by the presence of these strangers from North Africa, are forced to reassess their own habitus and comfort zone. The chapter closes with some remarks on whether Kabyles, Turks, and Germans can work together in reinventing the neighborhood they share, but leaves open the question of whether such a project is a realistic expectation.

Closely related to transnational migration and the problem of the social incorporation of migrants is the discussion of citizenship in chapter 4, "Citizenship: Statist, Cosmopolitan, Insurgent." Here, I engage with current debates about the theory of citizenship and try to relate these debates to an understanding of democracy as an intermittent historical project. The nature of the ongoing struggles for an expansion of rights combined with resistance to forces that restrict human flourishing provides a moral focus for the insurgencies of a nonterritorial citizenship. Insurgent citizenship is defined as a form of active participation in temporary social movements whose purpose is the defense of existing democratic principles and rights and the claiming of new rights, which, if enacted, would lead to an expansion of the spaces of democracy in any part of the world. It is a self-declared and voluntary citizenship, and its principal virtue is solidarity across all borders with those who are committed to these projects. In conclusion, I argue that we are beginning to live in a world of multiple citizenships with deep implications for our identities and loyalties.

Urban issues can be viewed from different perspectives and at different scales. With chapter 5, we turn to the smallest of scales, the city of everyday life with its focus on street and neighborhood. For people everywhere, the built environment with which they are most familiar and about which they care is charged with meanings. But these meanings don't enter into the official representations of the city, with their formal language of maps, graphs, diagrams, and statistics. I examine why the city of everyday life is absent from official representations of the city, why it remains hidden, and the difficulties that stand in the way of revealing its multiple meanings in planning processes. The city of everyday life is also a city of small spaces, and various attempts have been made to represent these spaces. But the meanings of this other city are often fleeting and evanescent. They are caught in gestures and gossip, whereas the official city stands in the service of power, and discourses of power are always difficult to challenge. Nevertheless, the city of everyday life has exploded into view, forcing itself on the attention of the city's power brokers. Examples of resistance as well as of participatory, collaborative, and counterplanning respectively from Mexico City, Pôrto Alegre (Brazil), Spitalfields (London), and Los Angeles are recounted. But difficulties remain, and people's right to the city continues to be contested.

In chapter 6, "The Good City: In Defense of Utopian Thinking," I construct a normative argument for a good city. The argument goes through four stages. In the first, some preliminary questions are considered: in setting out an account of the good city, whose city are we talking about? Can we legitimately assume that there is such a thing as a "common good" of the city? And in talking about the good city, are we primarily concerned with process, with outcome, or with both? And finally, how is a normative framework such as this to be thought of in relation to professional practice? In the second stage, I raise the question of a foundational value for the "good city." A principle of human flourishing is proposed and its wider ramifications are discussed. In the third stage of the argument, I propose a complementary guideline to assist us in assessing the performance of cities. This, I argue, is *multipli/city*, by which I mean an autonomous civil life free from direct supervision and control by the state. Finally, in stage four, I address the question of "good governance" in the city, proposing six specific criteria. My utopia, then, is not a detailed scenario of some universal realm outside of time. Rather, it is a set of criteria against which actual cities can be assessed *by their own citizens.*

The final chapter, "A Life in Planning," is an intellectual autobiography. Here I take a retrospective and critical look at my own work over the past fifty years. Reading it may recall the many "solutions" to urban and regional problems that have been proposed in this half century and provide a sobering background for the preceding essays. The chapter also illustrates the interdependence of theory and practice, in itself an abiding message as well as a personal commitment.

All in all, the essays in this book sketch out an ideological position informed by what Albert Hirschman (1971) has called a "bias for hope." The position I hold is for inclusive, democratic practices, for local citizen rights, for peaceful, multicultural diversity in the cities of this world, for cooperative rather than competitive solutions, and for meaningful intervention by states in the market economy to protect and further citizen rights. Given the enormous changes afoot in the world that are driven by technologies and global corporations, this is a modest—a minimum—agenda.

Surprisingly, perhaps, my hopes were buoyed during a recent visit to Guangzhou in southern China. Guangzhou is an ancient city with two thousand years of history that is now being reborn. It is an enormous one-hundred-mile city, beautiful in parts, exuding great vitality. Its young people are open to the world. They have come here from all over

China because the city is a window to the world, because here, for the first time, they discover a freedom to be themselves they could only dream of in the rural backwaters of their vast country. True, political freedom is not yet part of their experience, but that is slowly beginning to change. It is thus to the enterprising, hope-filled people of Guangzhou that I dedicate this book.

1
The Prospect of Cities

Fundamental Urbanization

Some fifteen years ago, when I was teaching at UCLA, a newly arrived Master's student from Ahmedabad cocked her eyebrows in shocked surprise when I suggested to her that, in its settlement patterns, the world was becoming inevitably an urban world. What proof did I have, she demanded to know. At the time, nearly 80 percent of India's population was classified as rural. There was still a living memory of Ghandi who had thought of reviving India's rural economy in ways that would avoid large-scale urbanization. From an Indian perspective, my prognosis seemed very shaky indeed. Of course, I had no solid proofs for my prediction. But I did have a theory and associated data from Berkeley demographer Kingsley Davis, a theory he called the urban transition. It was based on a simple S-shaped growth curve, starting from less than 5 percent urban in 1800 and terminating asymptotically three centuries later at around 80 percent (Davis 1972, 1973). I'm not sure that this settled the matter for my student, who went on to study political ecology with a dissertation on the lower Himalayan forest communities (Rangan 2000). But we do have two more decades worth of statistics now, and they show unequivocally that the urban transition will not be reversed. India's urbanization is proceeding apace at around 3 percent annually, with the UN projecting an urban population of around 45 percent in another quarter century. China's trajectory of around 4 percent per annum is even more spectacular. By the year 2025, the People's Republic is projected to have 55 percent of its 1.5 billion people living in cities. As for the world as a whole, the estimated urban

1

population will be 61 percent of a total of 8.3 billion (all data from Habitat 1996).

Willful attempts at ruralization, such as in Mao Ze Dong's China or Pol Pot's Kampuchea, were thus never more than temporary reversals. And so today I repeat the assertion I made to my student from Ahmedabad: We are headed irrevocably into a century in which the world's population will become, in some fundamental sense, completely urbanized. Following this logic, if there were 2.6 billion urbanites in 1995, we can reasonably expect that number to more than triple over the next hundred years to perhaps 8 billion. This prospect is worth pondering.

Long-term projections such as these hinge on certain assumptions and imply a particular way of looking at the world. The most important assumption, perhaps, is that global capital will continue to expand and consolidate its hold on the economy. This does not mean, however, as anthropologist Arjun Appadurai reminds us, that the world is becoming culturally homogenized (Appadurai 1998). Contrary to some people's expectations, the world is not in danger of cloning, say, an Australia, Germany, Britain, or the Netherlands—countries that have present urban populations in excess of 85 percent, and each of which is historically and culturally distinctive. Similarly, each node in the network of cities has its characteristic historical profile—culturally, politically, economically— and its future cannot be charted like the reductive S-curve of the urban transition. Nevertheless, linkages among cities can be expected to get stronger. And even though a borderless world is certainly a fantasy, that of an increasingly transnational world is not. As an institution, the powers of the nation-state may be weakening, but the state is far from dead. The number of UN member states—now in the neighborhood of two hundred—continues to go up. But most of them are states in name only, lacking any sort of real sovereignty in a world of ever greater interdependencies (Boniface 1999).

In short, even when we look in greater detail at only one or a handful of cities, we are forced to adopt a global perspective. Appadurai is, therefore, correct when he asserts that even though localities are, in one sense, globally produced, each locality has a particular history and geographical setting, and its trajectory is path-dependent, offering only limited choices at certain historical junctures. Even so, local responses to global challenges are decisive for the future of cities and preclude any sort of easy prophesying. In any event, prophecy is not my business. What I hope to do in the following chapters is to dwell on a small number of issues that I regard as crucial for public policy in a rapidly urbanizing world. Neither their selection nor any of their particulars hinges on a specific teleology for the century ahead. I shall make only three basic assumptions: that the expansion and consolidation of global capital will continue, that the urban transition will all but be completed over the next several decades, and that city-mediated, increasingly transnational relations will continue to be strengthened.[1]

Three Meanings of Urbanization

Before proceeding, however, the processes of urbanization need to be examined more closely. The broad concept of urbanization has in fact three distinct, if interrelated meanings, all of which are, in one of their dimensions, spatial. The first and most common meaning and the one that has given rise to the model of the urban transition is *demographic* and refers to the increasing concentration of people (relative to a base population) in urban-style settlements at densities that are higher than in the areas surrounding them. There is a measurement problem here, of course, and how we draw the boundaries around the urban cluster will make a difference in the numbers. For Max Weber (1958), for example, the city was a walled settlement, but whatever the historical merits of this view, the contemporary city is not so readily delimited, and different countries employ a gamut of criteria, from demographic to political. Some use administrative boundaries, others a variety of auxiliary markers. Furthermore, distinctions are commonly made among urban, suburban, and ex-urban areas. As for cities above a certain population size, *metropolitan* is the term most often used to describe a large and interdependent cluster of urban spaces.

However, the term I prefer is *city-region*. Every urban core needs a surrounding regional space to sustain itself. This is space for its future expansion and for all those space-extensive activities that a large city needs, from airports and landfills to industrial districts and areas of intensive agriculture, to open space recreation and water reservoirs. Traced by these criteria, city-regions typically extend outward from a core for a distance of roughly one hour's commuting time, or fifty to one hundred kilometers. Using this concept of an extended urban region requires that we reexamine the *demographic definition* of urbanization as a particular density configuration of human settlements. Although a definition based on population density may still stand for the urban core (or cores, since many large city-regions now have more than one center), it requires the complementary concept of a functional region that even though it is typically far less densely settled, nevertheless contributes significantly to sustain the urban complex as a whole. I won't attempt a formal statement of this addendum, but it is one that we will have to keep in mind, for it has major implications for both land use and governance.

The second meaning of urbanization is *economic*. Here the reference is to economic activities that we normally associate with cities, such as manufacturing, construction, trades, and services. That would leave primary activities (agriculture, livestock, forestry, fisheries, and mining) as the residual of a rural economy. But I believe we should challenge this residual approach and broaden our criterion beyond labor-force participation to include as well the economic organization and capitalization of the primary sector. As the rate of labor-force participation in primary activities dwindles, primary production is becoming big business, increasingly multinational in scope, with rationalized methods of production that more and more resemble those of an industrial enterprise of the Fordist variety. A Kansas farmer with a university degree, hooked up to the Internet and a fax machine, with a barn full of expensive machinery, who keeps strict accounts and sells his grain on the Chicago Mart is no longer meaningfully engaged in anything we might want to call "rural life"; in an economic, if not a demographic sense, he is as fully urbanized as any medium-size manufacturer in Topeka. The main difference is that his business is space extensive. The same can be said of businessmen-farmers in Holland who grow flowers in temperature-controlled glass houses and simultaneously air-freight exotic flowers from Kenya whose cultivation is strictly supervised by the importing firm. All other so-called primary activities could be subjected to a similar test. How are they organized? How much capital do they use? How specialized is their production? How much labor of what types do they employ? Who sets the terms of contract? My point is that residual rural activities are disappearing from more and more parts of the world, and that economic urbanization is gaining as the redundant surplus of labor moves from countryside to city in search of a better livelihood. From a perspective of fifty to one hundred years, the erasure of the traditional category of rural would be a reasonable assumption.

The third meaning of urbanization is *sociocultural* and refers to participation in urban ways of life. Here we must be careful not fall into the trap of culturally specific biases. Are there some categories of the socio-cultural urban that are universal? I would argue yes. For example, to be urban is to be literate, which in turn implies a certain level of educational attainment. Literacy has been associated with urbanism since Babylonian times. Another sociocultural expression of the urban, closely related to literacy, is being knit into communications-intensive networks, which are today no longer confined to local or national settings (Smith and Guarnizo 1998). The city has always had specialized spaces, which are the nodes of such networks: streets, public squares, coffeehouses, tea rooms, wineshops, pubs, restaurants, and now cybercafés, all of which exist to facilitate people meeting and talking with one another. If we are to believe Habermas (1989), places such as these brought the first (bourgeois) public spheres in Europe into being. Today, communications-intensive networks are extended worldwide through the electronic media, from cellular telephones to the Internet, reconfiguring the urban into what William Mitchell (1995) calls cybercities. To be connected to these virtual cities means to become informed, to see (or at least imagine) multiple worlds rather than merely the familiar faces of one's family and immediate neighbors. The words, sounds, and images that travel over these networks create new desires and fantasies, and with expanding consciousness of what is possible, people arrive at new levels of political awareness and, among other things, begin to glimpse the possibility of claiming new rights as human beings and citizens. They join up to assert and struggle for these rights, in social movements, labor unions, and political organizations. And as the individual is weaned from communal obligations to a more trenchant assertion of individual rights and citizenship, traditional loyalties and customs are loosened and reconfigured into new patterns.

Perhaps I have said enough to suggest that sociocultural urbanization is a dimension that, like the economic, is no longer exclusively associated with the city as a built environment, though it is linked to it, but extends outward from the core into nonurban space in ways that are occasionally startling (Tacoli 1998). Satellite dishes dot the Brazilian rain forest (Browder and Godfrey 1997). Indigenous people who only fifty years ago were labeled primitive by European anthropologists studying their "mentality" now hold intercontinental congresses to devise common strategies in their separate struggles for collective rights. Aborigines paint canvasses in the Australian outback, which are then exhibited in coastal city galleries to great public acclaim. The far is brought near, and the near is far removed. The global and the local are joined in ways that are mutually transforming (Wilson and Dissanayake 1996).

The Skein of the Urban

As the skein of the urban steadily advances across the surface of the earth, its vertical dimensions are layered to produce a new global topography of the urban. Calibrated differently, demographic, economic, and sociocultural urbanizations do not necessarily coincide in space. There are heavily populated areas that are urbanized both economically and in a sociocultural sense, but have no sizeable cities. Many years ago, I called such areas "agropolitan" and found contemporary instances in the deltas of the great river systems of the world, particularly in China and India (Friedmann 1981). On the other hand, there are cities, especially but not only in Africa, which are weakly urbanized in economic terms, and where the bulk of the urban labor force works precariously in informal trades and services (Rakodi 1997). One result of this uneven articulation is the rapid disappearance of what we are still accustomed to calling rural areas. To be sure, in much of the developing world, subsistence peasantries remain dominant. But their incomes are earned increasingly outside of agriculture, and even in remote villages, young and old will gather around a television set in the evening to follow soap operas, the news, and other entertainments that are produced thousands of miles away. Cityward migration within a single country, and transnational migrations even more so, will only speed up and intensify this process of transforming peasants into proletarians, introduce new social inequalities, and create new relations of power in even the poorest regions.

Yet the disarticulated layering of the three dimensions of the urban is not a random process, and the places that have the highest measure of urbanization in all three senses—the peaks of the urban landscape, so to speak—are typically also the major nodes of the transnational system and are clearly conjoined to an existing global system of economic power. Although efforts have been made to map this new configuration of power, none have been completely convincing, because the data sets that would either confirm or contradict them simply don't exist. Even so, it may be useful to consider at least one such mapping in detail and speculate on the ways it might be changed over the coming decades.

World City Hierarchies . . .

In a paper first published in 1986, I suggested a complex spatial articulation based on a concept of world city (Friedmann 1995a). Although references to world cities now abound even in the popular press, a certain ambiguity has always surrounded this concept, which can either refer to a limited class of cities that play a leading role in the spatial articulation of the global economy, or designate a dimension of all cities that are variously integrated with this system, from strong to weak. I believe that these two meanings can be reconciled by positing a *global hierarchy—a hierarchical system—of cities* in which every city occupies a position that reflects its relative importance in the articulation of the global "space of flows" or, to put it more plainly, its relative economic power.

At the top of this hierarchy we find a very small number of global financial centers: London, New York, and Tokyo (Sassen 1991). As we descend from these pinnacles of power, we can identify multinational financial centers (Miami, Frankfurt, Singapore), centers that dominate large national economies (São Paulo, Paris, Sydney, Seoul), and important subnational or regional centers (Osaka-Kobe, Hong Kong, Vancouver, the Rhine-Ruhr conurbation, Chicago). In all, I identified some thirty leading "world cities" that reflected the spatial reach of their economic and financial articulations. We can catch a glimpse of this "reach" by looking at the dominant linkages of the global airline network. Figure 1.1, prepared by David J. Keeling of Western Kentucky University, clearly shows the triadic structure of the world-cities network in the early nineties. This urban hierarchy is obviously truncated because, in fact, there is no city anywhere that is not articulated, however tenuously, into the global system. But below a certain threshold, the individual importance of these cities in the overall accumulation process is relatively small.

Any such mapping must be approached with caution, however. For one thing, we can decide to change the income threshold, raising or lowering it, or adopt different criteria for identifying them, thereby changing the number of so-called world cities. For another, the topography of world urbanization is constantly changing. For example, projecting ourselves several decades into the future, we would be greatly surprised, I think, if China and India, for example, were to remain without major world cities of the kind I have described. Now that India has

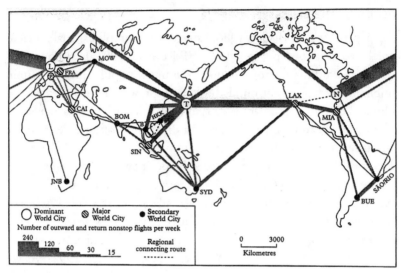

Figure 1.1. Dominant linkages in the global airline network. From Keeling 1995. Reprinted with permission of Cambridge University Press.

begun to open up to the global economy, Mumbai (formerly Bombay) is slated to be the country's first "world city" (Shaw 1998), and as the "dragon head" of the Yangtse Valley, Shanghai is similarly poised. Within the next two or three decades, places such as Bangalore and Tianjin will perhaps also rise into the hierarchy of world city power.

This hierarchy is certainly not written in stone. Over time, some cities will drop from the list, and others will join. A great deal depends on how particular cities respond to external challenges—for example, to new technologies that put a range of industries on which their wealth was formerly based out of business. Today's world is full of "rust belt" cities—in Germany, Russia, the Ukraine, Spain, the United Kingdom, America, China, Korea—that a globalizing economy has made redundant. Some contemporary answers to threatening rust-belt status have been gambling casinos and mega-sporting events (Melbourne), world-class museums (Bilbao), "hip" new industries based on biotechnology or pollution instrumentation (Ruhr Valley), and even the speculative building of a "golden gateway," such as in East Shanghai. However, not all strategies work, and some cities, unable to rally themselves successfully, continue to disinvest in their future.

Despite high capital mobility, the reordering of the world-city hierarchy is a gradual process. Ultimately, it is a hierarchy of power, and capital is not infinitely mobile but large parts of it are embedded in brick, mortar, and steel and, more importantly, in the place-based social and cultural relations that are stressed by current regional theory.[2] Tokyo has been engulfed in a national crisis for more than ten years, but given the continuing viability of its major financial institutions, the city continues to share top rank with London and New York as a truly globe-spanning metropolis. Nor is the power of world cities exclusively economic. On one hand, and especially where national capitals are concerned, the central state will do whatever it can to shore up and defend the position of its key city or cities. Because it is a city of global importance financially, New York was not allowed to bankrupt itself. And the central bureaucracy ensconced in Tokyo has no intention of presiding over the disestablishment of the imperial city.

Each world-city node articulates a subsystem of the global economy that is subordinate to it. We may call this its space of accumulation. This idea allows us to speak of global (primarily financial), multinational, national, and subnational (regional) spaces of accumulation. It is interesting to observe that there are stirrings of secessional desire in some of these regional cities, with Montreal, Milan, and Barcelona in the lead. Nor was Hong Kong simply reabsorbed into China in July 1997. Under the catchy formula "one country, two systems," it successfully negotiated its present status as a Special Administrative Region, retaining its own law courts, currency, semidemocratic political system, and so forth. Clearly, some regional cities no longer wish to be burdened with subsidizing the more backward parts of their own country (Milano → Mezzogiorno; Barcelona → Estremadura, Galicia, and Andalucia) and are looking for a way out by claiming greater autonomy from their national centers (Keating 1999).

By the middle of the twenty-first century, a mapping of world cities will show many additions, perhaps another twenty or thirty, commensurate with the immense scale of the global economy we can expect at mid-century. But what of the rest of the world, the weakly urbanized spaces that are, so to speak, off the global map? They comprise the invisible world periphery, and we should pay more attention to it than we do.

. . . and World Peripheries

World periphery is really a figure of speech more than an analytical concept. Yet we need the term to identify the diversity of peripheries that in fact exists. Regions and countries bypassed by global capital and perceived as largely redundant to the processes of accumulation, except possibly as a source of strategic raw materials, are part of this congeries of places. Peripheral regions are, by definition, poor and powerless. Their populations are not mobilized around a project of national/regional economic development and have other concerns. A rough, nonsystematic typology of world peripheral regions might look something like this:

1. *Living correctly in the world.* Revolutionary societies that assert and seek to impose only one correct way of being in the world. They may be of either religious or secular inspiration, portraying the global capitalist economy as Satanic, their Manichean other. The best-known example is postrevolutionary Shiite Iran, which has recently been joined by Afghanistan's Taliban regime. The ongoing, intermittently violent struggle for an Islamic state in Algeria has the same ideological basis. On the secular side, if one can call it that, examples would be Peru's Shining Path crusade, which has been brought under control, and Pol Pot's unlamented vision for Kampuchea.

2. *Naked struggles for power.* Contending groups, sometimes ethnically or class based, whose principal object is to seize the state apparatus. Recent instances include Somalia, Liberia, and Sierra Leone (in all three countries, war led to the collapse of the state), and Angola and Fiji.

3. *Closed military dictatorships.* Strongmen regimes that seal off their countries from all "contaminating" influences while brutally repressing all internal dissent and opposition, such as Myanmar (Burma) and North Korea.

4. *Secessionist struggles.* Ethnic/religious groups seeking greater autonomy for themselves either within larger, multinational societies or as sovereign nation-states under their own flag. Northern Ireland, Corsica, Euskadi, Chechnya, Kosovo, East Timor, Aceh/Sumatra, Irian Jaya, Kashmir, Kurdistan (Turkey, Iraq, Iran), Palestine, Sudan, Sri Lanka, and Tibet are some of the locales of currently ongoing struggles.

5. *"Destroying the Other."* Genocidal outbreaks of ethnic cleansing that seek to eliminate demonized groups from the aggressor's field of

vision and may be combined with territorial claims. The bloodletting in Rwanda and Burundi and the continuing ethnic violence in the former Yugoslavia are two tragic instances of recent memory. So-called communal conflicts in India (Hindus against Muslims) and Indonesia (Muslims against Christians) also belong here, but for all of their deadly violence, their national context is different, and they require a different interpretation.

6. *Pariah states.* States that, at one time or another and for varying reasons, are shut out from the global circuits of capital as a form of punishment. Cuba, Iran, Libya, Iraq, North Korea, Afghanistan, and (formerly) apartheid South Africa are well-known instances of recent memory.

This is only a partial typology, and the examples are not meant to be exhaustive. Many peripheral states, for example, are relatively free of violence and have not been politically isolated. Virtually all world peripheries, however, can be characterized by their *inward gaze.* Whereas world cities (together with their respective spheres of accumulation) are increasingly outward looking (and reluctantly prepared to live with difference that inevitably accompanies an attitude of world openness), world peripheries, largely shunned by global capital, concentrate their energies on political tasks within their own borders. Where they have not disintegrated, peripheral states are typically led by strongman regimes, rely on the military for support, practice torture and other forms of terror against their own populations, and are usually so corrupt that journalists sometimes stigmatize them as kleptocracies. Their armies are reasonably equipped with sophisticated weaponry that can now be purchased on the open market, and their political elites are not infrequently cultured, educated persons, some with advanced degrees from abroad. So, the violence of world peripheries is not, for the most part, because of peasant struggles for land, but because the struggle is focused, with all the technological instrumentation available in global markets, on the control of cities.

The violence is episodic (though it can sometimes last for decades, as it has, with terrible consequences, in the Sudan), but when it is over, the poverty that was there from the beginning remains, and there is new poverty as well: among the survivors of the killing fields, refugees that have fled to the cities or into borderlands, and in what is left of the destroyed cities and pillaged villages and fields. What was once a vibrant, if poor society is now in disarray. Homes have been burned. A neighbor could be someone who raped and killed a loved one. Public services are in a state of chaos. In extreme cases, the state may collapse altogether, leaving only regional warlords (or, in a few cases, as in Kosovo or East Timor, a hapless United Nations) fitfully in charge.

World peripheries generate two kinds of migration: internal, to the major city or cities of the region, and external, to the core areas of the world economy. In the former, the migrants' future is bleak and, for most, social reproduction takes place within what Clifford Geertz, writing of Java, called the bazaar economy—that is, a division of simple, everyday tasks into ever smaller, more specialized segments, each of which contributes to a bare subsistence (Fass 1988). Attempts by government to control cityward migration or even to reverse the flow of migrants from city to countryside, as in Maoist China, have been spectacular and tragic failures. However thin the periphery's global linkages may be, they are always greatest in the major cities, and this is where people go when they are hungry and adventurous. Some who are sufficiently clever or ruthless will eventually make a fairly decent living by local standards. The rest will not.

As for those who go abroad, they may or may not reach their goal, depending in part on whether they carry legal documentation. But once arrived, they quickly merge with the local subproletariat as construction workers, sex workers, domestic workers, sweatshop labor, and street hustlers, performing all manner of dirty jobs that the natives of the place refuse to do (Berger and Mohr 1975). Increasingly, women are part of this stream. All but invisible to the population at large (but not to the police), migrants fight against odds to establish a legal beachhead for themselves and their families. Despite occasional xenophobic outbursts, life for them is not without hope, and so they stay (Harris 1995; Uçarer and Puchala 1997).

Meanwhile, in the world periphery, life continues, though, given population growth and resource depletion, on an increasingly precarious basis. Emigration helps, but it is never enough. Remittances from abroad may help to ease the blinding despair of poverty. Nongovernmental, voluntary organizations and religious charities will alleviate it for a few. Dwindling international aid is diverted into the pockets of the kleptocracy. Global capital may make a fleeting appearance, funding mines, plantations, timber operations, or an occasional factory employing young, female workers to sew T-shirts or assemble baseballs, profitable but minor commodities for the international market. Overall, however, whether measured in terms of individual endowment, social organization, natural resources, environmental resources, and economic infrastructure, the wealth-producing capabilities of world peripheries are on a downward-spiraling path.

Entropy/Negentropy

This downward-spiraling path is more than a metaphor. It signifies an entropic social process that, after reaching a certain threshold, may become irreversible. Outside of its specific application in molecular physics, entropy can be conceived of as a measure of the *steady deterioration in social organization, the built environment, and natural resource wealth.* According to Nobel Prize–winning physicist and philosopher, Erwin Schrödinger (1992 [1945]), life forms flourish so long as *negentropic* flows of energy overcome the steady degradation that is always ongoing in the universe and from which no physical process is exempted. Negative entropy, according to Schrödinger, is a form of energy that feeds into and makes possible complex organic structures and ensembles. Essentially, it is a carrier of information and order.

> Every process, event, happening—call it what you will—in a word, everything that is going on in Nature means an increase of entropy of the part of the world where it is going on. Thus, a living organism increases its entropy—or , as you may say, produces positive entropy— and thus tends to approach the dangerous state of maximum entropy, which is death. It can only keep aloof from it, that is, alive, by continually drawing from its environment negative entropy—which is something very positive. What an organism feeds upon is negative entropy. Or, to put it less paradoxically, the essential thing in metabolism is that the organism succeeds in freeing itself from all the entropy it cannot help producing while alive. (71)

In the case of individual life forms, entropy, which is a measure of *disorder,* wins out in the long run, resulting in the death of the organism. But individuals do not live in isolation from each other, and a population of individuals, organized into social ensembles, is inevitably contained within a set of larger ecologies with which it is in constant exchange. Life forms are therefore open systems that, when they are sealed off from air, sunlight, water, and food, will die.

I believe that these two physical processes—entropy and negative entropy—apply not only to individual life forms but also to the larger ensemble that we call society. Unless self-organized societies are continually energized around what I am tempted to call a *civilizatory project* leading to more complex forms of organization and greater predictability, entropy takes us farther and farther along a road to collective self-destruction. Or, as the current, more familiar discourse has it, isolated societies that are on a downward-spiraling path are embarked on a trajectory that, over the longer term, is unsustainable.

Without reference to physics but intent on explaining capitalist development, the Austro-American economist Joseph Schumpeter focused his research on the energizing role of entrepreneurs (Schumpeter 1934, 1950). As a mode of production, Schumpeter thought, capitalist accumulation could only be understood as a historical process of what he called *creative destruction.* As a dynamic system of social relations, capitalism is a ruthless destroyer in which old structures are replaced by more powerful competitors, more efficient forms of production, more appealing commodities. It is easy to see how the concepts of entropy and negative entropy can be inserted into Schumpeter's model that is based on a succession of disequilibria that every few decades toll the bell for an era in the grip of entropic decline, even as it announces the arrival of new culture heroes (entrepreneurs), thus heralding another cycle of capitalist accumulation. These cyclical transitions are compressed into relatively short, intense bursts of ruthless innovation, dominated by bundles of new technologies, both hard and soft. In the core areas of the global economy, negentropic energies somehow succeed in overcoming entropic degradation, though for how long, no one can be sure. But on the world periphery, which in geographical terms is not far removed, the balance of forces is quite the other way around, and "development" now comes with a negative sign, because the new forces (and the entrepreneurs that are supposed to energize the process) never appear in sufficient numbers.

Moral considerations aside, all would be well if cores and peripheries were sealed off from each other. But, of course, they are not, nor can they be. Urbanization is a set of universal, if geographically uneven processes; the store house of natural resources on the world periphery is needed for the exorbitant needs of the rich countries at the core of the world economy and are followed by transnational migratory streams from the periphery to the center, where they constitute a proletariat that is not always welcome and typically maintains close social, economic, cultural, and political ties with their originating regions (Smith and Guarnizo 1998). What we have, then, is not two hermetically sealed-off spheres, one ascendant, the other in decline or, as some economists would have it, caught in a "low-level equilibrium trap," but the single world-system posited by historians such as Fernand Braudel (1992) and Immanuel Wallerstein (1974).

If we accept the interconnectedness of core and peripheral regions, then what happens in the various peripheries of the world system is a matter of prime importance for those of us who live in the central, energizing, and controlling cores of the system. A sustainable development must be forged in the face of the positive entropy the system continually produces—its long-term tendency toward increased randomness and disorder. The pain of this whirlwind of creative destruction can be lessened, but it cannot be avoided. When degradation builds up in any part of the world, even in world cities, it should be a matter of general concern, because entropy spreads like a cancer and is capable of destroying positive developments until the system as a whole is engulfed in crisis.

To know all this does not provide an answer on what to do. Knowing only tells us that we cannot afford to sit passively on the sidelines, watching the world peripheries go up in flames (and, for that matter, also the peripheries at the core of our own cities), because what happens "out there" will one day like a boomerang return to strike us.

The Language of Time

I don't want to leave the impression that there is nothing we can do. By posing the problem of the world periphery as being caused by global capital—though admittedly, peripherality may sometimes be the preferred option, witness Iran's (and now also Afghanistan's) theocracy—I would seem to be suggesting that much of the periphery is merely being victimized and should rise up, demanding justice in the court of world opinion. But moral outrage will not solve the problem of the downward-spiraling path, because in the end there is not just the one problem of weakness and decline; problems are numerous and must be seen in all of their particularity, and as a matter of local responsibility *in the first place*. The power may not always be there, but the information is available. And if it is true that good decisions are made where the information is richest (and where the capacity exists to interpret it correctly), power should be devolved to that level.

But, unfortunately, the world won't stand still while we are trying to fix it. The dynamics of core/periphery relations are ongoing and highly variable. The next century will see immense changes of all kinds. We are likely to experience a number of technological waves that will at least be as far-reaching in their implications for social and economic transformation as those we have been through over the past one hundred years. Nor can a global catastrophe on the scale of World War III be ruled out on a priori grounds.

Of this, though, I am certain: The balance of entropic and negentropic energies in the world system cannot in any simplistic fashion be reestablished in favor of the second, by spurts of increased foreign aid, a more effective UN Peace Force, or some other magic bullet for poverty and disorder. Complex problems call for approaches that are in no way less complex than the problem itself. Intuitively we already know this, and throughout the world, efforts are being made to devolve power, to make the exercise of power more accountable, to democratize power, to change the forms of governance at all significant intersections of power. Instead of a hedgehog state that knows only one thing, to paraphrase Isaiah Berlin (1953), we need a lot of clever foxes trying to figure out what to do. Not all of them may be as clever as we would like them to be, but to rely on the hedgehog that knows only one "big thing" would surely be fatal.

Lest we get lost among metaphors, let me explain: by foxes, I mean a local/regional response capability, with territorially based political communities proceeding by way of trial and error and demonstrating a willingness to learn from their own and others' mistakes. As for the hedgehog, it has one and the same solution for all the problems of this world. At the dawn of the twentieth century, a Polish linguist introduced the world to a new language he called Esperanto. He hoped that a common language would help to heal the world's ills. But the world did not rise to his challenge, and the ills are still with us. What we need now, at the beginning of the twenty-first, is not the reductive grammar of an artificial language (or of a master discourse such as neoclassical economic theory). What we need instead is *a heightened willingness to listen to a multiplicity of voices* and to learn and draw conclusions from them for our own practices. However imperfect, we need to gain an understanding of the problems that beset us from a diversity of perspectives, without attempting to reconcile multiplicities with each other, allowing each narrative to contribute whatever it can. Local or regional "takes" on an issue are not necessarily the only valid ones. Nor are the expert "takes" of expensive outside consultants. In attempting to work out solutions to a problem that is perceived locally, *all* of the information that time permits must be brought together, and when the clock stops, someone must assume the political risks of a decision. But for this strategy to work, localities must be empowered to act on their own behalf; if they are not, surely the hedgehog will win by default.

Even a radical devolution of powers, however, doesn't absolve us of thinking systemwide on several planes. In fact, the one requires the other. The more decentralized things are, the more we need central powers to balance and coordinate systemwide changes and ensure a greater measure of equity in the distribution of resources. But here, too, a multiplicity of perspectives is critical to successful management.

Perhaps I have said enough to suggest that a high priority for the century ahead is the rethinking and reconstruction of global governance, the division of powers and responsibilities among collective actors, the forms of networking, the territorial and nonterritorial institutions we need for a sustainable planet. This gigantic undertaking has already begun; we should think of it as a journey of exploration, the mapping of new land.

2

City Marketing and Quasi City-States: Two Models of Urban Development

As I am writing these lines, banner headlines scream from Melbourne's leading daily, *The Age,* expressing shocked dismay at allegations of corruption in the selection of host cities for the 2000 Winter and Summer Olympics, respectively Salt Lake City and Sydney. The stories claim that key members of the International Olympic Committee (IOC) were bribed and given other favors by the promoters of the local venue. There are calls for investigations, resignations, and other forms of punishment for the presumed offenders on both the giving and the taking side. The five rings must not be tarnished; the "purity" of Olympic sportsmanship must be preserved, write the pundits.

All this hullabaloo is, of course, little more than show, since it is by now widely acknowledged that the Olympics, far from being merely (primarily?) about athletic prowess, has also become, at least since the 1984 games in Los Angeles, big business. The Olympic games not only draw the world's attention to the host city, but also leave, it is hoped, hundreds of millions of dollars in the pockets of local merchants, hoteliers, and other providers. The games also serve to advertise sponsors' wares in a big way, from skis and running shoes to Coca-Cola. To land the Olympic games, a city is prepared to spend vast sums of taxpayer money to spruce itself up, upgrade its sports venues, and make other "improvements" in its infrastructure that, it is hoped, will be converted to civilian use once the games have moved on. Against this massive outpouring of public funds, itself a boon to the local construction industry, what are a few ten thousand dollars of spending money for a handful of needy IOC members, a university scholarship for one or another of their sons or daughters, a bit of female entertainment for those lonely

19

nights away from home, free first-class travel to distant places, and so on? Isn't all this part and parcel of what's now known as city-marketing? And isn't city-marketing what all cities must engage in if they are not to be sidelined from the circuits of global capital?

These musings led me to think about city-marketing as an urban development model and to contrast it with what to me seems a more promising approach. I call it the model of a quasi city-state. The two models are contrasted in Table 2.1.

Table 2.1. Two Urban Development Models

	Model 1: City-Marketing	Model 2: Quasi City-State
Action space	core city	city-region
Time frame	long-term payoff	short-term payoff
Scope	maximize economic growth	optimize multiple objectives
Primary development impulse	exogenous	endogenous
Mode	competitive (zero-sum)	collaborative (networking)
Power base	narrow/technocratic	inclusive/democratic
Sustainability	poor	good

Any distinction such as this one is, of course, an artifice intended to serve primarily a didactic purpose. Some may object that city-marketing is just a tool, one among several for promoting urban development and that it isn't a model at all, while others will point out that in the contemporary world, bona fide city-states such as Singapore cannot convincingly serve as the basis for a general model.[1] Nevertheless, the two approaches are significantly different from each other and help to bring out strategic aspects of urban development.

Let me first run down the left-hand column of Model 1 with which, after this analysis, I will no longer be directly concerned. The model comes close to stylizing current "best practice" (Kearns and Philo 1993). The *action frame* here is chiefly the core city stripped of its outer suburbs and immediate hinterland. The *time frame* is typically short-run political advantage, such as attracting global capital that will—so it is hoped—improve the competitive profile of the city and generate jobs and income. The model's *scope* is in the narrowest sense economic, and other concerns, such as social or environmental, tend to be sacrificed to serve short-run advantage. The *primary impulse* of this development model is assumed to lie beyond the city's control and, much like South Pacific cargo-cults, is exogenous. At the same time, the *mode* of development is seen in starkly competitive terms. Because there is only so much global capital to go around—this seems to be the reasoning—if your own city doesn't latch on to it, some other city will: city-marketing is an unforgiving zero-sum game. Hence the usual offerings on the altar of transnational capital are low wages, a compliant labor force, "flexible and responsive" local government, and all sorts of giveaways—tax breaks, free land, subsidies, and (of course) those little "favors" for the CEOs of multinationals or their delegates. The *power base* of urban development in Model 1 is quite narrow, consisting primarily of local business interests acting hand in hand with city government and transnational capital. Other interests are either effectively ignored or placated with symbolic gestures. City-marketing is a model promising short-term material payoffs for some and long-term damage for most of the rest. It follows that the *prospects for a sustainable development* are poor since, by definition, sustainability concerns the *longue durée*.[2]

All of these elements are inverted in Model 2, the quasi city-state development model. The choice of name is perhaps not the most felicitous one. Nevertheless, I decided in its favor, because it suggests a considerable degree of autonomy with respect to the region's future, because it emphasizes the role of the state rather than the corporate sector, and because it suggests the incorporation of a hinterland as part of the state formation, whatever form this might take. To bring out the key features of this model, I address five specific questions. The first concerns the governance of city-regions; the second asks in what measure city-regions can be said to be proactive on their own behalf; the third addresses sustainability; the fourth examines the notion of an endogenous development; and the last explores the relation between competition and collaboration. In conclusion, I return to the two models, but with this difference: In place of merely advocating Model 2, I will ask the question, What can cities do to move away from the currently fashionable approach of Model 1 to a form of endogenous regional development?[3]

On the Governance of City-Regions

In some ways, our conceptual language is much too blunt to capture the elusive, multifaceted dynamics of urban development. The statistical concept of urban is of only limited use: the concentration of a population above a certain threshold size and living at densities that are relatively higher than settlements in the surrounding (rural) areas. There are other, equally deficient definitions based on, say, administrative criteria. Specifying the concept of "urban" still further, some economic criteria may be added, such as the requirement that the population engage in predominantly nonagricultural work (see chapter 1).

All this analysis is straightforward enough in a context where urban areas are contrasted with rural ones. But the latter designation is, of course, an equally imprecise and, for the most part, empty category, not least in societies where the great bulk of the population is no longer devoted to farming, where farming itself has become a transnational business, and where freestanding small towns and villages have become an endangered species. Some European planners have proposed a new category of *neorural* to capture the phenomenon where land-based production systems, ecological protection, and quality of life coalesce in new combinations (Gulinck and Dortmans 1997). But the term could as easily have been *neourban.*

I will not attempt here to untangle the various meanings of these concepts that are, after all, in everyday use even when their scientific definitions remain contested. Instead, I want to turn to the notion of *city-region* as I propose to use the term. By city-region, I mean a functionally integrated area consisting of both a large urban core and a contiguous region that serves this city's multiple needs and provides a space for its expansion. As shown in Figure 2.1, the needs of a large contemporary city are many and complex.[4] Within this complex, the traditional distinction between urban and rural ceases to be meaningful. The whole of the city-region has, in fact, become a new form of urban landscape.[5]

City-regions on this scale typically overlap with multiple jurisdictional boundaries of governmental and administrative units that often act at cross purposes, making concerted action difficult. The awareness that large regions of this kind require some arrangement of common governance is, in itself, nothing new (Sivaramakrishna 1996). Many cities in Western Europe (Berg et al. 1993; Lefèvre 1998), North America (Sharpe 1995), and Asia (Laquian 1995) have wrestled with this problem since at least the 1950s, though none have been very successful. Representing one end of the spectrum, large American cities typically exhibit extreme fragmentation. General purpose governments are typically small, jeal-

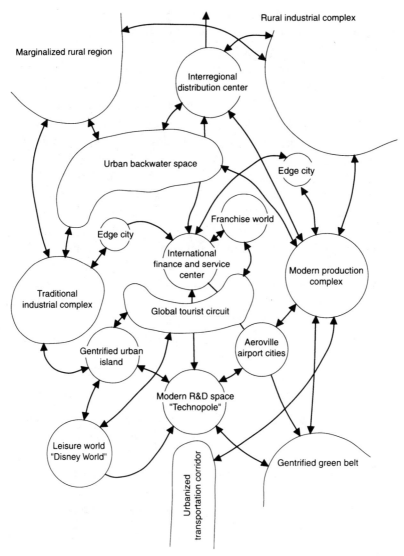

Figure 2.1. The spatial structure of the European city-region in the 1990s. From Kunzmann 1996. Reprinted by permission of Taylor & Francis, Ltd.

ously guarding their prerogatives as they fiercely compete for tax revenues, fiscal transfers, and jobs. Where regional services need to be coordinated, they are usually provided by counties and single purpose administrative agencies for transportation, air-quality management, and so forth. To call this a system of checks and balances is to give it more credit than it is due. In practice, it is a system incapable of timely and concerted action.

At the other end of the spectrum are the governance structures of major Australian cities (Murphy and Wu 1999). Australian municipalities, called Local Councils, exist at the sufferance of their respective states. It is the several state governments that are responsible not only for strategic and statutory planning, but also for many other critical urban functions. The elected government of Victoria, for example, presides over a state of 4.5 million people of whom more than 70 percent reside in the officially designated metropolitan area of Melbourne. The rest of the population is dispersed over a large area in smaller cities and towns and rural settlements. But what is called "country Victoria" principally serves the needs of metropolitan Melbourne and its port. By my definition, Victoria qualifies as a quasi city-state. The Commonwealth government in Canberra has very little say about what happens in Victoria. It is the several governments of the confederated states that hold the real power over local developments in Australia.

In Western Europe and Canada, the approaches to metropolitan governance have been more experimental and fluid. An excellent overview study by Christian Lefèvre (1998) describes recent efforts at forming metropolitan authorities:

> Metropolitan governance highlights values of negotiation, partnership, voluntary participation and flexibility in the constitution of new structures. In doing so, it presents us with a radically different idea of the institution [of metropolitan governance]. It is no longer presented at the start, created in advance, ready-to-use, but appears as the result of a constitutive process. It is the process which radically transforms yesterday's metropolitan model. Metropolitan governance does not consider the institution to be pre-established—on the contrary. The objective to be achieved (roughly speaking the form and content of the metropolitan authority) is not fixed in advance but becomes the product of the system of actors as the process unfolds. Thus, the process has its own dynamic, fed by the actors themselves. But this feeding is not left to chance; it is done through specific forms and negotiated procedures which frame and punctuate the process. Unlike the classic metropolitan model where the process of constitution was generally short but where implementa-

tion proved . . . defective, the process here is long, and may stop or slow down at any time, but the result seems less uncertain because the legitimacy of the institution is produced by all the actors during the process of constituting the metropolitan government. (18)

Lefèvre's formulation captures the idiosyncratic processes of today's experiments with metropolitan (or city-regional) governance. But these processes are a great deal more complicated than he suggests. To begin with, I would question whether their objective is simply the formation of a "metropolitan authority," as he suggests. Metropolitan governance is not a good in itself, nor is it merely a question of efficient service provision, which may or may not be subject to economies of scale. Rather, I would argue that behind the exercise of regional governance must stand a *vision of the good city*, even one that is fiercely contested (Friedmann 1998; see also chapter 6 in this volume). But whose concerns shall inform this vision? The city of the poor or the rich? The city of business or of civil society (see chapter 5)? Surely, this is a matter of inclusiveness in the representation of Lefèvre's actors. To bring together local officials and business interests in a "partnership" is one thing, but the further inclusion of "civil society" gives rise to a very different regime. And although constituting a system of metropolitan governance is important in itself, the powers retained by the smaller territorial units that are integral to the region are equally important. In the European Union, this question of the "territorial division of powers" is often discussed under the *principle of subsidiarity*, which refers to the delegation of powers to the lowest level of governance compatible with effective and efficient performance. But in practice, this principle isn't of much help, and its meaning remains ambiguous. Finally, there are the matters of transparency and democratic accountability in governance without which any system inevitably gets stuck in a quagmire of corruption. Evidently, then, "metropolitanization" ends up being a highly charged political process with very different outcomes for different cities and players.

Can City-Regions Be Collective Actors?

How the problems just enumerated are resolved in practice will have major implications for whether city-regions can be thought of as collective actors. Some time ago, I attended a conference where someone in the audience raised precisely this question: Does it makes sense to speak of the city as a collective actor? Isn't it true, the speaker seemed to be saying, that to claim cities as actors is just another instance of the "spatial fallacy" that attributes agency to space rather than people? Cities, the "corrected" argument would go, are merely *sites* where interests and ideologies are politically contested. My own answer to this question will take me back to an argument about city-regional governance.

In nondemocratic societies, an unquestioned assumption is that the ruler has the right to speak in the name of the realm. He or she is the absolute sovereign. But in an increasingly interdependent world, there can be no such thing as absolute sovereignty. Its assertion by some contemporary tyrants goes typically hand in glove with the abject poverty of their subjects. Today's world is characterized by its relative openness, connectedness, and increasingly democratic ethos. These are matters of degree, but the broad direction of the trend is clear. The idea that it is "the people" who should be the final arbiters of governance arrangements and their practical outcomes is steadily gaining ground.

Michael Storper (1997) has suggested that one of the advantages of cities over other forms of settlement is the daily talk in face-to-face encounters among their business elites. But it isn't only the expense-account lunch that brings people into the public sphere. The talk is everywhere, in pubs and bars, in cafés, in restaurants for the well- and the not-so-well-off, on street corners and park benches. It is a ubiquitous entertainment, engaged in with great gusto by most people. A lot of the talk, of course, is gossip about people and personalities. But this is simply our way to cut to the heart of the larger issues that concern us—the price of food, the transportation mess, new buildings going up in an old neighborhood, air and water quality, wayward youth, the corruption of politicians, and so forth. And all this talk is ultimately reflected in the ever-shifting kaleidoscope of public opinion. At election time, it results in a vote.[6]

With all this in mind, I believe we can say that cities and regions can indeed be seen as collective actors *to the extent that their form of governance is plurivocal and inclusive,* and when those who speak and act on the region's behalf do so with the full legitimacy of a democratic process.[7] But there is one additional requirement without which all the "small talk" of people in bars and on street corners doesn't amount to more than a gloss on the doings of the powerful. Good governance also requires leadership to articulate a common vision for the polity, build a strong consensus around this vision, and mobilize the resources necessary for carrying it out.

Having raised the elusive question of vision, I would now like to look more closely at one dimension that any compelling vision for a city-region must address: the long-term sustainability of its development. I confess a certain reluctance to invoke the mantra of sustainability, which by now is on virtually everyone's lips, as one and all profess their undying devotion to Mother Nature.[8] My understanding of "sustainability," however, is of a different sort, and to convey this understanding requires a detour into the economics of development.

Sustainable Development and the Creation of Regional Wealth

The idea that exports are at the base of a region's economy, propelling it to ever greater prosperity, has become part of the accepted folk wisdom among politicians and academics alike. One of the first formulations of this theory was by the American historian Douglass C. North (1955). Eighteen years later, Douglas Paauw and John C. Fei (1973) reformulated this doctrine in terms of national economies, with particular application to Southeast Asia, where it would soon be known as the strategy of export-led development, paving the way to the market fundamentalism decried by finance guru George Soros (1998). The strategy privileges trade over production and posits a virtuous circle of balanced trade in the context of a competitive interregional economy and division of labor. What this theory doesn't tell us is why trade should beget trade over the long run, why all regions are bound to gain from unregulated trade in global markets, who profits from this trade, how exports are produced, and what happens when stubborn deficits show up on the balance sheet in place of the hoped-for but ever-elusive and receding surplus. Without answers to these questions, the export-led theory remains incomplete, and development strategies based on it are likely to generate a host of unintended consequences.

What happens when a region's growth is stunted, and its interregional trade is balanced at very low levels or, more likely, runs a long-term deficit, with imports outpacing exports by a large margin. In this case, the region becomes a candidate for subsidies or transfer payments from elsewhere (the national treasury, Brussels, bilateral aid, the World Bank) and is likely to begin drawing down its initial fund of wealth-creating resources by a process of systematic disinvestment and neglect. Investments in at least seven interrelated resource complexes or forms of capital are essential to sustaining a city-region's ability to produce a trade surplus over the long haul.

1. *Human capital,* including all the things that nurture our ability to grow into healthy and productive human beings: good nutrition, housing and viazble neighborhoods, health care, and education.

2. *Social capital,* which is a robust, self-organizing civil society deeply engaged with the everyday life of its communities.

3. *Cultural capital,* or the city-region's physical heritage and the distinctiveness and vibrancy of its cultural life.

4. *Intellectual capital,* including the quality of the region's universities and research institutions and what Japan calls its "living human treasures," its artists, intellectuals, and scientists who embody the city's creative powers.

5. *Environmental capital,* which includes those qualities of the physical environment that are essential for sustaining life itself, such as the air we breathe, the water we drink, and the capacity of the land to sustain permanent human settlement.

6. *Natural capital,* or the region's natural resource endowment, such as land, landscapes, beaches, forests, fisheries, and mineral deposits whose use is for production and enjoyment.

7. *Urban capital,* commonly referred to as urban infrastructure, which includes facilities and equipment for transportation, energy, water supply, sewage treatment, and solid waste disposal or, in a more general sense, the built environment.

These seven tightly interwoven resource complexes constitute a city-region's major productive assets. Their benefits are calculated in the long run and in social terms; that is, they are measured against broad societal goals and values. When a region—and more specifically a city-region—fails to invest sufficiently in its assets because of continuing trade and budgetary deficits, or because hyper-rapid growth has put enormous pressure on regional assets, or for whatever other reason, they begin to degrade. Disinvestment can be read off the landscape: heavily polluted and health-impairing environments, land poisoning, speculative over-investment, aging "rust-belt" industries, rivers that are open sewers, the steady depletion and contamination of groundwater resources, land subsidence, persistent water and power shortages, the spread of under-serviced slums and shantytowns, social disintegration, poorly maintained economic infrastructure, and the degradation of formerly attractive landscapes into eyesores. It is a long and unhappy list that characterizes all too many cities. In the United States, systematic disinvestment has produced the bleak cityscape of Detroit. In Mexico, the national capital is a sinking city in both the metaphorical and literal sense (Pezzoli 1998). Reports from the former Soviet Union and from Iran suggest similar stories of decline. And in Southeast Asia, notable examples of deteriorating cityscapes include Rangoon, Bangkok, and Jakarta.

Unfortunately, the relationship between asset degradation and regional fortunes isn't always clearly understood. The two circuits of regional development—regional wealth-creation and intercity trade—must be kept in a rough balance (Thomas et al. 2000, chapter 2). Production for export, put in place by transnational capital, does not, of itself, lead to a sustainable development. Or to put it more bluntly, city-regions cannot hope to procure a sustainable development from outside themselves. To be sustainable, development must be based firmly on their own resource endowment.[9] The frenzied competitive search for global capital that seems to motivate so many city-regions around the world has just the opposite of the intended effect. It tends to drain a region's most precious assets for long-term development. Unless appropriate measures are taken, and the necessary investments are made, sustainable development is jeopardized.

Poor city-regions with low or, more likely, negative trade balances may think that they can afford to neglect the circuit of wealth creation so long as they offer financially attractive deals to foreign investors. But their philosophy of "grow now, pay later" is deceptively seductive. Disinvestment in wealth-creating assets has a hidden cost, which should be counted in whenever local governments, in a celebratory mood, boast of the dollars committed by multinational concerns in their cities. Although some disinvestment can be recovered later, there is no assurance that the circuit of intercity trade will continue to flourish without constantly attending to the condition of city-regional assets.

The Question of an Endogenous Development

I want to pause here briefly to meditate on the related question of an endogenous development. To be sustainable, I said, the development of city-regions must be firmly based on their own resource complexes; it cannot be imported. This inside/outside dichotomy is unavoidable, but it is far from being universally accepted.

Let me begin with what would seem to be a statement of the obvious: All development must be localized somewhere—in a country, region, or quasi city-state. To the extent that development refers to specific investments, say, in a chemical plant, its localization is a given. But how should we assess this investment from the standpoint of a sustainable development? Suppose it is a chemical plant whose toxic effluents destroy fisheries and impair human lives. Even to raise this question is to ask something about the meaning of development itself, what it is, and how it should be measured. *Development* is clearly not so much a technical term as it is a normative concept, and what indicators should be used to measure it is a normative question as well. It is also one of the oldest, unresolved questions in the business.[10]

The story of development indicators is a complex one, and I don't want to enter into a detailed discussion of this topic here. But without opening up a Pandora's box of controversy, two things can be said about a philosophically defensible measure of "progress." Following the line of argument given in chapter 1, the process of capitalist development is one of "creative destruction," in the sense that for any benefits received, some costs will always be exacted from someone, somewhere; moreover, costs and benefits are never equally distributed. An authentic measure of development will, therefore, have to take these costs into account so that changes can be reckoned on a *net* basis. But who is to make such a judgment, or rather series of judgments, including what is to be counted as "development" and over what period of time; what indicators should be used; what sort of costs are incurred where and by whom; how these costs should be apportioned; and how a congeries of unequally distributed costs and benefits, not all of them tangible, may be compared against each other to determine whether the outcome is "development" with either a positive or a negative sign? For all the cleverness of statisticians, the resolution of these familiar dilemmas is so complex that, in the final analysis, it must take place in a political forum. But a political forum requires a territorial system of governance. In a democracy, the answer to the question of who is to make a judgment about development is the affected citizenry of the territory in question. Despite globalization and its notorious "space of flows," development is always localized and its meaning in a political sense is territorially bounded. It is only with respect to such a territorial base that we can speak of development as either endogenous or exogenous, as being generated either from within or from without.[11]

In the Anglo-Saxon world, beholden as it is to "market fundamentalism," not much is heard these days about an endogenous development. The marketeers' focus is rather on the microeconomics of the firm and the flows of commodities, information, and money through global markets unrestrained by government interventions. According to them, development can be reduced to the traditional technocratic measures of economic growth, and it is competitive markets that ultimately decide how much development distills out for each locality. The question of wealth-creating resources at regional/urban levels is only lightly touched upon, if at all; the glittering vision is of a fluid "borderless world" (Ohmae 1995), with capital flowing to those sites where profits are expected to be greatest.

In view of this widely applauded ideological disappearance act, the question of an endogenous development is in need of rehabilitation. As a start, two notions about a territorially based development have to be dispelled. The first is that in a world of global markets, the state in all of its forms has become more or less superfluous and that, whatever residual functions it may still have, could probably be better performed by private firms. The second is that all things that are good for development (as defined by elites) generally come from somewhere else in the borderless world, especially from powerful transnational corporations and financial institutions that are forever in search of the most profitable deal.

Concerning the widespread idea that the state has been weakened to the point of superfluity. If we assume, as I believe we must, that democracy is better than any known alternative for providing a political framework in which life can be lived to the fullest, the state (and specifically the local state) is needed to ensure that a democratic consensus can be arrived at about the meaning of territorial development and, more specifically, about a development that is sustainable. Once decided, this will involve the husbanding of and investment in the region's wealth-creating resources—human, social, cultural, intellectual, environmental, and all the rest. Because results are reaped only in the longer term, this is primarily a state responsibility. Continuing along these lines, we can safely assume that a quasi city-state—that is, a city-region with a marked degree of autonomy over deciding its own future—that has managed its wealth-creating resources well, showing high performance levels in each cluster, is also likely to attract outside capital to itself and will be on its way to becoming an important trading city.

Concerning the belief that development capital must necessarily be imported. To clarify my position, let me say at the start that, of course, capital from beyond the local region will always be needed, even when the approach to development is predominantly endogenous. The issue is not outside capital as such but what else is needed for a sustained development understood as a territorially based process supported by its citizenry in both political discourse and practice. It is here that we come to a crucial problem for endogenous development: Is such a development also capable of generating enterprise and innovation, or will it suffocate under the weight of inertia, local bureaucracy, and inward gaze? In the end, will not city-regions have to depend on outside technologies and the innovative drive that goes with them?

The centrality of innovation (at least in the technical/economic sense) is nothing new, of course, and can be traced to Joseph Schumpeter's work on business cycles (1939). His iconoclastic views on long-wave cycles and entrepreneurship have been resurrected in recent years, as has the earlier work of Alfred Marshall (1920) on innovation. More recent studies have also been of European origin, such as those of Philippe Aydalot and David Keeble (1988), Denis Maillat (1991) and Jean Claude Perrin (1993) on innovation milieux.[12] Maillat, for example, describes the concept of a local innovation milieu as follows:

> If we wish to shape a theory of local dynamism, we must specify the role of the milieu. It is the milieu, not the enterprise, on which the analysis must focus. From there we should determine the extent to which the milieu generates and maintains an innovation process.
>
> The milieu must be envisaged in such a manner that it has significant action on the manner of giving life to an innovation process. The milieu is not a warehouse from which one obtains supplies, it is a complex which is capable of initiating a synergetic process. From this point

of view the milieu cannot be defined merely as a geographical area, it must be envisaged as an organization, a complex system made up of economic and technological interdependencies. In our view, the concept of milieu refers to a coherent whole in which a territorial production system, a technical culture and protagonists are linked. The coherence between the different protagonists lies in a common mode of apprehending situations, problems and opportunities. The spirit of enterprise, organizational practices, corporate behavior patterns, ways of using technology, apprehending the market and know-how are both an integral and constituent part of the milieu. (1991, 113–14)

The literature on innovative milieus has been critically reviewed by Michael Storper, who calls the milieu a "context for development which empowers and guides innovative agents to be able to innovate and to coordinate with other innovative agents" (1997, 16–17). Suggestive as this concept is, Storper faults it for its failure to reveal "what it is about innovative regions that is essential to contemporary capitalist development" (17).

In his monumental work *Cities in Civilization,* Peter Hall provides capsule accounts of innovative milieus in six cities: Manchester, Glasgow, Berlin, Detroit, San Francisco/Palo Alto/Berkeley, and Tokyo/Kanagawa. The six studies cover different periods of time and yield a wealth of information. But in the end, these stories turn out to have more particularities than commonalities, thus confirming Storper's skepticism about innovative milieus as an explanatory heuristic (Hall 1998).

Still, it is hard to abandon the concept altogether, particularly in the context of endogenous development. I recall a conversation with the planning director of Chile's National Planning Office in the latter part of the 1960s, when he bemoaned the lack of entrepreneurship in his country. The state had tried to fill the enterprise gap during the years of World War II with a para-statal development corporation (CORFO). But as a powerful government agency, the corporation was not inclined to take large risks and generally erred on the side of safety. Companies in which it had a financial interest (most of them substituting for imports) were all more or less insured against failure. The privatization process ruthlessly initiated by the military dictatorship that followed the brief interlude of the Popular Front under Salvador Allende, seemed to open up opportunities for vigorous enterprise in ways that Chile had not known before. This is not to praise a military dictatorship nor the neo-liberal ideology it espoused. But the fact is that the country is today one of the most dynamic small economies in Latin America. Is there an "innovative milieu" in the Chilean capital, Santiago, with its six million people? I don't know. But I believe that an endogenous development—which is what Chile had until the 1980s—is not condemned to remain without entrepreneurial spirit forever.[13]

The development of quasi city-states must lead from internal local strength to global involvement. It must not shut itself off from the world but reach out, and one of the ways to reach out is to link up with other city-regions in the pursuit of common objectives. These linkages give rise to intercity networks suggestive of both collaboration and competition. It is the collaborative part that I would like to stress here, with particular reference to intercity networks.

Competition through collaboration: The formation of intercity networks. In the early 1990s, the European Commission reported the existence of thirty-seven collaborative intercity networks (Kunzmann 1995). One of the first of these and, in some ways, the most interesting, is Eurocities, which got its start in 1986 with an explicit political agenda: To press for a European-wide urban policy and thus for the formal recognition by Brussels of cities as significant centers of subnational governance. In addition, the founding cities hoped to increase the transfer of knowledge, experiences, and best practices among themselves and to facilitate the implementation of practical projects. Last but not least, the network would assist cities from outside the European Union (EU) to integrate themselves into it and support their "continuing progress towards democratic government and a market economy." Membership is open to democratically elected city governments, as well as to their "economic and scientific partners" (chambers of commerce and universities, for example) in cities having a regional importance, with a minimum population of 250,000 and "an international dimension." By mid-1997, Eurocities had grown to include sixty full-member cities, sixteen associate-member cities (from beyond the EU), and eleven economic and scientific partners (Eurocities 1995, 6).

The Eurocities publication, *A Charter of the European Cities,* reveals a good deal about this oldest of contemporary intercity networks. The charter was specifically addressed to the European Commission in an attempt to rewrite, or rather amend, the basic treaty of the union. Its preamble is a remarkable statement of a political tradition that reaches nearly a millennium into the past.

Cities are one of the characteristic features of European civilization. Their ancient history, their tradition of autonomy and pluralism and their ability to blend diverse cultures into a real local community have given rise to several developments of significance in the world: from the period of free communes and cities through the principle of self-government to the very idea of citizenship. The variety of political, cultural, and social experience of European cities has given them an exceptionally rich and diverse quality of life. (Eurocities 1995, 6)

Here, in a few sentences, we have a heroic appeal to history, municipal autonomy, cultural diversity, the communal tradition, democratic governance, and citizenship. A number of more substantive statements elaborate on this revealing declaration (summarized from Eurocities 1995, 6–9).

Cities are a basis of European integration. Cities root citizens in their institutions and traditions. They are also the first and essential political and institutional point of contact for those who choose to move, whether EU citizens or not, in a Europe where immigration and cultural and ethnic pluralism are increasingly widespread. Local authorities in cities can play a vital role in developing the dialogue between society and the system of democratic representation, in leading the fight against racism, xenophobia, and intolerance and ensuring that the benefits of city life are available to everyone.

The principle of local self-government. Despite having evolved far beyond its intergovernmental origins, the EU has not yet come to terms with its responsibilities as a truly supranational organization, necessitating intense cooperation with local and regional authorities as well as with member states. To do this, regional and local authorities must be recognized as essential levels of government, and the principle of local self-government must be considered as a basic right.

The principle of subsidiarity, or proximity. The Treaty of Maastricht was the first to clearly state the principle of subsidiarity and to address the institutional dimension of intrastate powers. Perhaps better described as the principle of proximity, it states that decisions should be taken at higher levels of government only when there are manifest reasons for doing so. Until now, this principle has still not been recognized as applying below the level of member states, however. Eurocities' aim is not the suppression or reduction of policies at European or national levels, but their coordination with those of local government and the activities of civil society.

Cities are partners in European policies. European cities wish to become partners with the national governments and community institutions in defining and implementing regional and urban policies. Cities have a vital interest in seeing concrete policies put in place on a number of issues, including (a) the development of trans-European networks linking cities to each other; (b) the combination of the development of these networks with the demand to spread the benefit of economic growth and maintain the environmental balance necessary to ensure their sustainability; and (c) the inclusion of the long-term aims of social cohesion and employment creation in all relevant EU policies.

European citizenship. Cities have an important role to play in the realization of European citizenship, specifically in developing local democracy, in guaranteeing the balance between the rights and responsibilities of all those who live in their communities, in promoting the equality of the sexes, and in enabling the active participation of citizens in the processes of government.

The challenge of social exclusion. The treaty must reflect the major preoccupation of urban governments with the problems of unemployment, poverty, and social exclusion. Cities want to see a greater emphasis on the union's duty to promote social cohesion and a more active commitment to combating disparities *within* communities as well as *among* regions and, above all, to ensure equal opportunities for all the citizens of Europe.

These six points constitute a powerful *political* agenda; they also assert the vital importance of the metropolis as an organized community and critical agent in European development, mediating between the suprastate of the EU and local citizens. Remarkably, the charter also encapsulates an ideology to which the nearly eighty European cities of this network have subscribed, a statement of what unites them beyond their frequently divisive economic interests.

I have discussed the Eurocities network at some length, because it demonstrates how an endogenous form of development under today's circumstances needn't lead to isolation and stagnation. On the contrary, intercity networking and an endogenous development go hand in hand, stimulating enterprise and innovations for all participants.[14]

Concluding Remarks

It is time now to return to the two models with which I began. Models don't purport to describe reality; they are "ideal types" useful for talking about the issues which they raise. Model 1 places the onus of development on external capital. The city here plays the passive role of a courtesan hoping to seduce outside investors who will shower material blessings on her. In this model the city has cut itself off from the surrounding region and is looking elsewhere. Its governing elites have only a rudimentary notion of urban development: capturing global capital, investing in speculative real estate and economic infrastructure, improving the city's international image and credit rating. Their time frame is generally the next few years. Enticements to outside capital must be paid for. With a tight budget as a base, chances are the city will go further into debt to please outside investors, neglect its social facilities, and underinvest in its future. And then there is always that nagging fear that in the competition for capital, your city remains vulnerable and may lose its clients to more attractive, more seductive sites. This is not the road to a sustainable development.

The focus of Model 2 is a central city politically articulated with its contiguous region. In contrast to the city-marketing model, its leadership is guided by a long-term strategic vision that enjoys strong popular support. Central to this model is an inclusive, working democracy. Power is decentralized, but there are mechanisms for strong decision-making at the center. The local state in this model is a proactive state that pays attention to the need to preserve and improve the quality of the region's wealth-creating resource complexes, while striving to encourage innovative thinking and practice without presuming to act as its own entrepreneur in every case. A city-region organized along these lines is not anxiety-ridden about its future. In its dealings with the outside world, it leads from strength. Quasi city-states can reach out to their similars, forming collaborative networks where the good of any particular region does not necessarily come at the expense of any other but increases the opportunities for all regions. In Europe, this outward-looking thinking has given rise to collaborative intercity networks extending from the Hanseatic League in the Middle Ages to the contemporary Eurocities. The first led to an immense flowering of cities in northern Europe; the second can achieve a similar cultural surge in the twenty-first century. This experience, I believe, holds important lessons for city-regions around the world.

3
Transnational Migration: Spaces of Incorporation

Of Freedmen and Metics

At varying times in the period of pre-Roman classical Greece, the city-state of Athens accommodated large numbers of resident noncitizens. Moses Finley estimates their numbers as a ratio to citizen males at between 1:6 and 1:2.5, which is to say, from 15 to 40 percent of all male residents of the city, excluding slaves, were either freedmen or metics (Finley 1973, 48). Only Athenian citizens were permitted to own land, and citizens were expected to participate in the public life of the *polis*. Noncitizens, most of whom were foreign born, engaged in trade, manufacture, and money lending, activities that were considered to be beneath the dignity of citizens. As Finley writes, "The citizen-élite were not prepared, in sufficient numbers, to carry those branches of the economy without which neither they nor their communities could live at the level to which they were accustomed" (60). Freedmen—manumitted slaves—and especially metics were thus essential to the well-being of the city, and so, of course, were the slaves. Athens was far from being a self-sufficient economy. Most important, two-thirds of its grain as well as the better sorts of wine had to be imported, the grain chiefly from the Crimea. Writing in the middle of the fourth century B.C.E., Xenophon even proposed a scheme for increasing the number of metics. He suggested that metics be released from the burdensome obligation of service in the infantry; admitted to the cavalry, which was now a merely honorific service; permitted, in the case of particular worthies, to buy building lots in the city on which to construct houses for themselves; and be given reserved seats in the theater. In addition, he thought that more lodging houses and hostelries should be built for them in the Piraeus, where most of them lived; that market officials should be offered prizes for the just and speedy resolution of disputes; and finally, and somewhat tentatively, that perhaps the state should build its own merchant fleet. Metics, he said, are one of the best sources of "public revenues," and so it was in the polis's best interest to attract them (in Finley 1973, 163).

I cite this example from antiquity because so many of its themes are familiar to us from our own experience, even down to the proportions in the population of freedmen and metics—our foreign-born—in some of the principal cities of the global economy. According to the *Far Eastern Economic Review*, Singapore's resident foreigners are estimated at 700,000 and account for more than one in five workers in this city-state (March 18, 1999, 54). Frankfurt's noncitizens now account for around 30 percent of total population, and for Los Angeles County a decade ago the corresponding figure for foreign-born residents was 33 percent; it is undoubtedly higher now. Other similarities are equally striking, such as the reliance on foreign labor for work considered "dangerous, difficult, and dirty" and thus "beneath the dignity" of native-born citizens. Or the worry, at certain times and places, on how to accomplish the city's work without foreign workers in the face of a rapidly aging and possibly even declining population (e.g., Japan). Assisted immigration schemes, not unlike Xenophon's proposal, were in full swing in the post–World War II era of Australia (Castles and Miller 1998, chapter 8). The denial of full citizen rights to even long-term foreign residents is alive and well in contemporary Switzerland (Castles and Miller 1998, exhibit 9.6 on page 234). The attempt to restrict the foreign-born to certain ethnic districts, such as the Piraeus, is a practice only too familiar to us, and not only in the United States (Marcuse 1989). And the moral contempt with which so many foreign migrants are still regarded reproduces Plato and other Greek and Roman literatis' condemnatory views of freedmen and metics for their "vices and evil ways" (Finley 1973, 60).

In this chapter, I focus on some aspects of transnational urbanism. This perspective has so far received little scholarly attention. Michael Peter Smith refers to it as "a new optic for guiding urban research" and argues that four contemporary processes contribute to the formation of transnational networks of social action: the discursive repositioning of cities in relation to nation-states in an era of globalization; the emergence of cross-national political and institutional networks; the facilitation by technology of transnational social ties; and the spatial reconfiguration of social networks that further the reproduction of migration, business practices, cultural beliefs, and political agency "from below" (Smith 2001, chapter 3). Within this broad framework, I selectively focus on two subjects: the formation of transnational communities and spaces, with examples drawn from the U.S.-Mexican borderlands, the Turkish and Kurdish diasporas in Germany, and the world of Chinese professional migrants on two continents; and the incorporation of transnational migrants into cities and the resulting conflicts.

Transnational Migrants, Cities, and Spaces

Migration across national frontiers is normally studied from a perspective of national policy (see, for example, Castles and Miller 1998, among countless others). As Saskia Sassen points out, nation-states, jealous of their sovereignty, focus on borders and individuals as principal sites of control (Sassen 1998, chapter 2). Yet most migrants, insofar as they are not streams of refugees driven from or fleeing their homelands (the latest victims being Kosovite Albanians and East Timorese) end up in a relatively small number of cities that occupy strategic positions in the global system. German residents without a German passport, as they are sometimes referred to, constitute 8.8 percent of the country's population but make up 30 percent of Frankfurt's. In the United States, two-thirds of the 20 million foreign-born residents in the early 1990s were concentrated in only five states and, within these states, predominantly in the major "world cities" of Los Angeles, New York, Miami, Chicago, and Houston (Friedmann and Lehrer 1997). The same is true of Asian city-regions. Greater Tokyo's share of total registered foreign population in Japan was 39 percent in 1997 (Machimura 2000). According to the *Far Eastern Economic Review,* in Singapore, more than one in five workers is a resident foreigner (March 18, 1999, 54).

Transnational migration is thus a preeminently urban phenomenon that poses multiple problems for city governments, from housing and land use to the management of interethnic relations. Cities that harbor a large number of foreign residents—legal and illegal, short term and long term, heavily endowed with "human capital" as well as "simple labor"— I refer to as *transnational* cities. These cities occupy strategic nodes in an interregional, global network defined, in the first instance, by economic relations. Via transnational migrants, however, they are also tied to thousands of communities of migrant origin, some little more than villages, others of a distinctly urban character. These ties are primarily social in nature (in a way that global money markets are not), though they are involved in economic transactions, such as remittances, which play a critical role in the foreign exchange balance of many receiving countries.

This dual characteristic of migrants—an uncertain home in the host city and multistranded ties to their communities of origin—has given rise to the concept of a *diaspora*. Originally used to describe the situation of Zionist Jews in their millennial hope to reestablish themselves on the soil of their distant ancestors in Palestine, its meaning has been extended to embrace other migrant groups, such as overseas Chinese, who maintain social, cultural, economic, political, and emotional ties of varying intensity with their ethnic homelands. Diasporic communities create a *transnational social space* that links places of residence with networks of families, friends, and associates in the localities where they originated, sometimes several generations earlier. Transnational migrants are thus "at home" in two or more places simultaneously; some may even hold dual citizenship. Yet, it is also true that they may be securely at home neither in the city where they live nor in the imagined community of their homeland. This feeling of being adrift, of not truly belonging anywhere, is not an unusual experience among transnational migrants and may explain their strong attachment to ethnic neighborhoods in transnational cities, where Koreans live with Koreans, Turks with Turks, and so forth, in an attempt to drown out their sense of being lost in a world that has become estranged from them (Nair 1999).

In this chapter, I examine three very different examples of diasporic urban communities. They illustrate a number of issues that typically arise in a context of transnational migration without claiming to cover the full range of related phenomena that still need to be carefully identified and studied (for further examples, see Smith and Guarnizo 1998). My first story is drawn from the U.S.-Mexican borderlands and concerns the forging of a common socioeconomic space through the migrant circuit between Monterrey and Houston. The second story is about the Turkish and Kurdish diaspora in Germany and concentrates on the quasi-political organizations among them that link them directly with the politics in their country of origin. The third story concerns professional Chinese migrants whose frequent moves from country to country have earned them the epithet "trapeze artists." Men and women on the go, their business or profession requires them to be specialists in mobility. These stories, it seems to me, raise important questions about the shifting meanings of place, identity, citizenship, and loyalty.

Transnational Communities: The Migrant Circuit Monterrey-Houston

This is the story of Don Joel, who one day in 1979 decided to leave his native Monterrey, metropolitan capital of Nueva León, and cross the border, five hundred miles to the north, to Houston, Texas.[1] It is also the story of a transnational community held together by powerful social ties on both sides of the border. Upon arriving in Houston, Joel worked initially as a lathe operator in a small machine shop with ties to the local oil industry. His father and two of his eight brothers had preceded him there and helped him get his first job. Before long, Joel met the woman he would marry. Doña Rosa was an American citizen, which allowed Joel to apply for a resident green card. In due course, he received a card. In 1982, only three years after arriving in Houston, Joel and Rosa started a small business, one of many such businesses in the area that transport money, letters, goods, and people between the two cities. Fifteen years later, their business was still thriving.

By 1997, they owned two vans that made the Houston-Monterrey run twice weekly. Initially, their place of business was outdoors at one of the parks in a Mexican neighborhood of newcomer migrants to Houston, but after several years, Joel and Rosa were able to afford a small space in a Mexican restaurant, renting for $350 a month. Only two employees are not members of the family—they load up the vans and alternate with Joel as drivers. At the other end of their transport business, in Monterrey, Joel installed himself in a house he bought for his father. His local staff there includes two brothers-in-law, a sister, and a nephew whose task is to distribute the money, letters, and packages to the homes of recipients throughout the metropolitan area. For these deliveries, they use two older vehicles. The bulk of their work, however, is concentrated in only two of Monterrey's eight barrios with which they are intimately acquainted and where, in turn, they are well known.

Every Friday night and Monday afternoon, a van departs Houston for its long journey south. Actual driving time is ten hours, but the vehicle may be held up at the border for an additional two or three hours. On a typical Friday evening, men will gather at Don Joel and Doña Rosa's transport enterprise to leave their money and other goods for delivery in Monterrey the next day. Friday is payday for many of these men, and part of what they have earned during the week is regularly dispatched to their families. Money is handled exclusively by Joel and Rosa. The precise amount is entered into a registry, and the money is placed into an envelope with the address of the intended recipient. Receipts are not handed out; the entire operation is based on personal trust. Even so, the amounts are substantial. According to Joel, the average remittance (in cash!) is $200, but actual amounts vary from $70 to $400. (Fees are charged according to the amount of money being sent, beginning with $10 for up to $300.) Thus, over a typical week, Joel's vans will transport roughly $40,000, rising up to $60,000 during certain times of the year, such as Easter or Christmas. These figures suggest that as much as $2 million may be transmitted by only this small family business, and there are many others competing in the same line of work throughout the Houston area. In addition to cash, Monterrey migrants also send goods such as clothing and shoes, iceboxes filled with chicken, milk, and orange juice, satchels of corn tortillas, television sets, toys and bicycles, armchairs, candles and lamps, air conditioners, and tools for car repair, which are faithfully dispatched to Monterrey. Some of these items, originally acquired in flea markets and used clothing stores, are undoubtedly resold at a profit in Mexico.

Monterrey recipients are mostly young mothers with small children and infants as well as aging parents and grandparents. For them these weekly or biweekly parcels and letters from husbands, fathers, and brothers confirm emotional ties that help to weld these social networks into a living reality. Occasionally, over long weekends and holidays, some of the men will make the trip south in one of Don Joel's vans to visit with family. Or they will call long distance. At other times, there is a return flow of goods traveling north, mostly food packages containing local delicacies, and even medicines, which in Mexico are easier to obtain without a prescription.

The many-stranded ties that bind the Mexican migrant families of Monterrey and Houston into a transnational community are not a passing phenomenon. Boys grow up in Monterrey dreaming of one day working in Houston like their fathers or older brothers. Going north is for them a rite of passage. Some, like Don Joel, will eventually marry there and have children of their own, even as their extended family continues to live in Mexico. Others will shuttle back and forth between the two cities before deciding where they will settle. Some of them may hope to operate a transnational enterprise akin to Joel's and Rosa's, a business that operates with a minimum of overhead and a maximum of social capital, or trust. Over time, they will become bilingual, speaking a Spanish peppered with American expressions and English with a strong Mexican accent. Some will eventually acquire American citizenship, even as they continue to hold a Mexican passport. Others, born in the United States, will make frequent trips to visit their grandparents on the other side of the border. In this fashion, the Monterrey-Houston migrant circuit is evolving as a transnational life space in which foods, language, traditions, and popular customs acquire hybridity. The local expression for this is "Tex-Mex" and is a proud subculture of its own.

Diasporic Politics: Quasi-Political Organizations of Turkish Migrants in Germany

A very different story of transnational community is that of quasi-political organizations in the Turkish diaspora in Germany. The so-called Turkish diaspora is not uniformly Turkish, however, and a distinction must be drawn between ethnic Turks and Kurds. The latter, although citizens of Turkey, are not ethnically Turkish and claim a separate ethnonational identity. Of the 1.8 million Turkish citizens in Germany, fully one quarter are ethnic Kurds. Their largest organization is the Association of Kurdish Workers for Kurdistan. A more militant organization is Birkan, a close supporter of Abdullah Öcalan, the former leader of the secessionist Kurdish Workers Party (PKK) currently on trial in Turkey.[2]

Political and religious factions are common among diaspora Turks. Many older residents who have lived in Germany for a long time struggle for their political rights and dual citizenship. But in the language of Nermin Abadan-Unat, the majority of Turkish associations represent "nationalist, cultural enclaves with a minimal interest in German society" (1997, 243).

A quick look at some of the major Turkish associations in Germany provides an insight into diaspora politics, which, in this case, reflect the close connection that exists in Islam between religion, politics, and the conduct of everyday life (Jonker 1997).[3] In 1997, 1,341 such associations were reported, nearly all of them highly politicized. Although some funds for social integration are provided by the federal government, they can only be accessed locally. Collective initiatives on the part of umbrella organizations depend to a large extent on individual contributions and the financial support of Islamic countries, not least from Turkey itself. By the mid-1990s, major umbrella organizations included the following:

- *Extreme right-wing nationalist (secular) organizations.* Although establishing branches of foreign political parties is prohibited in the Federal Republic, the ban was overcome by the establishment of associations such as the Greater Ideal Association, the Turkish Community, and various Turkish student and youth organizations. All of these eventually united under a single umbrella, the Federation of Turkish Idealist Associations in Europe (ATÜDF). Centered in Frankfurt, ATÜDF boasts 170 local member associations throughout Germany. According to Abadan-Unat, the federation cooperates closely with the renamed party of Alparslan Türkes, the National Action Party. The ideology of this federation is based on an extreme form of nationalism, which rejects social integration with Germans to prevent ethnic Turks from becoming a "secondary race" (Abadan-Unat 1997, 243).

- *Religious and religious-political organizations.* Up until the early 1980s, Islamic Cultural Centers (IKMB) represented the largest religious movement in Germany. Backed by followers of the Süleymanli sect of Turkish Islam, which fought against Atatürk's secular reforms fifty years earlier, this umbrella organization has its center in Cologne from where it controls over three hundred mosques and local associations throughout the Federal Republic. Its most important characteristic is its negative attitude toward cultural integration. School subjects such as music, arts, and sports are declared "un-Islamic," and members are prohibited from engaging in social contacts with "infidel" Germans.

  The most powerful Turkish religious organization is the National Vision Organization of Europe (AMGT). Established in 1976 as a branch of the National Salvation Party, later renamed the Welfare Party, this organization is also headquartered in Cologne and claims 110,000 members and sympathizers in Germany alone. In general, its political agenda is to fight secularization. Attempts at sociocultural integration in Germany are defined in the hyperbole of political discourse as treason toward Islam. The Welfare Party's leading news outlet, *Millî Gazete,* is published in Germany as well as Turkey.

- *Small separatist organizations.* The Union of Islamic Associations and Communities (ICCB) was established in 1984 by Cemalattin Kaplan, it represents a dissenting wing of the National Visions Association. After losing his nationality in Turkey for dissident activities, Kaplan settled in Cologne and started to build his own organization. He advocates an Islamic Turkish Republic on the model of Iran, and pleads for the reintroduction of the *sharia* (Islamic law) and the replacement of the Turkish script by the Arabic alphabet. The organization is largely self-supporting.

  Another dissenting faction is the Union of Turkish-Islamic Cultural Associations (TIKDB). This association split off from the secular, rightist-nationalist ATÜDF and focuses on the preservation of the national and cultural values of the Islamic faith. Politically, it supports the right-of-center Motherland Party in Turkey, which became the ruling parliamentary party in 1997.

- *The official, government-supported organization.* The Turkish Islamic Union for Religious Affairs (DITIB) was created to counterbalance the spread of "fundamentalist" Islam in Germany. Linked to the Turkish Ministry of the Interior, the union embraces 700 local chapters with a claimed membership of about 90,000. It also enjoys the support of 215 Turkish civil servants who are on detail to Germany, and all of whom are graduates of divinity schools and thus familiar with Islamic theology.

Nearly two million Turks and Turkish Kurds are living in Germany but are not *of* Germany. Very few so far have opted for German citizenship. Yet, their numbers continue to increase through births, family reunification, asylum applications, and illegal migration. Emotionally, they are oriented toward their homeland. Clustered in Turkish urban neighborhoods where they have evolved a separate religious, cultural, and commercial life, they are living a self-imposed "island-like" lifestyle (Abadan-Unat 1997, 247). Homeland politics has migrated along with them, and different ideological currents are now struggling for the minds and souls of the Turkish and Kurdish diasporas. In Germany, *homeland politics has become a transnational politics.*

This is not to say that, particularly among the third generation, many Turks as well as Kurds wouldn't prefer to live a peaceful, secular life in a multicultural Germany. Indeed, according to Tietze (1997), if one converses with young men rather than only reading the pronouncements of umbrella organizations, a great variety of views on the question of integration is revealed. But the pull of family, religion, ethnicity, and community is a powerful one, and many young Turks are drawn by their idealism toward the idea of a reborn Islam that, they hope, will be given political form in an idealized homeland that many of them have perhaps never even visited.[4]

Trapeze Artists: Chinese Professionals and Businessmen on Two Continents

Over a decade ago, Taipei wits coined a new term to describe the transnational existence of some Chinese, primarily from a professional and business background. *Kuangzhong feiren* (trapeze artists) are residents with established homes in more than one country, often with dual citizenship and carrying multiple passports. These *kuangzhong feiren* tend to have extended families and networks of friends and associates on both sides of the Pacific (Hsing 1997; Wang 1998; Cheng and Hsia 1999; Ong 1999; Tseng 2000). Professionals and businesspeople of whatever nationality are a famously privileged and mobile group who often know their way around national regulations that govern the entry of less fortunate migrants. In many countries, citizenship is up for sale. In the decade leading up to reunification with China, for example, many wealthy Hong Kong residents succeeded in establishing themselves in Australia, New Zealand, and Canada, even as part of their families continued to live and work in the colony, now the Special Administrative Region (SAR) of the People's Republic. More recently, a similar exodus of ethnic Chinese has occurred from Indonesia, from where they have fanned out to Singapore, Australia, and North America.

The Far Eastern Economic Review reports an instance in the formation of these trapeze artists. After the Tiananmen incident in 1989, the U.S. government granted the more than 50,000 Chinese students in the United States the right to remain in the country. Of this group, many went on to obtain advanced degrees in computer science and electrical engineering. Today, the story continues, "they form the nucleus of a talented new generation of information-technology entrepreneurs that is forging commercial links with China." Chen Hong is one of them. A 1982 graduate of Hian Jiao-tong University, Chen remained in the United States in the post-Tiananmen amnesty, and obtained his doctorate in computer science from the State University of New York in 1991. Today he is chairman and chief executive of GRIC Communications, which links Internet service providers across countries. According to Chen, many of his friends are returning to China. "They have become very successful because of their connections in the U.S.," he says. "You are going to see a lot of people like us being hired back to head information-technology companies in China in the future" (March 11, 1999, 50–52).

Trapeze artists shuttling back and forth between Taipei, San Francisco, the Silicon Valley, and Chinese coastal cities are now helping China's drive to become a major economic power in East Asia. Citizenship has for them primarily a utilitarian character. As the network of *guanxi* relations of trust and reciprocity spreads ever more densely across the Pacific, it comes down to little more than a North American passport or resident card.[5]

What do these stories tell us? First of all, they are urban stories. And if I am right in saying that, in the coming decades, some fifty or sixty cities worldwide will come to play major roles in spatially articulating the global economy, it is many of these same cities that will also be transnationalized in the sense of having, say, from 20 to 40 percent of their population living in diasporic communities at the very heart of the global system. A relatively small but growing proportion of this population will be trapeze artists who move among these cities outside the official categories of migration. Professionals and business managers, they constitute a new transnational class that is always welcome, because their services are essential to the conduct of global business (Sassen 1998, 15–16; Ong 1998). Members of this class tend to be people without strong attachments to place. They are "at home" in international airports and hotels, the "non-places" so well described in Marc Augé's provocative essay of some years ago (1995). Permanent expatriates, their families are scattered globally. Tseng Yen-Fen concludes his trenchant essay on Taiwanese capital-linked migration with these words:

> By studying the migration of Taiwanese entrepreneurs along with their overseas investment, we are able to see how people are living and thinking transnationally. As members of the transnational diaspora they live daily lives depending on multiple and constant interconnections across national borders, their public identities are often configured to more than one nation state. . . . Some assume a more cosmopolitan identity, disconnected from any particular state, that makes them think of themselves as global citizens. To this group of people, nationality is a utilitarian matter

signaling little emotional attachment. Others might prefer a transnational identity that is based on constant interconnections between host country and homeland. It would be interesting to learn in what micro-level fields various types of identities are created, maintained, and even disrupted. (2000, 162)

Transnational migrants with more modest educational and/or financial endowments tend to be considerably more grounded than this class of high flyers. They are represented by my stories from the U.S.-Mexican borderlands and the Turkish and Kurdish diasporas in Germany. The Monterrey-Houston axis is one of many such linkages in the borderlands gradually evolving into a new Mexican-American (hybrid) subculture. The tale of Don Joel's small transport business, a key link in the bipolar transnational locality of Houston-Monterrey, tells us that those who leave their villages, towns, and cities for the strategic nodes of the global economy do not necessarily leave family, friends, and social networks behind but, undeterred by the fortified national border, maintain enduring social ties with them. For official purposes, they may be treated as "immigrant" residents in Houston, but in fact they continue to live "transnationally." Ask them where they are from, and they will probably give you contradictory answers, depending on where and by whom they are being interrogated. *Modern urban nomads, their true home is the circular journey between.* A large proportion of Houston's population continues to be attached to Monterrey, even as many families in the second city have loved ones in the first. Over time, the circuit becomes routinized, and the question of where one belongs has no final resolution.

My second story must be read somewhat differently. Turkish and Kurdish minorities are doubly marginalized in Germany. Not being of German "blood," they will always be seen as aliens regardless of their formal citizenship status. And as Muslims, they have inherited a thousand-year history of conflict with the Christian West. It is no accident that Turkish membership in the European Union, though long desired by Turks, has been tenaciously resisted by Europeans. Turks and Turkish Kurds continue to be treated as outsiders in Germany. Under these circumstances, it is not surprising to find diasporas that are self-organized through quasi-political associations that, in many cases, are based on local mosques and have intensely nationalistic aspirations. *Marginalization on the German side is thus reciprocated by the self-exclusion on part of the marginalized.* And so it happens that Turkish politics are played out not only in Turkey but increasingly on German soil as well, where the issues are, respectively, independence for the Kurds in a state of their own and the transformation of the secular Turkish state into one modeled on a reading of the Qur'an and Islamic traditions. The dangers posed for the Turkish state by these politicized diasporas have led the government to organize its own umbrella association under the tutelage of several hundred officials skilled in the rhetoric of Islamic theology. Turkish and Kurdish communities in German cities are thus ensconced in ethnic enclaves where Islamic clergy command considerable influence over the mental world and conduct of their coreligionists and where the national politics of Turkey is never far away.

Incorporating Migrants into Transnational Cities

I turn now to my second major but closely related topic, the incorporation of transnational migrants into receiving cities. This is a greatly understudied and poorly understood subject. Migration studies typically work within a national policy framework, where the strategic sites of control are the border and the individual (Sassen 1998). But once transnational migrants have succeeded in entering national space, the problem of how to respond to their presence devolves to the receiving cities. Incorporating transnational migrants confronts city officials with a host of issues that have to do with communication and language, employment, social services, housing and urban design, land-use planning, education, health, the justice system, political representation, and last but not least, interethnic relations. Only a handful of studies have so far addressed these issues (Chua 1991; Watson and McGillivray 1995; Friedmann and Lehrer 1997; Lehrer and Friedmann 1997; Sandercock and Kliger 1998). And yet they are issues that must be confronted, as local governments respond to a wide range of demands, deciding on policy as they go along.

I would like to illustrate this with a story about the city government of Kawasaki, a small municipality in the Tokyo metropolitan area. The study from which I have drawn this story begins with the following quote from a senior city official:

> Since about 1988 or 1989, lots of foreign workers have come to Kawasaki. At that point, the city decided that foreigners living in Kawasaki are local citizens, and that consequently, the same as Japanese local

citizens, we had to ensure their access to city services. (Tegtmeyer Pak 2000, 244)

In the context of official Japanese policy, which, according to Katherine Tegtmeyer Pak is to "control 'foreigners' as a category of persons understood as potential threats to the integrity of the nation" (255), this statement must appear, at least to Tokyo bureaucrats, as verging on the subversive. But, in fact, it is largely a pragmatic response on the part of a local government to the rapid influx of transnational migrants. Between 1985 and 1996, registered foreign residents in Kawasaki nearly doubled, rising from 10,841 to 19,496. The inclusion of undocumented migrants might well have doubled and tripled these numbers, but those who work illegally in Kawasaki are not objects of official attention by city hall.

In response to pressure from the city's long-established Korean community and the municipal administration's awareness that something needed to be done to maintain harmony between immigrants and local neighborhoods, an International Office was set up in Kawasaki to coordinate service delivery to transnational migrants. Here is how one government document described the new level of consciousness:

> As the number of resident foreigners has rapidly increased in the last few years, differences in customs and culture, and misunderstandings based on language have brought many puzzles and issues of mutual misunderstanding to the attention of local government and the community. . . . In doing our best to ensure that local citizens accept foreigners as members of the community without delay, we have set up Japanese language classes and clubs for foreigners who use the City's International Exchange Center and neighborhood community centers in order to improve communications between foreigners and local citizens. (Tegtmeyer Pak 2000, 251)

In the four cities of her study (of which Kawasaki is one), writes Tegtmeyer Pak,

> most city governments provide maps, information about local government offices, community newsletters, and guides to daily life in Japan in a range of foreign languages. Japanese language instruction opportunities are also increasingly available through local government for minimal fees. . . . In some cases, the classes are offered through the city's quasi-public International Exchange Association, other classes are available at

local city-run community centers . . . in either case, they are likely to be taught by volunteers who receive some training by the city. . . . Another increasingly popular way to overcome the language barrier is to offer consultation services to foreign residents. . . . In those cities which have seen rising numbers of foreign children enrolling in local schools, more extensive programs of supplementary classes and tutoring in Japanese language are being implemented. . . . Kawasaki has gone so far as to establish a Foreigners' Advisory Council, which enables representatives from the foreign population to participate in a regular ongoing forum, ensuring communication with local bureaucrats and politicians. Other examples of this perspective are the support of hundreds of local governments for efforts to grant the vote at the local level to long-term foreign residents, and the decisions by many local governments to abolish the nationality requirements (propagated by the national government) for most local administrative positions. (252)

What is clear from this account is that even in Japanese cities, where the presence of foreign residents is still at an early stage on the long road to becoming truly transnational cities, the beginnings of a movement at the level of local government to provide essential services to transnational migrants are already becoming visible. Except for the activities of a handful of nongovernmental organizations, civil society in Japan is not yet greatly aroused by the issue of migrant workers from abroad. Nor has there been a pronounced political backlash to the foreign presence despite a recent upsurge in national feeling. What does emerge from this and other accounts is that the complex processes of incorporating transnational migrants must be resolved primarily in the spaces of everyday life.

If we penetrate into these spaces, however, the policy models that are so contentiously debated around the world don't quite seem to fit. Stephen Castles and Mark Miller, for example, divide countries into three broad categories, based on three generalized models for the incorporation of migrants (1998, 244–50).

- *The differential exclusionary model* is found in countries in which the dominant definition of the nation is that of a community of birth and descent (examples: Germany, Austria, Japan, Gulf Oil States).

- *The assimilationist model* proposes that migrants will be absorbed into the society through a one-sided process of adaptation: immigrants are expected to give up their distinctive linguistic, cultural, and social characteristics and become indistinguishable from the majority population (examples: France, Britain, the Netherlands, the United States, Australia up until about 1970). This model, currently embattled, is sometimes replaced with a softer version of *integration*. But the final goal of integration is still the incorporation of migrants into the dominant culture.

- *The multicultural or pluralist model* implies that migrants should be granted equal rights in all spheres of society, without being expected to give up their diversity, though usually with an expectation of some conformity with key social values (examples: Canada, Sweden, Chile, and Australia from 1970 onward).

The authors present these models as ideal types, pointing out that actual policies are invariably subject to the vagaries of politics and swings in public mood. The present conservative coalition government in Australia, for example, which came to power in 1996, has been at pains to avoid using the language of "multiculturalism" partly fear of a political backlash to increasing migration from Asian countries. Although a number of multicultural programs that were begun under the previous Labor regime are still in place, their future remains uncertain. The debate about multiculturalism also continues to rage inside and outside the American academy. Although the presence of distinctive ethnic communities in U.S. cities is generally accepted, the role of the state is not seen as ensuring social justice for immigrants or providing for the maintenance of ethnic cultures. At the other extreme of the spectrum, in Japan, a major rethinking is currently underway about the presumed ethnic homogeneity of the Japanese people. The outcome of this rethinking process may have major implications for shifting Japanese policies away from the differential exclusionary model (Fukuoka 1998; Douglass and Roberts 2000).

Yet, for all the heat they engender, the models proposed by Castles and Miller are not especially helpful for coming to grips with the three instances of transnational migration I have described—the migrant circuit between Monterrey and Houston, the ethnopolitics of Turks and Kurds in Germany, and the world of Chinese business and professional elites and the incorporation problems they pose. We saw migrants from Turkey who, in response to their marginalization within German society, but for their own reasons as well, are opting for self-exclusion, even as their numbers continue to increase. In the case of the transnational communities along the Mexican-U.S. border, cultural "hybridity" rather than assimilation is the long-term outcome of transnational relations. And Chinese trapeze artists, building a brave new cyberworld across the Pacific, are in many cases living in a nonplace world that seems to lie outside any policy model altogether. The phenomenon of transnational migration has thus become a good deal more complicated than was once the case.

Living with Difference: The Difficult Role of Habitus

Transnational migrants are often perceived as strangers whose very presence poses a threat to the way of life and sense of self/identity of the host society. This is an inevitable source of conflict, usually local but readily blown up to national and even international proportions by the media. It is also one of the major difficulties facing planners and activists who, on a daily basis, must confront and deal with the many interrelated issues of the successful incorporation of migrants into the local society. Pierre Bourdieu's seminal concept of a field-specific *habitus* may help us to understand one of the root causes of this difficulty and so perhaps also to learn how better to manage it.[6]

The habitus of concrete practices requires a "social field" that has both structured these practices and has, in turn, been structured by them. According to Bourdieu, societies are composed of a large number of relatively autonomous, linked, and overlapping social fields. Some of them, such as a specific social class or, for that matter, the Algerian Kabyles—a village people of ancient lineage—are vast and encompassing, while others are more narrowly, though still quite broadly, defined. Examples would be the contemporary "worlds" of the university, artistic production, science, and medicine. According to Bourdieu, each field is structured by relations of power among the individuals and institutions that occupy the strategic positions that exert control over the field as a whole. The object of these power holders is to keep the "game" going. The game itself is a form of agonistic competition among the players in the field for the accumulation of "symbolic capital," another key concept in Bourdieu's lexicon. It is this constant striving for influence and power that is the real stake of the game. Specific rules must therefore be enforced to prevent the game from deteriorating into chaos.

Corresponding to each social field is a characteristic habitus that gives each of the players a "pre-reflective, infra-conscious mastery" of the field (Bourdieu and Wacquant 1992, 19). Bourdieu defines *habitus* as the "durable, transposable, structured (and structuring) dispositions of individuals" (Bourdieu 1990 [1980], 53). Specific to given fields, the habitus must be learned. It manifests itself as a pattern of practices so tuned to the rules of the game that to be in the field and taking part in the game is to feel comfortable and "at home" (Bourdieu and Wacquant 1992, 128). It is what one does. By the same token, practices tolerated and even appreciated in one field, say in a Melbourne workingman's pub, would be shockingly out of place in an upscale restaurant only a few paces away, where the same practices would make everyone, not least the intruders, feel ill at ease.

The term *dispositions* is critical to the definition of *habitus*. We could say that the habitus serves as a kind of template that generates strong, normative *probabilities* of actual practices that are considered normal, acceptable conduct within a given field. According to Bourdieu, the habitus serves as a "generative principle" that makes possible, but also sets limits to, the "free production of all the thoughts, perceptions, and actions inherent in the particular conditions of its production" (Bourdieu 1990 [1980], 55). Thus the blanket term *practices* covers forms of behavior, speech, bearing, posture, manners, eating conventions, aesthetic preferences, as well as ways of seeing and interpreting the world. Always gender-specific and sometimes age-specific as well, the habitus is acquired in early childhood and continues to evolve on the basis of new experiences throughout one's lifetime. Though inscribed in the individual human body, it is a collective phenomenon in the sense that a certain habitus must be shared by all the players in a specific game. The tendency is therefore for the collective habitus to be preserved over relatively long periods of time. But because the field is subject to multiple influences, both within and outside itself, it will inevitably undergo a slow process of change, so that what used to be acceptable practices within a given field, say three or four decades ago, are no longer acceptable conduct now.

Consider now the case of Kabyle village society in its transition to a transnational migrant society. Bourdieu undertook extensive anthropological studies of Kabyle society during the latter half of the 1960s, a work that resulted in his first major book, published in French in 1972 and, five years later in an English translation, *Outline of a Theory of Prac-*

tice (Bourdieu 1977). The Kabyles are an ancient, predominantly agricultural, tribal people of North Africa, whose center is the rugged Kabylia region of Algeria. Forming one of the larger divisions of the Berbers, they are known for their fierce resistance to the successive conquerors of the region and were in the forefront of the struggle to drive the French colonial government out of Algeria. Slow to adopt both Muslim religion and Arabic speech, they still retain, in the central and southern parts of Algeria, their vernacular language.

The Kabyles are a phallocentric, highly regulated society that finds its legitimacy in a cosmic worldview based on the binaries of light and darkness, outside and inside, and dominant/virile and subordinate/receptive. Bourdieu's "The Kabyle House or the World Reversed," (in 1990 [1980]) gives both the flavor of his writing and a glimpse into the world of the Kabyles in their mountain strongholds.

> The interior of the Kabyle house is rectangular in shape and divided into two parts, at a point two-thirds of the way along its length, by a small openwork wall half as high as the house. The larger of the two parts, some fifty centimeters higher and covered with a layer of black clay and cowdung which the women polish, is reserved for human use. The smaller part, paved with flagstones, is occupied by the animals. A door with two wings gives access to both rooms. (270)
>
> The lower part of the house is the place of the most intimate secret within the world of intimacy, that is, the place of all that pertains to sexuality and procreation. More or less empty during the daytime, when all the (exclusively female) activity in the house is centered on the fireplace, the dark part is full at night, full of human beings and also full of animals, since the oxen and cows, unlike the mules and donkeys, never spend the night outdoors; and it is never fuller than in the wet season, when the men sleep indoors and the oxen and cows are fed in the stable. The relationship that links the fertility of the humans and the fields with the dark part of the house . . . is here established directly (274). . . .
>
> At the centre of the dividing wall, between "the house of the humans" and "the house of the animals," stands the main pillar, supporting the "master beam" and the whole framework of the house. The master beam (*asalas alemmas,* a masculine term) which extends the protection of the male part of the house to the female part, is explicitly identified with the master of the house (274–75). . . .

In contrast to man's work, which is performed outdoors, women's work is essentially obscure and hidden . . . : "Inside the house, woman is always on the move, she bustles like a fly in the whey; outside the house, nothing of her work is seen." Two very similar sayings define woman's estate as that of one who can know no other abode than the tomb: "Your house is your tomb"; "Woman has but two dwellings, the house and the tomb."

Thus, the opposition between the women's house and the men's assembly, private life and public life, the full light of day and the secrecy of night, corresponds exactly to the opposition between the dark, nocturnal, lower part of the house and the noble, brightly lit, upper part. The opposition between the external world and the house takes on its full significance when it is seen that one of the terms of this relation, that is, the house, is itself divided in accordance with the same principles that oppose it to the other term. So it is both true and false to say that the external world is opposed to the house as the male to the female, day to night, fire to water, etc., since the second term in each of these oppositions splits, each time, into itself and its opposite.

The house, a microcosm organized on the same oppositions and homologies [qualities of similarity in structure, form, or function] that order the whole universe, stands itself in a relation of homology to the rest of the universe. But, from another standpoint, the world of the house, taken as a whole, stands in a relation of opposition to the rest of the world, an opposition whose principles are none other than those that organize both the internal space of the house and the rest of the world and, more generally, all areas of existence. Thus, the opposition between the world of female life and the city of men is based on the same principles as the two systems of oppositions which it opposes to one another. The application to opposing areas of the same *principium divisionis* that establishes their opposition ensures economy and a surplus of consistency, without involving confusion between those areas. (276–77)

The world of the Kabyle house is indeed a World Reversed!

Imagine now a number of Kabyle families as they move from their mountains aeries to the city. To make the contrast as stark as possible, let that city be Frankfurt, Germany. At first, only the men made the move at a time when Germany was importing large numbers of *gastarbeiter* (guestworker) from abroad. The work and the pay were good, and after some years, the men decided to bring their families from Kabylia to join them. Once in Frankfurt, they and their families moved into tenement flats that had absolutely nothing in common with their dwellings back home. The cosmic order that had always given meaning to their lives was now shattered for good.

Kabyle men worked on construction jobs and had picked up enough German phrases to get by in their daily work. Their children, if they were old enough, were sent off to school, where they soon became fluent in the Frankfurt vernacular, although at home they continued to speak their own language, increasingly peppered with German expressions. But what about the women? What was their place in the new setting?

The tenements where the newcomers lived stood in an old Frankfurt neighborhood of older working-class Germans intermixed with a sprinkling of Moroccan and Turkish guestworker families. A few local shops catered to the *Ausländer,* or foreign migrants, but to get to a mosque, they would have to take public transport for a suburban location. Initially, what would eventually grow into a small Kabyle community found accommodations through personal connections, but once a beachhead was secured in the neighborhood, others soon followed. The Kabyles tended to cluster together, as did the Moroccans and Turks, glad to find people like themselves, and similarly disoriented, with whom they could talk, recalling familiar scenes from the old country and pouring out their pain, and who could help one another cope with this new life. Occasionally, their kids would come home from school with tearful tales of chicanery and harassment inflicted on them by their German schoolmates. But who was there to complain to and set matters right? Their children's teachers spoke no Arabic, their menfolk had to report to work every morning, and the women, vaguely fearful, couldn't even begin to contemplate contacting the school authorities to protest the rowdy waywardness of their children's tormentors. It was scary enough for them to venture out onto the street to buy ingredients for their next meal, in an area where hardly anyone spoke their language and where they, themselves unable to read Arabic not to mention incomprehensible German, might easily lose their way. Danger seemed to lurk everywhere. For instance, there was the threat of being "at the mercy" of male shopkeepers whose hair was blond and whose blue eyes looked on the black-clothed women with intentions they were unable to read. Come evening, their menfolk, tired from work, would return home, expecting the familiar dishes of Kabylia, but they would often be obliged to make do with whatever was set before them. The flavor had gone out of their food.

Now imagine that one day, a young woman from the city's Office of Multicultural Affairs appears in the neighborhood, accompanied by an interpreter. She invites the Kabyle women to a welcome festival for newcomers from abroad to be held at the Römer, the city's main square. And she invites them to come dressed in their "native costume" and perhaps perform some village dances for the audience. The event would be popular, drawing thousands to the festivities. The Kabyle women would scarcely know how to reply to an invitation that, though spoken by the skilled interpreter in mellifluous Arabic, asked them to dance before the eyes of thousands of strangers. And perhaps they think to themselves, "Woman has but two dwellings, the house and the tomb."

I hope this imaginary journey has been sufficiently instructive to raise a number of questions. We have seen how the Kabyle habitus is strongly gendered, defining very clear roles and even physical spaces for both male and female. It is also evident that their habitus is deeply integrated with a view of the world, and indeed of the entire universe, which, though deeply patriarchal, confining women's place to the enclosure of the house, is a worldview so complete in itself that even the dwelling reflects it symbolically in its layout, domestic space being tightly controlled with regard to who may occupy it at what times and for what purpose. For all of its rigidity, it provides a strong sense of order and security for all members of the clan. The world is as God has ordained it. Outside forces are repelled, sometimes fiercely, and the culture remains intact. The great turning point in Kabyle life came with the Arab conquest in the eighth century, when Kabyles converted to Islam and began using Arabic as the new lingua franca of the region while retaining their own vernacular. Their strictly enforced habitus guaranteed that the social order of Kabyle peasant society would be reproduced down through the centuries, from one generation to the next. Cultural changes no doubt have occurred over the past twelve hundred years, but we know little about them.

Migration to Germany shattered this habitus once and for all. The tenement flats in cosmopolitan, multicultural Frankfurt allowed none of the practices to be maintained that had been central to their life in Kabylia. It is nevertheless interesting to note that transnational migrants in Frankfurt (as indeed in all transnational cities) tend, at least initially, to cluster in what we may call *affinity environments*. As distinct from ghettos, affinity environments represent a voluntary clustering of migrants in certain districts that, by virtue of their proximity to each other, offer material and cultural support and ease the psychological pain of coping with the strains of surviving in a city where none of the familiar cultural cues are present. Absent these cues, situations arise that can lead to a serious misreading by both newcomers and older resident populations of practices that, harmless and even well-intentioned in themselves, may easily be interpreted as hostile, leading to flare-ups of passion.

The adjustment of migrant families to their new life is mediated through gender, age, and education. The men work, leaving their dark, airless, and overcrowded flats in the morning, to return only at night. In this way, they maintain their dignity as Kabyle men: they are not house husbands "who brood at home like a hen in its nest" (Bourdieu 1990 [1980], 276). Men's place is out of doors, women's place is inside the home. But in a city like Frankfurt, Kabyle women cannot remain shut in. They have to run errands, use public transport, look after their small children, perhaps become involved with a Kabyle women's group. In this wider range of contacts, they must venture out into public space and learn its geography, its opportunities and dangers. Their inability to speak German, let alone read it, turns out to be a major handicap.

Kabyle children growing up in Germany are the real problem, however, especially the boys, since girls are more under the supervision of their mothers and are likely to be more inclined to submit to the rules of the patriarchal order in "exile." Marriage in the traditional manner may be arranged for them, and on reaching puberty, some of the girls may even be sent home to relatives in Kabylia to get them out of harm's way. But the boys assimilate rather quickly to their new surroundings and are powerfully attracted to the material youth culture of Germany. This brings them inevitably into conflict with their parents, who may still harbor thoughts of eventually returning to an ever more idealized Kabylia, and are likely to be "in denial" about the very real cultural disruption they have suffered.

And there is this further consideration. Many of the Kabyles' German neighbors are not particularly friendly toward the newcomers or, indeed, toward the other *Ausländer* living in the area, Turks and Moroccans. There are so many barriers to mutual understanding: physical appearance, religion, language, the smell of food and even of bodies. And there is also a feeling of resentment, because many Germans, especially among the unemployed, believe, rightly or wrongly, that it's the *Ausländer* who are taking their jobs away. Kabyle kids experience this resentment physically, hence their many tales of woe. Children want desperately to belong, but in the end, Kabyle boys have only each other. And so they form gangs that are up to all sorts of mischief, from graffiti to drugs, and they fight with (perhaps) local Turkish and Moroccan gangs that have come into existence for much the same reasons: rejection by Germans, poor performance in school (language, cramped quarters at home), frustrated material dreams, the need for some recognition by one's peers, and so on.

Youth gangs add a reality dimension to the neighborhood, where older German residents now have an objective reason to feel insecure and are threatened by muggings and street violence. Police presence is increasingly visible, and boys quickly learn that the German police are likely to see things mainly from a German perspective. After all, they have a habitus of their own. The result is that the number of Kabyle, Turkish, and Moroccan arrests is disproportionately large in Frankfurt.

In the opinion of many Germans, the Kabyles are intruders. Originally, they may have been brought to Frankfurt as guestworkers, but that was then, and this is now. It's true, they may have had the legal right to bring their families, but no one asked them to stay on and disrupt the peaceful neighborhood with its *Biergarten,* small grocery shops, and butchers. The character of the neighborhood has changed and, in the opinion of the German residents, much for the worse. Their grown-up children no longer want to live there, and are likely to move into "nicer" suburbs as soon as possible. And what began as a mixed neighborhood and an affinity environment for Kabyles, Turks, and Moroccans may, in the longer term, turn into a less benign foreign ghetto.

How are places, like our imaginary Frankfurt working-class neighborhood, severely strained by their insertion into the global economy, most powerfully by transnational migration, to be reconstituted? And is reconstitution, assuming it is desirable, a genuine possibility? This is the question I explore next.

Placemaking As Project?

In an excellent theoretical reflection on the "politics of place," Arif Dirlik argues the case for conceiving of "place as a project" somewhat along the lines of what the "modernist project" was in its dimensions of development, social analysis, and culture, only in a very different direction (Dirlik 1999, 43–56). For Dirlik, place is a topographically and ecologically situated, inhabited space, a locality whose boundaries are porous, but even so, a particular world, with its own historical memory and shared understanding of itself. I want to pick up on Dirlik's proposal, using my imaginary Kabyles in Frankfurt to further explore the meanings of habitus. In this next stage of our journey, I will give a more precise definition of *place* and a pragmatic meaning to *project* that differs significantly from Dirlik's use of these terms.

I have already referred, if somewhat obliquely, to the transnational character of Kabyle migration. In their (temporary?) and voluntary exile, the Kabyles are living simultaneously in two countries: the Algeria of their origin and the Germany of their work. In the latter, they earn money and raise their families, but their emotional home continues to be Kabylia in whose stony and unforgiving ground their culture has its roots, where their relatives continue to live, where their remittances go, and where they are politically engaged. In Frankfurt, by contrast, they are socially and politically excluded. Thus we may call Frankfurt a divided city, a place torn apart by migration from outside the EU.

Place and *place consciousness,* terms that have come into increasing use, tend to have a positive connotation, just as *placelessness* is generally regarded as what Gertude Stein is supposed to have said dismissively about Oakland, California: "There is no there there." In my own vocabulary, however, the subjective quality of a place, what can perhaps usefully be called its character, is neither good nor bad. Always a locality, but of uncertain dimension, its character is what it is. To borrow a terminology derived from Marxism, an Oakland or Frankfurt (or any specific subdivision of these cities) is merely a place *in* itself, not necessarily *for* itself. If it is to become the latter, that is, if it is to begin to think of itself *politically,* it must, for a significant part of its population, become a project.

The "home away from home" the Kabyles made for themselves in Frankfurt was gained at the expense of the "affinity environment" of the resident German population they disrupted, unintentionally to be sure, by settling into their neighborhood. It is this disruption of a finely tuned German working-class habitus that many among the German residents resent, and it is why they wish the foreigners would go away, preferably to where they came from. A place so torn apart will have the character that it does, a wounded, divided, conflicted place, but it will never be able to think of itself politically as a place *for* itself that is inclusive not only of Germans, but of Kabyles, Turks, and Moroccans as well. To become that kind of place, to mobilize itself around common objectives, will require something more than the rhetoric of multiculturalism.

In the late 1980s, a Social Democratic and Green coalition captured the Frankfurt City Council and, under the charismatic leadership of Daniel Cohn-Bendit, established the city's first-ever Office of Multicultural Affairs (Friedmann and Lehrer 1997). It was a valiant, if underfunded effort that, by a variety of ingenious means, attempted to institutionalize something like a *local citizenship* for residents "without a German passport." I followed the story for a number of years, until a more conservative council was elected and Cohn-Bendit departed for the European Parliament in Strasbourg. But my guess is that the antiforeign sentiment among many Frankfurters hasn't changed very much over the decade, and that the once so proud designation of *local citizen* has left a bitter aftertaste for a population that continues to be socially and politically pushed to the margins, much as was the case before the experiment with multiculturalism. When, as a result of the last federal elections in Germany, the Greens joined the Social Democrats, this time in a "red" coalition, one of the first moves they made was to launch a proposal that would make it much easier for aliens to gain German citizenship, including even dual citizenship. Initially, this brave attempt was hooted down by the conservative opposition even before it reached the federal parliament, making it abundantly clear that, as far as most Germans are concerned, citizenship is a privilege reserved chiefly for those of German ancestry ("blood"), and not for swarthy foreigners.[7]

I nevertheless maintain that the notion of a local citizenship—of granting local citizenship rights to migrant residents—has merit and is actually the basis for what must become a three-pronged approach to integrate transnational migrants both socially and politically in the spaces of everyday life. The aim would be to create an environment in which local places, now torn apart by migrant settlement, can be sutured and healed and begin to be proactive on their own behalf. Briefly, the three prongs are *special education* to assist foreign kids of both genders to overcome the learning difficulties they experience in their host city, supplemented by adult education programs, especially for migrant women; *job creation programs* in cities and regions suffering economic depression, specifically targeted at immigrants; and *restructuring local governance ar-*

rangements in ways that will give more visibility and voice to the excluded population and get them actively to participate in programs for the betterment of their own neighborhoods. None of these programmatic suggestions will be easy to implement, and results are not guaranteed. But in principle, they should help to foster something like local citizenship and pride in place that will go a long way toward healing the social body. Short of a multilayered approach such as this, wounded places will remain wounded, ghetto formation will almost certainly follow, and antiforeign feelings will seek to find expression in nationalist parties that, like Austria's Freedom Party and similar movements throughout the world, thrive on racism and may ultimately do great harm to our liberal democratic order.

Concluding Comments

There are several reasons why I have taken an explicitly transnational perspective on the phenomenon of cross-border migration. The language of transnationalism helps us to focus attention on social interaction in the context of both sending and receiving communities. It allows us to delineate a common sociocultural and political space joining two or more communities divided by international boundaries. It helps us to identify key cities in the global economic order that, by virtue of their strategic position, attract large numbers of transnational migrants whose social networks extend outward into transnational space, reconfiguring the web of global relations in new and unanticipated ways. Social, political, and cultural contacts are globalizing no less than economic relations but in ways that are particularized and not necessarily in conformance with the geography of capital. Finally, the concept of transnational leaves open the question of where migrants and their families will eventually settle, abandoning their sojourner status to become either immigrants or return to their homelands.

I have looked at two facets of transnational urbanism. The first had to do with the way that cross-border migrations link receiving cities with communities of migrant origin, creating a counterpoint to the Castellsian "space of flows" of information, money, and commodities. The principal focal points of these new linkages are the global cities of the world economy that, in the present optic, I called transnational. It is principally these four- or five-dozen cities around the world that are thus well along on the road to becoming denationalized.[8] Global control centers and switching points for capital "without a national sign," they are also trading centers with multiple international destinations and home to millions of migrants from abroad. But these transnational migrants do not leave their communities of origin behind but continue to interact with them in a variety of ways and with varying degrees of intensity. Denationalizing cities are thus slated to be the new "free zones" in a world of cities and candidates to become the quasi city-states of the future.

Second, I took a closer look at the problem of incorporating large numbers of transnational migrants into these cities. Because this is still a largely neglected subject, I concentrated on only one aspect of this process, the tensions that transnational migration inevitably provokes in the host society. Drawing on Bourdieu's twinned concepts of habitus/field and on his researches in Kabyle village society, I tried to show what happens when the patriarchal, Islamic Kabyles leave their mountain villages and migrate to a city such as Frankfurt, Germany. By their very presence in a German working-class neighborhood, however, the Kabyles challenge and indeed threaten the habitus of the older German population who, moreover, see the intruders as competitors for their jobs. At the same time, the Kabyles' own habitus is disrupted as they come into close contact with German society: men at work, women at home and in the neighborhood, and children at school. The result is a deeply conflicted and increasingly dysfunctional society and place, and what begins as an exercise in multicultural politics ends with a foreign ghetto. The only way to deal with this difficult situation, I argued, is to extend local citizenship in both its social and political aspects to the Kabyles, a project that would involve innovations in education, job creation, and local governance. At the same time, the imagined and real fears of the German population would have to be addressed.

In conclusion, I would like to plead for more research on the complexities of migrant incorporation into transnational cities. The questions that arise in this context are legion, and we are far from having an adequate theoretical framework for understanding the dynamics of successful incorporation. Before such a framework can evolve, however, many more detailed studies are needed. In the present climate of widespread hostility toward transnational migrants, both documented and irregular, the urgency to undertake such studies is great.

4

Citizenship: Statist, Cosmopolitan, Insurgent

Instead of seeking enclosures that will make freedom possible, we will have to orient ourselves toward a politics of flows and connections that takes us beyond where we are and decentres our own activities.
—Warren Magnusson, *The Search for Political Space*

Toward a Transnational Politics

During the past decade, under the authority of the United Nations, major world summits have convened on the environment, population, women, social development, and human settlements. Each of these official gatherings, in Rio de Janeiro, Cairo, Beijing, Stockholm, and Istanbul, was accompanied by a parallel "gathering of the tribes," an alternate "summit" convened by nongovernmental organizations (NGOs) and concerned individuals, in a kind of *salon des refusés,* such as were held in the latter part of the nineteenth century on the margins of Beaux Arts exhibits in Paris. What do these alternate summits represent, these tent shows, always more exciting, more colorful, and more polemical than the rhetoric resounding in the formal chambers where the machinery of the United Nations grinds out its high-minded declarations that, in search of the widest possible consensus, inevitably settle for the blandest version? Or let me ask a different but related question. How shall we think about activist membership organizations that operate on a global scale, such as Greenpeace, the Cousteau Society, Amnesty International, Médecins sans Frontières, the World Wildlife Fund, World Watch, Care, the American Friends Service Committee, and numerous others? Where, in the grand scheme of things, do they fit in? Do they speak and act for anyone but themselves? Or to take yet another and, in some ways, astounding example: What about the formation of the Pan-Indian movement in North and South America that expresses the shared identity of indigenous peoples in ways never dreamed of in the pre-Columbian past. This movement, as Warren Magnusson reminds us, "opened out as the 'first nations' of the Americas made contact with Australian Aborigines, Maoris in New Zealand, Pacific Islanders, Saamis, Inuit across the Arctic, and many others. The World Council of Indigenous Peoples, formed in the 1970s, gave an institutional expression to this enlarged entity" (Magnusson 1996, 297).[1] Is this world council some unique, unclassifiable event, made possible by modern technology, or does it have a deeper significance? And is this meaning not related to the "gathering of the tribes" on the margins of the United Nations Organization, or to the militants in the trenches of the struggle for, to use a cliché of the moment, a "more livable world"? Or yet again, think of the multiple organizations that sprang up in American cities at the time of the terrible Central American wars of recent memory to tell the truth about these wars, to receive, help, and protect the hundreds of thousands of refugees seeking asylum in the United States, and after the wars, to help rebuild shattered countries and shattered lives. Are they not also part of this global civic movement?[2] And if there is such a movement, what is its nature and deeper significance?

In this chapter, I argue that all of the examples I have given are best understood as instances of a nonterritorial, self-proclaimed form of grassroots citizenship that, in concerted "acts of resistance" (Bourdieu 1998) and in its claiming of new rights, constitutes a new form of *insurgent citizenship and practice*.[3]

This revisioning of the concept of citizenship departs radically from the only form of a universally acknowledged citizenship, which is a form of citizenship centered on the national state. As territorial entities, national states place obedience and loyalty to themselves above all other public virtues; in return, they are expected to afford some degree of protection to their subject "citizens." Virtually every living person belongs, as a citizen, to some national, putatively sovereign state. Rainer Bauböck (1994) calls this a nominal citizenship and argues that it serves merely as a classificatory device. In this sense, citizenship has nothing to do with democracy or with any specific enumeration of "rights."[4] One can be a citizen of a military dictatorship, a ministate such as the Cayman Islands, a kleptocracy such as the Republic of Congo, a Communist Vietnam, a democratic Taiwan that is not a member of the United Nations, and even a nonstate presided over by warlords such as Somalia. Most national states grant formal rights and privileges to their own citizens that are unavailable to others who may be living in the country. In fact, however, they are much more interested in extracting reciprocal obligations, not only obeying the law of the land (however arbitrary it may be) and paying taxes, but also serving in the armed forces when called on, and demonstrating appropriate respect for the state's leadership and the national flag.

Granted that, in the traditions of Western political philosophy, citizenship has a more trenchant and specific meaning. In this discourse, a *substantive* citizenship is linked to liberal democracy and a theory of citizen rights. In democratic formations, it is said, people are the ultimate sovereign, constituting the state understood as a political community, and they expect the institutions of the state to be accountable to themselves. As far as theory is concerned, such a state does not have a legitimate claim on its subjects. But in any actually existing state, the relationship between itself and its citizens is blurred. If it is not to their liking, citizens can try to reform and, in principle, even overturn the state; at the very least, they can change the faces of political office holders. But speaking practically, it is inevitably the state that holds most of the trumps in these situations, so that "throwing the rascals out" or reforming the state is never a simple task. Moreover, it would be a gross mistake to think that even liberal democratic states, such as Australia's, are fundamentally benign institutions solely dedicated to the well-being and concerns of their citizenry. Between citizen and state there is bound to be a permanent tension defined by relations of power (Arendt 1965, 251). In principle, all citizens are supposed to be equal in the eyes of the state and thus entitled to equal consideration. But in fact, they have constantly to claim rights that, even if enshrined in legislation, must be eternally defended against recurring attempts to restrict, erode, or deny them, whether for the population as a whole or for certain groups, such as women, children, prisoners, or others marked by certain ethnic characteristics. There is never anything permanent, much less universal about citizen rights.

The British theorist T. H. Marshall, whose work is the inevitable point of departure for contemporary debates on citizenship, thought that citizen rights in Western democracies had emerged in a linear progression, from civil rights in the eighteenth, to political rights in the nineteenth, and on to social rights in the twentieth century (1964). Given this triumphant march through the centuries, one could presumably project the conquest of cultural rights in the twenty-first century, and so on, culminating in a vision of cosmopolitan citizenship in some distant future that would be based on an encompassing set of human rights. But the real story has been quite otherwise. The social rights whose conquest in the form of the British welfare state Marshall celebrated in the years following the World War II have been all but buried under the impact of a more recent neoliberal philosophy and what Pierre Bourdieu calls its *idée force,* the ideology—the project—of globalization.

As regards political rights—the franchise above all—they have taken on a highly ritualized form. In the old liberal democracies—the United Kingdom, France, the United States—people no longer march to the voting booth with bounding enthusiasm and swelling pride. Almost everywhere now, politics and politicians are held in fairly low esteem by citizens who, in principle, should be its protagonists but who, in practice, have become victims of meaningless choices and saturation bombing by sound bites in the media. Around election time, pundits worry about political apathy, but citizens display little interest in the politics of the day, except perhaps as a form of entertainment. Their intuition tells them that there is little to be gained through a traditional politics of representation. And perhaps their energies should be directed elsewhere.

This argument, at any rate, is the one I should like to make. In an era in which a great deal of effective power has shifted away from national states to anonymous financial markets, multinational organizations, global business, and international institutions with worldwide reach, none of which are accountable to the *demos,* yet whose actions have enormous consequences for the life-chances of present and future generations, the sites of politics have acquired a new dimension. Benevolent authorities will never bestow a global citizenship from above. This much we know. The struggle for rights will have to be carried to where the action is. To Seattle, for example, to disrupt the closed process of the World Trade Organization.

In the next two sections, I engage the current debates about the theory of citizenship and try to relate these debates to an understanding of democracy as an intermittent historical project. The nature of the ongoing struggles for an expansion of rights combined with resistance to what David Held (1995) has called the *nautonomic forces* loose in the world provides a moral focus for the insurgencies of a nonterritorial citizenship. In conclusion, I argue that we are beginning to live in a world of multiple citizenships that hold deep implications for our identities and to what or to whom we are ultimately loyal.

Three Models of Citizenship

Marshall's seminal work on citizenship was firmly planted in the concept of the sovereign national state. More recent scholarship, however, has tried to come to terms with the changed spatial configuration of the world—its increasingly transnational character and the new geographies that have arisen from it (see chapter 3 in this volume). As a result, citizenship has become one of the livelier discourses in the human sciences, the stakes being the very meaning of contemporary citizenship itself. The idea of multiple citizenships, for instance, has been seriously engaged, though only a small number of states currently allow their own subjects to hold dual citizenship. Even in the European Union (EU), it is up to its member states to determine which of its nationals will have a right to European citizenship with its implications for cross-border travel, permission to work, voting rights, and so on (Bhabha 1998; Borja 2000). Similarly, there is growing recognition, particularly in Western Europe, of the need to extend a limited number of citizen rights to longer-term residents of cities, regardless of their nationality. Another hotly debated issue concerns the legal rights of transnational migrants, which bear directly on the life and livelihood of millions of migrants and their extended families across the continents (Bauböck 1994; Bauböck and Rundell 1998). Other agenda items include the construction of a transnational legal system that would set forth and ensure compliance with basic human and citizen rights, superseding national jurisdictions, and the important matter of collective versus individual rights.

The starting point for all of these debates is the common understanding that *citizenship* is a term designating individual and equal membership in a territorially defined political community. A major problem with this understanding is that for many of us, up and down and across social hierarchies, life is spilling over national frontiers, becoming increasingly transnational. National borders, of course, are still there, but are becoming more porous with each passing day. Moreover, the

growing interdependencies of life on the globe, and the near simultanei-
ty of information about events, regardless of where they occur, and information that reaches us with the uncanny vividness of being actually
there—in Kosovo, East Timor, Palestine—has created a space for imagined political communities that are unrelated to issues of territorial governance and are spatially unbounded. Such communities, or transient
polities, come into being whenever like-minded persons, determined to
engage issues that they perceive to exist in places that may be far away
but are close to their hearts, join with one another in politically relevant
practices. Their actions give rise to an *insurgent citizenship* (Holston
1999).

To set this puzzling matter into context, I attempt here to set out
briefly three models of citizenship that progressively loosen the bounds
of territoriality. I begin with the traditional concept of a *state-centered
citizenship,* follow with an account of an incipient *cosmopolitan citizenship* model, and conclude with the idea (and practice) of an *insurgent
citizenship.*

State-centered citizenship. This is the classical model and the one with
which all of us are familiar. For this reason, it will suffice if I merely
highlight certain structural features of this model as a basis for comparison with the remaining two (Turner 1992; Bauböck 1994; Kymlicka
and Norman 1995).

- Citizenship status is granted to individuals by a national state according to certain rules and principles. In most cases, citizenship is auto-
  matically acquired by either place of birth or descent, but it may be
  extended to noncitizens through a process of naturalization. Although
  citizenship is generally for the lifetime of the individual, it may be re-
  nounced (as when you elect to become a citizen of another country)
  or, in exceptional cases, revoked or otherwise limited by the state.

- State-centered citizenship entitles one to the rights and privileges of
  membership in a territorially bounded political community, at the
  same time that it imposes certain obligations toward the sovereign
  state that is its symbolic embodiment.

- State-centered citizenship is conceived primarily as passive or dor-
  mant, becoming activated at periodic intervals to elect the political
  agents by whom citizens will be represented and governed.

• The primary virtues of state-centered citizenship are obedience to constituted authority and unswerving loyalty to the state as the collective representation of the people constituted as a political community.[5]

Much of the discussion around this model has been about the question of democratic citizen rights, or what some have asserted as the excessive claim-making of citizens on the state. According to these writers, claim-making has led to a condition of *ungovernability*, as citizens are said to expect "too much" of their government, demanding too many privileges and entitlements, while being unwilling to shoulder a broader range of civic obligations in return (Janoski 1998). Still, "the right to claim rights" has been called the most fundamental right of all. Here is how Rainer Bauböck formulates this thesis:

> Citizenship is not only about negative liberties [that is, what I am free to do without interference by the state]. Political legitimation requires positive freedom and rights. In contemporary democracy, citizens acquire claims-rights towards the state which far exceed those of mere protection against violence. There can be no democratic legitimation of political authority without institutionalized forms of participation in civil society beyond the electoral process and without basic rights to protection against existential risks in market economies. (1994, 19)

But—and here we must leave the neatly segmented picture of state-centered citizenship—"communities defined by the range of allocation of these rights reach beyond nation-states. In this way, democratic citizenship questions the existing forms of segmentation, extends the space of politically organized society, and creates a complex map of overlapping memberships" (Bauböck 1994, 19).[6] With this "paradoxical" formulation, we enter the domain of cosmopolitan citizenship.

Cosmopolitan citizenship. This model, most fully articulated by David Held (1995) and his colleagues (Archibugi and Held 1995), pushes beyond state boundaries; nevertheless, it remains moored to a statist conception. Rather than attempting to paraphrase what, for the moment, remains little more than a vision, I quote from Held's formulation directly:

> The individuals who compose the states and societies whose constitutions are formed in accordance with cosmopolitan law might be regarded

as citizens, not just of their nation, communities, or regions but of a universal system of "cosmo-political" governance. Such a system connotes nothing more or less than the entrenchment and enforcement of democratic public law across all peoples—a binding framework for the political business of states, societies, and regions, not a detailed regulative framework for the direction of all their affairs. People would come, thus, to enjoy multiple citizenship—political membership in the diverse political communities which significantly affected them. They would be citizens of their immediate political communities, and of the wider regional and global networks which impacted upon their lives. This cosmopolitan polity would be one that in form and substance reflected and embraced the diverse forms of power and authority that operate within and across borders and which, if unchecked, threaten a highly fragmented, neo-medieval order.

Against the background of a cosmopolitan polity, the nation-state would, in due course, "wither away . . ." [meaning that] states would no longer be, and would no longer be regarded as, the sole centers of legitimate power within their own borders (as is already the case in diverse settings). States would be "relocated" within, and articulated with, an overarching global democratic law. . . .

Thus, sovereignty can be stripped away from the idea of fixed orders and territories and thought of as, in principle, malleable time-space clusters. *Sovereignty is an attribute of the basic democratic law, but it could be entrenched and drawn upon in diverse self-regulating associations, from states to cities and corporations.* Cosmopolitan law demands the subordination of regional, national, and local "sovereignties" to an overarching legal framework, but within this framework associations may be self-governing at diverse levels. A new possibility is portended: the recovery of an intensive and participatory democracy at local levels as a complement to the public assemblies of the wider global order; that is, a political order of democratic associations, cities, and nations as well as of regions and global networks. The cosmopolitan model of democracy is the legal basis of a global and divided authority system—a system of diverse and overlapping power centres, shaped and delimited by democratic law. (1995, 233–35; italics in the original)

Held envisions that the push for a gradual establishment of the cosmopolitan model will come from "outside" the national state through a network of regional and international agencies and "assemblies" that cut across segmented political space. Its impetus would come from "the development of transnational grassroots movements with clear regional or global objectives . . . the elaboration of new legal rights and duties affecting states and individuals in connection with 'the common heritage of humankind,' the protection of the 'global commons,' the defence of human rights and the deployment of force; and the emergence and proliferation . . . of international institutions to coordinate transnational forces and problems" (1995, 237).

All in all, this is a hopeful vision based on the idea of a democratic legal order with global reach. A legal order, however, is still a state-centered order, even if the national state is no longer its principal focus. And contrary to Held's assertion that the emerging cosmopolitan order will be democratic, his text gives no indication of why this should be the case, or even in what sense it would be "democratic." To be sure, social movements, embedded in civil society, exist and may advocate a supranational legal order, from human rights to a global commons; but it is not clear whether and to what extent this order, once it is entrenched in supranational institutions, would remain accountable, or to whom. Finally, it is not the case that a formal judicial order at some supranational level—supposing that one existed—will necessarily prevail in instances where it clashes with national interests. For instance, in a well-documented study on human rights in the era of Maastricht, Jacqueline Bhabha concludes that "despite the appeal to fundamental rights, attempts to translate this broad vision into concrete entitlements for citizens [of the EU] have been unsuccessful" (1998, 722).

Despite these unresolved issues, Held and his associates point us in the right direction. It is only because they fear fragmentation and desire to see certain principles enshrined in an overarching body of law that they overlook the virtues of the third model of citizenship which I call insurgent and which does not seek power for itself but an enlargement of the spaces of democracy.

Insurgent citizenship. The term *insurgent* used in conjunction with *citizenship* was originally suggested to me by James Holston:

If modernist planning relies on and builds upon the state, then its necessary counteragent is a mode of planning that addresses the formation of insurgent citizenship. Planning theory needs to be grounded in these

antagonistic complements. . . . : on one side, the project of state-directed
futures . . . and, on the other, the project of engaging planners with the
insurgent forms of the social . . . which are in important ways heteroge-
neous and outside the state. These insurgent forms are found both in
organized grassroots mobilizations and in everyday practices that, in different ways, empower, parody, derail, or subvert state agendas. They are
found, in other words, in struggles over what it means to be a member of
the modern state—which is why I refer to them with the term citizenship. . . . Citizenship changes as new members emerge to advance their
claims, expanding its realm, and as new forms of segregation and violence counter these advances, eroding it. The sites of insurgent citizenship are found at the intersection of these processes of expansion and
erosion. (1998, 47–48)

Holston's dialectical conception of citizenship is grounded in everyday experience. Before giving my own account of a radical, insurgent
citizenship model, let me briefly review the contributions of two other
authors who come at the same issue from very different theoretical perspectives. In a brilliant theoretical essay, "Outline of a Theory of Citizenship," Bryan Turner concludes that "citizenship does not have a unitary character" (1992, 47). In other words, the official understanding,
he argues, is inadequate to account for the process of democratization itself. He makes two fairly straightforward distinctions: passive and active
forms of citizenship, and citizenship "from above" and "from below."
Since the citizenship model "from above" is well understood—it is the
state-centered model discussed above—he spends a good part of his argument justifying its counterpart, which for him, as it is for Holston, is
an active and engaged citizenship grounded in civil society. I am inclined to call it a conflict model, since it lacks the specific dialectical
turn of Holston's conception, and Turner is more interested in typolo-
gies of citizenship than in a specific political practice.

My third antecedent is an essay by Chantal Mouffe, who argues in
favor of "a common political identity as radical democratic citizens"
(1992, 236). Despite a somewhat obscure writing style, her message is
clear: political communities do not exist as a banal geographical fact;
they don't have that kind of reality. Rather, they are "discursive surfaces"
or, more plainly, discourse communities (237). It is significant that
Mouffe uses the plural form here, suggesting a diversity of radical com-

munities committed to the liberal democratic principles of equality and liberty for all. To have the identity of a radical democratic citizen does not preclude one to have other identities and loyalties. Hers is a non-essentialist understanding of identity.

Mouffe's other relevant contribution here concerns the substance of a democratic politics. She is critical of both liberal (Rawlsian) and neo-communitarian perspectives. The first she rejects for being purely procedural, the second for harboring within itself the virtual impossibility of a modern consensual community at any significant scale. Her own view is that politics may become something other than a mere reflection of the prevailing hegemony. This set of conditions can be called the "common good" of the polity, an ethical bond that cannot simply be dissolved into a bundle of legal procedures for the pursuit of private interests. But as an expression of existing power relations, the constitution of the political community will always be contested. Politics, she says, is largely about the construction of the political community in which we desire to live, and this is a permanently unfinished project (234–35).

It is time now to offer my own formulation of the issue at hand. Let me define *insurgent citizenship* as a form of active participation in social movements or, as we may also call them, *communities of political discourse and practice,* that aim at either, or both, the *defense* of existing democratic principles and rights and the *claiming* of new rights that, if enacted, would lead to an *expansion of the spaces of democracy,* regardless of where these struggles take place. Following Mouffe, I argue that such movements constitute temporary polities that are held together by the ethical bond of its members' commitment to one another and to the purposes of the movement itself. It is these nonterritorial movements of resistance and claiming that represent the dialectical other to the formal citizenship "from above."

In this sense, let me characterize *insurgent citizenship* in the same way as I did the state-centered model earlier:

- Insurgent citizenship is self-declared and voluntary. This is what defines it as being "from below," that is, from the classes of commoners, and recalls for us the Rousseauvian tradition of popular sovereignty that culminated in *The Declaration of the Rights of Man and Citizen* of 1789. Parisians storming the Bastille needed no state to adorn them with the sobriquet of citizen; it was by their actions that they declared themselves as *citoyens* and *citoyennes*.

• Insurgent citizenship is achieved through active participation in *temporary, nonterritorial political communities engaged in a dual struggle:* the defense and preservation of existing human and citizen rights and the claiming of new rights.

• To be an insurgent citizen is to be active in projects that, in the broadest sense, are aimed at the *expansion of the spaces of democracy.*

• The primary civic virtue of insurgent citizenship is solidarity across all borders with those who are committed to these projects. This sense of solidarity is best expressed by the Spanish *compañero/compañera,* suggesting a personal commitment to a common undertaking.

This idea of a citizenship contingent on membership in a temporary, nonterritorial sodality is at odds with received notions of both citizenship and democracy, where the latter is understood as a form of territorial governance (Dahl 1989). It is therefore necessary to establish the contrary idea of democracy as an unfinished and intermittent project.

The Unfinished Project of Democracy

Democracy, writes the distinguished political philosopher Sheldon Wolin, "is a project concerned with the political potentialities of ordinary citizens, that is, with their possibilities for becoming political beings through the self-discovery of common concerns and modes of action" (1996, 31). And a little further on in the same essay: "Democracy was born in transgressive acts, for the demos could not participate in power without shattering the class, status, and value systems by which it was excluded" (37).

For Wolin, as for Hannah Arendt (1958) who exerted a strong influence on his thinking, democracy is less a system of governance than a mode of being in the world, a way of acting in both word and deed. It is only by being political—and in this both writers are unashamedly Aristotelian—that we become human in full measure. More specifically, to be political is to be physically present in a public arena where one can be *seen and heard* on matters affecting the common life of the *polis.* Central to Arendt's vision is that, as human beings, we are endowed with the power of speech. It is only through speech, as opposed to mute violence, that politics is actualized. "Violence itself," she declares, "is incapable of speech" (Arendt 1965, 9). Through their emphasis on nonviolent action, Wolin and Arendt both advocate an existential form of democracy. Democracy comes to life whenever we take a stand in the public space of appearance. It is a standing *with* and *against*. Historically speaking, these moments are rare. It is in this particular sense that democracy may be called an intermittent project.

Let me illustrate this idea with Arendt's account of what she refers to as the "lost treasure" of the revolutionary tradition (Arendt 1965, chapter 6). Driven by the febrile enthusiasm of the Parisian *demos* caught up in revolutionary beginnings, forty-eight so-called sections of the Parisian Commune came together as self-governing bodies in 1789 to form the Commune of Paris, which would subsequently play a decisive role in the ensuing events.

Side by side with these highly localized municipal bodies, a great number of spontaneously formed clubs and societies—the *sociétés populaires*—came into being. In the words of Robespierre, their aim was "to instruct, to enlighten their fellow citizens on the true principles of the constitution, and to spread a light without which the constitution will not be able to survive" (cited in Arendt 1965, 242). Here, then, according to Arendt, was a luminous moment in the history of democracy. But the moment passed. Elected to the Committee on Public Safety, which he soon came to dominate, Robespierre set out to destroy the many local assemblies that had rapidly spread throughout the whole of France. Now that he himself was in power, their task would no longer be the "discussion and exchange of opinions, mutual instruction, and information on the public business, but to spy upon one another and to denounce members and nonmembers alike" (250).

The spontaneous formation of self-governing councils, *soviets* and *Räte* would characterize subsequent historical moments marked by popular uprisings (265–66). Arendt lists the following:

- In 1870, when the French capital, besieged by the Prussian army, spontaneously reorganized itself into a federal body that would form the nucleus for the second Parisian Commune government the following year.
- In 1905, when the wave of spontaneous strikes in Russia developed a political leadership of its own, and the workers in the factories

organized themselves into *soviets* for the purpose of representative self-government.

- In the February revolution of 1917 in Russia when, despite different political tendencies among workers, the organization itself, that is, the *soviet,* was not even a matter for discussion. It was assumed to be the obvious, natural form.

- In 1918 and 1919 in Germany when, after the defeat of the army, soldiers and workers in open rebellion constituted themselves into *Arbeiter- und Soldatenräte* (Workers and Soldiers Councils) demanding, in Berlin, that the system of councils become the foundation stone of the new German constitution.

- In the autumn of 1956, when the Hungarian revolution produced the council system anew in Budapest, from whence it spread to the rest of the country.

These councils, comments Arendt, "were always organs of order as much as organs of action, and it was indeed their aspiration to lay down the new order that brought them into conflict with the groups of professional revolutionaries who wished to degrade them to mere executive organs of revolutionary activity" (1965, 266).[7]

Despite their heady moments of flourishing in France, Russia, Germany, and Hungary, these councils were, in each and every case, suppressed as democratic fora and replaced by a unitary system of national power. But as an idea the council system survived and continues to inspire and regenerate itself in always new contexts. It is fruitless to debate whether, in this or that particular historical circumstance, a more positive result might have been possible, and with what consequences for the succeeding course of events. The inspiration is of a different sort. Thomas Jefferson's "elementary republic of the wards," which belongs to the same family of democratic ideas though it was never put into practice (Arendt 1996, 254; see also Friedmann 1973a); the two Paris Communes; the Russian *soviets*; and the German *Räte* all had this in common: they were self-generated popular assemblies—spaces of appearance—where the *demos* could be seen and heard. They were small, autonomous, self-governing, and linked to one another across cities and regions in what today we would call a network pattern.

With only small modifications, this organizational model describes many of today's "new" social movements, which, like the council system, work through a dual cellular-network structure. Because they do not themselves seek the power to govern, they are neither territorial nor designed for permanence, but are capable of acting in both small places and at large anywhere in the world, being thus coterminous with the reach of global capital and its institutions. Contemporary communication technologies make it possible to coordinate their actions across a large number of sites simultaneously. Insurgent citizenship arises from membership in these movement organizations and from participation in their projects (Carroll 1992).[8]

What remains is to delimit the normative parameters for movement actions, to be certain that their aim is, indeed, to "enlarge the spaces of democracy" and/or resist attempts to erode the gains already made. For not all social movements are democratic in their intents and practices, and many subvert freedom. An insurgent citizenship can only be assured through participation in movements that conform to a democratic ethos.

The Daily Struggle against "Nautonomy"

But how will we know whether a social movement or association from within civil society actually works to preserve and expand the spaces of democracy? A simple and straightforward answer would be that any political practice that promotes democratic values such as collective self-determination, substantial equality, and political participation would qualify. Although one could easily add to this list of high-minded values, a formulation that limits itself to declaring its purposes in the grand manner serves chiefly to divide rather than unify those who would act in their name. The "yes" and the "no" of political practice are not symmetrical with respect to each other. By this I mean that it is far easier to forge agreement on what is to be resisted than on the vision at the end of the rainbow. Thus, it is easier to know the common enemy in wartime than what to do once the task of peaceful reconstruction begins. America's war aims in World War II were couched in vague and tepid phrases such as "Preserving the American Way of Life," whereas rallying public opinion against the brutal aggressions of Nazi Germany and imperial Japan helped to cement the Allied Powers, even when, on ideological grounds, they were deeply divided among themselves.

In applying this logic to the question of democracy, I find David Held's concept of *nautonomy*—meaning the negative of autonomy— particularly helpful.

Where relations of power systematically generate asymmetries of life-chances they may create a situation which can be called "nautonomic." Nautonomy refers to the *asymmetrical production and distribution of life-chances which limit and erode the possibilities of political participation.* (Held 1995, 171; emphasis in the original)

According to Held, life-chances, which is to say, our prospects to fully share in the "economic, cultural, or political goods, rewards, and opportunities" available in a community, have a social origin: they are produced and distributed unequally. It is this inequality that limits and erodes the possibilities of citizen participation. What I call the possibility of "human flourishing" (see chapter 6 in this volume) thus appears as a function of relations that lead to the systematic disempowerment of large numbers of people on the lower and lowest rungs of the social order.

Held's focus here is on the life-chances of individuals rather than on collectivities or groups deprived of their fundamental right to human flourishing because of certain ascribed characteristics, such as gender, "race," migratory status, and other markers used to marginalize entire populations. His aim is to construct a theory of individual rights around a small number of crucially important "sites of power" that include the body, welfare, culture, civic associations, the economy, coercive relations, and legal and regulatory institutions (Held 1995, 192–94). Held defines power broadly as the capacity of social agents and institutions to maintain or transform their social or physical environment. Power is thus about the *resources* that underpin people's capacity to act, and the *forces* that shape and determine the exercise of this capacity (191). Having successfully claimed rights clustered around each of these seven sites of power, individual citizens would, in Held's view, be enabled to "participate on free and equal terms in the regulation of their own associations" (191).

Held's approach to the multiple and interlocking nautonomic forces in the world, and the daily struggles against them (as well as for the conquest of new citizen and human rights), has much in common with my own discussion of a theory of dis/empowerment (Friedmann 1992). Rather than using a rights framework, however, my point of departure was the production of the "life and livelihood" of households (rather than individuals) and the cluster of resources essential for their flourishing: housing, surplus time above what is required to produce a given level of living, membership in organizations, social networks, tools of production (including good health), financial resources, knowledge and skills, and information pertinent to the application of knowledge and skills. Each of these eight clusters is simultaneously a *site of struggle* to enable poor households to improve the circumstances of their lives. I called it a struggle for social empowerment, and emphasized the need eventually to move from social to political empowerment, thus joining forces with Held's project for expanding political rights and resisting their erosion. In other words, my dis/empowerment model may be seen as providing the *material basis* for a political struggle in a world where 40 or more percent of the population are living on the edge of starvation, a condition that would seem to make a mockery of democratic aspirations.[9]

At the strategic level, what I have referred to as the daily struggle against relentless nautonomic forces requires, first, an understanding of which groups are disempowered, in what specific ways, and why their condition is what it is. It is not particularly helpful, for instance, to proclaim a universal ethics of environmental care (which is an easy thing to do) when the specific problem at hand is rather the unhealthy physical surroundings of urban squatter communities next to vermin-ridden garbage dumps in the anarchic proletarian suburbs of Rio de Janeiro or Metro-Manila. To act in this situation, what is needed, as a first step, is a *concrete and critical understanding* of why there are still large numbers of squatters in these cities, why they are located where they are, and why their situation persists. Only when we have gained such an understanding can insurgent counterpractices hope to be effective (Douglass 1995; Douglass, Ard-Am, and Kim 2002).

Principles of Insurgent Practice

I admit that the preceding is but a small and, from a structural position, insignificant example, but it helps to illustrate a number of normative principles of an insurgent practice.

- Insurgent practice must always be focused on specific groups whose life-chances are collectively at risk in particular circumstances of time and place.

- A concrete and critical understanding must be obtained of the structural, that is, nautonomic, forces that systematically deny these populations the fundamental right to human flourishing and full political participation.

- The problem must be attacked simultaneously at all scales, from microlocal to global, at which pertinent nautonomic forces operate. This requires drawing up strategies that are appropriately tailored to each scale.

- The diverse practices of insurgent citizens are articulated through loosely networked, temporary sodalities, or solidarity groups, that range from community-based mobilizations to NGOs, churches, students, academics, international organizations, private foundations, and so on.

- Insurgent practices must aim simultaneously at a number of different but related problems: the local squatter population and their insalubrious environment, the gradual empowerment of squatter citizens through self-organization and the betterment of their physical surroundings, the more generic problem of housing for the large numbers of people who would otherwise remain homeless, the human right to adequate housing, and the still wider aims of human flourishing that involve both material foundations and political rights.[10]

- Insurgent practices operating at all interlocking sites of power must engage the many agencies of the state and statelike formations without which no lasting solutions can be found. Insurgent citizenship in intersecting, overlapping sodalities is nonterritorial, and so are the interlocking sites of power whose ultimate reach is global. But the problems that must be attended, like the squatter settlements of Rio de Janeiro and Metro-Manila, are always on the ground and for that very reason subject to territorial relations of power and control.[11]

To many well-intentioned people, the idea of an insurgent practice is unappealing. Some are put off by the adjective *insurgent,* cherishing an image of a citizenry that is law abiding. Others, less concerned about rhetorical devices and generally sympathetic to social movements, may not think of themselves as activists, preferring a more quiet life. Still others—and they are more than a few—will counter with the familiar trope, "Who wants to spend all their evenings and weekends in meetings?" For the most part, all of these objections are misplaced. Insurgent practices need activists in the trenches, but they need many others as well. Those who raise issues of justice and rights in public forums, who write about them, who donate their time and money are all needed. The practice of insurgent citizenship at different scales is an established historical fact, and whether one joins a particular cause is a matter of personal decision. Insurgent citizenship is never a question of numbers.

A Multiplicity of Citizenships

The engagement of the state in insurgent practice, to be against the state but also with the state, returns us to the beginning of our inquiry. It is a necessary reminder that the national state, and thus state-centered citizenship as well, is here to stay, even as pressures across national frontiers to expand (and defend) human and citizen rights are on the rise. The world is rapidly moving toward a time when the citizenship of individuals will no longer be centered exclusively in a single state. Where transnational and national citizenships overlap, as they do in Europe, and where Euro-citizens have acquired the franchise to vote in local elections regardless of their nationality, prefigures this multiplicity. In addition to these three levels of citizenship—local, national, and transnational—it is likely that bi- and even trinational citizenship will become more common reflecting, for many of us, the increasingly transnational character of our lives. And adding to this, the visionary cosmopolitan citizenship toward which David Held and his colleagues are working is also likely to gain ground, particularly in the area of human rights (Archibugi 1995).

Although a multiplicity of citizenships is thus virtually assured, some of them will be little more than nominal. With advancing globalization, for example, there is a surging desire among people who feel themselves to be oppressed minorities in larger states to assert more specific collective identities, whether of an ethnic, religious, or historical sort and to press for greater territorial autonomy, perhaps even statehood. The case of the Ruthenians is paradigmatic. An east Slavic people ensconced in a sliver of land lodged between the Ukraine, Slovakia, Hungary, and Romania, Ruthenians have always worked as farmers and woodcutters in the Carpathian foothills. Today, as many as one million ethnic Ruthenians are nominally citizens of the Ukraine, with smaller minorities in the surrounding countries and have begun their own autonomy movement (Ash 1999). Ruthenians are not alone in their quest. As Timothy Garton Ash informs us, the Web site of the Unrepresented Nation and People's Organization (UNPO) includes "a list of almost fifty [groups], starting with Abkhazia, Aboriginal Australians, and Alcheh/Sumatra, then on to East Timor, Kurdistan, Nagaland, and Tibet. And in the middle, Kosova—the Albanian spelling of Kosovo" (1999, 55). Some of these groups will surely, in time, receive some sort of recognition as autonomous regions with their own governments or as independent states. Yet this autonomy, and even more emphatically, any potential "sovereignty," will have primarily a symbolic value. Such mini-, micro-, and quasi-states will have little power to provide effective protection for their nominal citizenry who may have to be satisfied with the trappings of a national anthem and symbol: for the Ruthenians, a flag of yellow and gold stripes with a red bear prancing. The protection of their citizens will have to depend largely on the continued good will of powerful neighbors, international agencies, and emerging cosmopolitan law.

All of these forms of citizenship, whether nominal or substantial, are in one way or another state-centered, even where the state is multinational as it is in the EU. Alongside this formal structure of citizenship, however, there is the continued growth of an *active, nonterritorial citizenship of insurgent practices* in support of the material foundations for political participation, for the expansion of human and citizen rights, and for the defense of rights already achieved but inevitably vulnerable. Based in the transterritorial sodalities of social movements or self-identified political communities, and deeply rooted in social formations significantly free from direct state intervention, insurgent citizens are continually generating a politics-from-below that, though often extremely local, tends to operate at all pertinent scales, all the way up to the as yet unrealized cosmopolitan world order (Falk 1995). To become a self-declared citizen in this sense requires nothing more than to become politically engaged in ways that may range from small political talk with friends and neighbors expressing concern over an issue, to making monetary contributions, to political advocacy and a lifetime of activism. In the daily struggle against nautonomic forces, all the evidence points to the crucial importance of a civil society that is constantly on the alert to defend and expand the spaces of democracy.

5

The City of Everyday Life: Knowledge/Power and the Problem of Representation

Landmarks of a New Generation

In 1992, the Getty Conservation Institute conducted a study of Los Angeles "landmarks," their relationship to the city's history, and their use. This was the year of the great civil disturbances in the city, and the folks at the Getty thought that perhaps officially designated landmarks might not be all there was to know about L.A.'s image. A creative idea occurred to them. Why not ask young people—kids—from the city's many ethnic neighborhoods to photograph landmarks they themselves would identify, and then talk about them. A young professional photographer, Lauren Greenfield, was invited to direct the project, and the results of the project were published two years later, as *Picture LA* (Beley et al. 1994).

Having scoured the city's schools and community centers, Greenfield selected eight young people between the ages of ten and eighteen from diverse community and ethnic backgrounds. Each of them was provided with a basic point-and-shoot camera. They were given elementary instructions on the use of the equipment and were set the task of shooting Los Angeles "landmarks." In her introduction to the book, Greenfield writes,

> For over twelve weeks, the photographers worked independently in the field with the help of Jessica Karman, Juliann Tallino, and myself (as well as family and friends). We facilitated their creative impulses with transportation, moral, and logistical support. In the field, we understood that our role was to accompany and encourage the photographers without interfering with their vision or intuition. . . . For the first

month, the photographers worked individually without meeting each other or looking at prints of their work. . . . Later, we came together as a group five times in a series of critiques and field trips. During the critiques, the photographers shared stories about their experiences in the field and were intrigued by each other's landmarks. . . . We also organized field trips to some of L.A.'s designated landmarks to raise the awareness among the photographers of places that reflected the city's history and culture. (Greenfield 1994, 5)

In all, more than five hundred rolls of film were processed from which Greenfield selected the photos for the published volume. Accompanying the pictures is a selection of quotations by the young artists talking about their work.

What's a landmark? I think it is something that you see every day and it's there and will never disappear. It's like a part of you. It represents you and where you live and how you live and what area you live in and the people that live around there. It can also represent something beautiful, something that you never really see and you never really feel until you see it—and it totally changes you.

—Raul Herrera, 18 years old

A landmark is different for everyone, I think it's something you have grown up with and seen all of your life.

—Abbey Fuchs, 16 years old

Without landmarks, there would be no history. . . . Without history, what do you have to look back on? Like memories. Life is based on memories.

—Osofu Washington, 16 years old

When you destroy a landmark, you destroy some of other people's history.

—Sabrina Paschal, 14 years old

If people can understand our landmarks, they can see things from our point of view.

—Osofu Washington

I would like to show everybody the historical landmarks and how they can help us, so we can save them and they won't be junked up and mess up the children's future.

—Daniel Hernandez, 10 years old

These statements are expressions of an untutored, spontaneous philosophy, a result of what for these young people was a voyage of exploration and discovery. In the process, they also discovered something about themselves and their city. Escaping from the Getty's formalistic concept of a "landmark" ("a conspicuous object that marks a course or serves as a guide . . . an object that can be used to define a locality"), they produced a wide range of landmarks of their own, from a backyard basketball net to the awesome geometry of L.A.'s freeways, from the inside of a barbershop in a south-central African American neighborhood to a graffiti-covered tunnel of an invisible Los Angeles River. In the book there are landmarks showing the destructive fury of the recent earthquake that sheared freeways in two, and of storefronts burned and looted during the "multicultural uprising" following the Rodney King verdict. Both were perceived as "turning points" in the history of the city.

Look again at the brief quotations about landmarks from our young artists. Raul said a landmark, "it's like a part of you." And Abbey said, "A landmark is different for everyone." A landmark, then, is not an "object" as the dictionary would have it, but a subject-centered meaning inscribed on the physical environment. But through the act of communication—through a photograph, for example—meanings can be shared. This point is taken up by Osofu ("Without landmarks there would be no history") and Sabrina ("When you destroy a landmark, you destroy some of other people's history").

An even deeper perception emerges from Osofu's remark that "if people can understand our landmarks, they can see things from our point of view." Osofu Washington is an African American. So the "people" in this sentence refers to whites, and he expresses his hope that with projects such as the Getty's, the chasm in understanding that separates white from black in Los Angeles might be bridged. Ten-year-old Daniel echoes this plea for mutual understanding. He realizes both the fragility of the web of meanings to which the landmarks project is dedicated and its ultimate importance to kids like himself growing up in the ethnic ghettos of the city: "So [the historical landmarks] . . . won't be junked up and mess up the children's future." Landmarks are essential to people's sense of who they are.

Posing the Problem

The Getty Conservation Institute probed serendipitously into a city that, most of the time, remains invisible and mute. Call it the city of everyday life. The lived spaces of the city are sometimes directly experienced, as, for example, the skateboard plaza in downtown Melbourne is experienced by the athletic youngsters who gather there on afternoons and weekends; at other times, they form merely the familiar background for what we routinely do: shop, catch the bus, walk the dog, and so on. The city of everyday life is composed of the multiple meanings with which we invest the built environment. Some of these meanings arise from intensely personal associations; others are more widely shared. Some meanings abide for centuries; others are ephemeral. It is true that we usually outgrow the meanings of places where we have passed the years of our childhood, but later we may be drawn back to them to re-experience them with the eyes of an adult. For gifted writers—a James Joyce, Marcel Proust, or Richard Wright—those places are an inexhaustible well of memories from which they draw their art. For all of us, the city where we live holds a panoply of meanings, but these meanings rarely inform the plans that reshape urban space. Usually, they are swept aside by the power brokers of the city, because they are thought to be irrelevant for the grand purposes of city building.

The city's power brokers work with authoritative representations of the city that take the form of graphs, maps, diagrams, models, and statistics. These modes of representation—the planners' stock-in-trade—are widely believed to be objective, "a little machine for producing conviction in others" (Rose 1999, 36–37). They are abstract, reductive, and static renderings of the city. Often they are embedded in documents that carry the force of law or serve as blueprints for construction. They are emblematic of scientific and professional authority. In the exhibition center of Berlin's Potsdamerplatz—tagged during the 1990s as the world's largest construction site—the severely sculptured heads (in imitation bronze!) of the architect-designers of this strategic urban site survey their handiwork with a weighty arrogance worthy of Ayn Rand's *Fountainhead*: the architect as god. These are the men (and they are all men!) who have created this city within a city ex nihilo, and the "info box," as Berliners call it, is their Pantheon. From the first-floor balcony, visitors can see the city slowly rising from the dust and din of clanking cranes, and only marvel. One doesn't argue with a god.

This, then, is the "official story" and it is overlaid on the city of everyday life, rendering it invisible. Plans and related documents rarely acknowledge the landmarks of ordinary folks, except perhaps through an occasional faded photograph of a neighborhood that was erased and now seems merely quaint. Its sepia tones suggest a rapidly receding memory of a past that has been swept away (Hayden 1997).

So why doesn't the city of everyday life ever become part of the "official story"? And what difficulties do we face in wanting to give it a legitimate standing? Lisa Peattie was the first to draw planners' attention to these problems (1987), and this chapter is inspired by her work.

But before I attempt to answer these questions, I must take you on a brief theoretical detour.

The Theory of Small Spaces

The small spaces of the city are the lived-in, experienced spaces of everyday life. To write this sentence would have been impossible but for the work of Henri Lefebvre, the preeminent French philosopher of *la vie quotidienne* and *l'espace vécu* whose seminal writings have influenced generations of urbanists on both sides of the Atlantic (Lefebvre 1968; 1974; 1996). For the specific meaning of small spaces, however, I turn to three American authors: Kevin Lynch, Christopher Alexander, and William H. Whyte. All of them did their major work during the 1970s.

Whyte's delightful but little-known exploration, *The Social Life of Small Urban Spaces* (1980; see also Whyte 1988), is a perfect starting point. Methodically, meticulously, Whyte observed and recorded people's behavior in streets and squares and in the tucked-away city parks of Manhattan and a number of other cities. He wanted to know what makes these places attractive to people, and why other spaces, though designed for public use, aren't used. Such knowledge, he hoped, would help urban planners and designers to make the city a more attractive place to live. Whyte observed of Paley Park, a minipark in Manhattan popular with New Yorkers, that

> passers-by are users of Paley, too. About half will turn and look in. Of these, about half will smile. I haven't calculated a smile index, but this vicarious, secondary enjoyment is extremely important—the sight of the park, the knowledge that it is there, becomes a part of the image we have of a much wider area. (If one had to make a cost-benefit study, I think it would show that secondary use provides as much, if not more, benefit than the primary use). If one could put a monetary value on a minute of visual enjoyment and multiply that by instances day after day,

year after year, one would obtain a rather stupendous sum. (Whyte 1980, 51)

Paley Park, so goes Whyte's argument, has entered New Yorkers' consciousness as one of the many small events that makes life pleasurable. And yet, the enjoyment it affords is registered only on William Whyte's cameras for the particular days when they were trained to capture images of the park. They register a fleeting, ephemeral pleasure—a brief smile—that tells us that the park is a significant addition to people's valued image of their city. Take away the park, and their everyday lives will be diminished.

Kevin Lynch's work is probably more widely known than Whyte's (Lynch 1973; 1981), yet both were concerned with how we experience the city, and how our experiences can be made visible. Whyte used cameras as his tool of observation, Lynch preferred the sketch maps he would ask people to draw. From these maps, he distilled a visual language and design vocabulary to analyze how well the city's image worked for people's sense of place and direction.

With his first major book, *The Image of the City* (1973), Kevin Lynch launched a research program into the construction of these so-called mental maps. He hoped that professionals would use them as a way of taking the meaning of the city's small spaces out of the subjective sphere, rendering objective people's sense of place by using the abstract language of planning, enabling designers and others to manipulate and hopefully improve these spaces. Mental mapping continued to be a major preoccupation of his. "Most difficult of all, perhaps, and quite at the heart of the city experience," he wrote years later, "is to find some objective way of recording how residents think about the place in their minds: their ways of organizing it and feeling about it. Without some knowledge of this, one is hard put to make an evaluation, since places are not merely what they are, but what we perceive them to be" (1981, 354).

Christopher Alexander's philosophical *The Timeless Way of Building* (1979) is the last of this trinity of groundbreaking American works that, along with Lefebvre's extensive writings, set out a theory of small spaces. According to Alexander,

> We must begin by understanding that every place is given its character by certain patterns of events that keep on happening there. . . . These patterns of events are always interlocked with certain geometric patterns

in the space. Indeed, . . . each building and each town is ultimately made out of these patterns in the space, and out of nothing else: they are the atoms and molecules from which a building or a town is made. (1979, 55 and 76)

For Alexander, the confluence of behavior and physical object—which he calls events—is the primary datum of the built environment and the source of our experience with it. "Those of us who are concerned with buildings tend to forget that all the life and soul of a place, all of our experiences there, depend not simply on the physical environment, but on the patterns of events which we experience there" (1979, 62). "All the life and soul of a place"—that is precisely the city of everyday life. And larger patterns are built up from smaller ones: "The larger patterns which are needed to define the whole, can be created piecemeal, by the slow concrescence of the individual acts" (1979, 496).

This organic philosophy—concrescence, or a growing together, a term borrowed from biology—bears a striking resemblance to a well-known theory of incremental policy change through sequences of mutual adjustment among actors, which engaged many planners thirty-five years ago (Lindblom 1965). Both theories, however, suffer from a fundamental flaw. Small systems are parts of larger ones, to be sure, *but the larger system has its own dynamics*; it is not merely a result of gradual "concrescence." A theory like Alexander's, whose only story is how the built city evolves from minute events into larger physical patterns, can never be a theory of urban form as a whole. The shape of cities and regions is determined by forces that are larger—national policies, for example, or global markets.

What message do these decades-old theories of the city of small spaces have for us today? A synthesis of this impressive array of individual works—informed by Heideggerian and Marxist philosophy, urban sociology, urban planning, and architecture—is not possible. Each author opens a small window unto a landscape, and each sees something very different. My own take is by a more circuitous route.

Valence, a term used in psychology, refers to the attraction or aversion an individual feels with respect to a specific object or event. As we walk city streets, spaces either attract or repel us, put us at ease or alert us to possible dangers, give us a feeling of repose or awe, remind us of who we are and have become or warn us from crossing dangerous thresholds.

The experienced city is a dense web woven of such valences or meanings with which we endow its geometry, especially the intimate spaces of social reproduction and places of work, along with the pathways that connect them. In this perspective, the city is not merely a node of capital accumulation (which our large cities certainly are) but also a set of particular places that are lived-in, experienced, and charged with meaning by their inhabitants.

Many of these meanings come to be shared and, to this extent, they lose their unfathomable subjectivity, becoming factual by a sort of truth-by-consensus. Not that all of the city's residents will inscribe the same valences on their environment. The visible city is rather a palimpsest of shifting meanings that are always in flux and frequently overlap, coincide, and collide with one another. And notwithstanding the notable efforts of Whyte, Lynch, and Alexander, these meanings are exceedingly difficult to represent authoritatively.

Master Narratives and Other Stories

I return now to the questions I posed at the beginning of this chapter: Why doesn't the city of everyday life ever become part of the "official story"? And what difficulties do we face in wanting to give it a legitimate standing? In most cities around the world, the "official story" is devised by the power brokers of the city. Most of them are men. It is a story typically driven by a desire for power and material gain. For many among the power brokers, land is primarily a potential source of profit, and therefore they privilege economic growth, capital accumulation, and globalization over social, cultural, and environmental concerns. The small, lived spaces of the city are for them chiefly a diversion from the all-absorbing business of making money (and gaining status) out of city building.

A telling example is a recent publication issued by the Australian State of Victoria's Department of Infrastructure, which oversees the physical planning for the entire state, including metropolitan Melbourne. The document is a glossy brochure filled with statistical tables, graphs, and pie charts, with the catchy title *From Doughnut City to Café Society* (State of Victoria Department of Infrastructure 1998). Ostensibly, this handsomely produced publication reports on demographic changes for the metropolitan area as revealed by an analysis of the 1996 census. It tells the story of a "turn-around" in the traditional pattern of settlement.

During the post–World War II period, Melbourne expanded rapidly into its outer suburbs, as more and more families were able to realize their "dream" of a large house on a quarter-acre suburban lot. Inner-city areas were emptying out and becoming derelict, thus the phrase *Doughnut City*: suburban growth, inner-city decline. But by the mid-1990s, significant changes in this trend could be observed: empty nesters were starting to move back into the city, young people were tending to marry later, white-collar were replacing blue-collar jobs, and "yuppies" were living in apartments close to where the action was. Medium-density development was beginning to replace the quarter-acre lot. And so "Café Society" was born.

The city's power brokers were keen to promote this conversion, and they pushed major projects to reinforce this trend. They built Australia's largest, most opulent casino-hotel cum entertainment palace overlooking the Yarra River. They undertook a huge redevelopment scheme in the former Docklands off to one side of Melbourne's central business district where, they hoped, the world's tallest building would rise 120 stories into the sky, thousands of elegant marina-oriented housing units would line the waterfront, a multipurpose state-of-the-art stadium would attract 80,000 people to its year-round events, and a science-technology park would help to round out this image of "Victoria on the Move." They also assigned contracts for the city's first privatized system of toll roads, foreshadowing the demise of the city's traditional system of streetcars; and they were determined to turn Melbourne into an international sporting capital with events like the Australian Formula 1 Grand Prix (Sandercock and Dovey forthcoming; Dovey and Sandercock forthcoming).

The Department of Infrastructure publication made only passing reference to these projects, but the way the data were presented made it fairly obvious whose interests were being served. The four local council areas that constitute Melbourne's inner city are, in fact, quite small, comprising less than 8 percent of the metropolitan population. These same areas are also the economically most privileged: 44 percent of their population work in managerial, administrative, or professional occupations, 20 percent have advanced degrees, and 11 percent earn more than a thousand dollars per week. They also harbor a remarkably young population: a full quarter is in the twenty- to twenty-nine-year-old age group. The rest of metropolitan Melbourne, or 92 percent of the population, are rendered invisible; they are not part of Café Society. They continue to live their ghost lives in the middle and, above all, the outer suburbs, and among them are many immigrants.

The report is littered with twenty-five-year demographic projections, a notoriously inaccurate species of projection, especially for small areas. But no methodology is given, and inherent uncertainties in the projections remain unacknowledged. Instead, a five-year "trendlet" of migration inversion from suburbs to the inner city is projected as irreversible for the next quarter century, because the political task of the publication is to persuade Melbourne's opinion makers to accept its logic. In his public pronouncements, the Minister of Planning had nothing but derisory remarks about the people he called "wheelie binners" (residents of leafy suburbs who roll their garbage containers out to the curb for weekly pick-ups), who are forever "whingeing" (complaining) over the government's lack of attention to their needs. He seemed to be saying, Why don't they, too, join the trek to the inner city and the glamorous Café Society on the south bank of the Yarra?

With their attractive publication, Victoria's Department of Infrastructure constructed a new master narrative for the city's power brokers, which leaves scant room for argument. Substantive objections would quickly get lost in a maze of technical rebuttals about demographic projections, the inclusion or exclusion of certain local council areas from the "inner city" and so on, ad infinitum. Knowledge here is clearly at the service of power.

My second question concerns what I perceive to be the very real difficulties of authentically representing the city of everyday life. The problem is this: The reductive language of maps and statistics is, in the event, quite useless. Meanings are formed by experience and are shared in the small talk of everyday life. As a rule, this talk carries little weight with planners and engineers. It is as lightweight as William H. Whyte's photographs of fleeting smiles. And even if we were to eavesdrop on the small talk of neighborhoods, we would soon discover that the words *not* spoken are often more important those that are. Silence forms the shared background of understandings over which words ripple like waves. Moreover, the stories people tell one another are unlike the stories meant only for the ears of strangers. The first are often alive with feeling, gaining such power as they have from the tone fall and color of passionate speech, whereas the stories told to strangers tend to be more formal and are pitched to reveal as much as to conceal.

A small number of city landmarks are assimilated to the "official story," becoming icons of city marketing: the Eiffel Tower, Sydney's Opera House, the Golden Gate Bridge, Frank Gehry's Guggenheim Museum Bilbao. But the landmarks of ordinary people, as we saw in the Getty photo project, are hidden in the small spaces of everyday life, in backyards and barbershops. And when they are not simply taken for granted, that's what their talk is about. The difficulty, then, is twofold: on one hand, to sort out purely personal, idiosyncratic meanings from those about which there is wider agreement and, on the other, to make shared meanings sufficiently audible to be counted as serious statements about shaping urban neighborhoods.

Enter Civil Society

Some of the ways to accomplish these purposes are well understood; others less so. They all involve a degree of mobilization and/or organization on the part of civil society. Perhaps the most familiar of these ways is *popular struggle–protest–resistance*. Keith Pezzoli gives a detailed account of an urban resistance movement in Mexico City (1998, chapter 9). In the 1980s, the Mexican government tried to stem the overspill of popular, self-built housing into a so-called ecological zone, the Bosques del Pedregal, high up in the mountains encircling the city to the south. But it was not only a matter of saving the ecology of the area. There were also powerful private interests involved that saw the very same "ecological zone" as the perfect location for villas and upper-class residential developments. The local communities mobilized against threatened dislodgment and were soon joined by sympathizers from the city, many of them university students. With many ups and downs, the struggle has continued for over two decades, and it is not yet over. But the people of Bosques del Pedregal are still there, and their first priority—housing and a hold on the land—has been achieved.

Another and quite exceptional mode of accommodation between civil society and power brokers is illustrated by the southern Brazilian city of Pôrto Alegre. This story turns on a *participatory mode* of municipal capital budgeting that has been successfully implemented for more than a decade (Abers 2000). Acceding to power with the support of popular movements in 1989, the Brazilian Workers Party set out to reform the city's traditional clientilistic politics. Its first priority was to ensure that more of the city's limited resources would go toward improving daily life in the settlements of Pôrto Alegre's working-class suburbs and toward projects that were identified with the help of the people living there. An elaborate system of consultations was worked out over the next several years and led to significant accomplishments, not least in the form of urban governance. As many as fifteen thousand people might be involved in any given budget year, attending literally hundreds of neighborhood meetings to debate local priorities for municipal investment. For everyone concerned, not least for the bureaucrats in the city administration, this was an extraordinary educational experience. Roads were paved and schools and clinics were built, largely in accord with people's considered wishes, though the final decision remained with city council, and negotiations were constantly taking place. Since its first incumbency, the Workers Party has been reelected to office twice, proof that people are reasonably content with how their government is doing its job.

A less dramatic example of a form of *collaborative planning* comes from Spitalfields, a predominantly Bengali neighborhood in London's East End, abutting the city (Lo Piccolo 1999). Spitalfields is one of the poorest, most overcrowded areas in London and was picked by the Thatcher government as a prime target for gentrification and redevelopment. Initial protests led to the formation of the Spitalfields Community Development Group. A slowdown in the urban economy during the early 1990s tamed developers' rapaciousness and created an interregnum during which intensive negotiations between the community and developers took place. The Bengalis, especially along Brick Lane, the main thoroughfare running through their neighborhood, were not interested in merely stopping the "invasion" but of exploiting it for their own purposes. New, more ample housing was needed for their numerous extended families. The unemployment rate had to be cut by at least half. New facilities, such as a bazaar, that would serve this multiethnic community needed to be built. To implement these initiatives, a trust fund was set up, with contributions from the developers. In these various ways, collaborative planning helped to bend redevelopment in ways that would enhance rather than destroy the local community. And, as in Pôrto Alegre, the story continues.

Finally, a brief note about what I would call *counterplanning*. By counterplanning I mean a form of planning at the initiative of and carried out by the residents of a neighborhood, though generally with professional (and financial) outside help. The following story is taken from a personal communication from Professor Anastasia Loukaitou-Sideris of UCLA's School of Public Policy and Social Research (1999; see also 2000). She writes,

> I worked with seventeen UCLA students on a comprehensive project that helped Pico-Union residents develop a plan for physical and economic revitalization of their community and streets. This is a very low-income immigrant area which has, however, some very motivated residents [most of them from Central America] and local institutions. They were able to attract a $350,000 grant from the Los Angeles Neighborhood Initiative. We worked with local residents, merchants, churches, PTAs, and school children and brought them together in an effort to crystallize some vision for this neighborhood, which has never appeared in official plans and policies. The exciting thing is that implementation of some of the work has already started and will continue for the next couple of years.

Acts of resistance, as well as participatory, collaborative, and counterplanning are some of the forms of involving civil society in giving expression to its sense of what's important in the city of everyday life. Each of the four stories involves the mobilization of sectors of civil society and a capacity and willingness to negotiate with the power brokers of the city. They are stories of community empowerment where initial weakness is transmuted into strength. Not all stories, of course, end on this upbeat note, and worldwide, there are probably more failures than successes. Historical conjunctures, personalities, and luck all contribute to outcomes. But, as the *I Ching* advises, "Perseverance matters." These stories never seem to end, even when our accounts of them do. They simply merge with the flow of life.

The Right to the City

Whatever we may think of Alexander's biological metaphor of concrescence, it is probably true that most people would prefer gradual change to changes that are unexpected, sudden, and massive, especially when it affects the intimate spaces of their habitat. The gradual transformation of their lived spaces has many origins, including technology, demography, the land market, and migration. Given sufficient time to adjust, changes of this sort are seen to be part of normal life.

But when change comes all at once, without forewarning, it is a violent act that severely disrupts shared meanings and the social relations on which these meanings depend.[1] Examples abound. So-called squatter removal from self-built housing in Third World cities is a particularly reprehensible practice. The construction of major thoroughfares through residential neighborhoods is equally disruptive. The wholesale razing of old housing stock to make way for office buildings and upscale apartment blocks is another variant of the same story. And so is the cumulative location of unwanted facilities—prisons, garbage incinerators, landfills, chemical storage tanks—in poor people's neighborhoods, a well-known strategy adopted by the state as it seeks locations that are least likely to offer effective resistance.

In all these instances, "invasion" typically arrives without prior notice. Those who are its victims are frequently the most vulnerable, least organized parts of the population. As far as the city's power brokers are concerned, these folks are little more than a bothersome obstacle to what appears to them as self-evident progress. Land clearance schemes, gentrification, redevelopment must go forward for the "general good" of the city, regardless of the pain they inflict on others, whose implicit "right to the city"—*le droit à la ville* in Henri Lefebvre's memorable phrase—goes unacknowledged. Yet the pain, the grieving, the rage caused by these disruptions are not scaled according to income or social position. Poor people feel every bit as distressed, disoriented, and disempowered over the sudden loss of meaning as would those who live in high-security villas and condominiums if a similar fate should befall them (Marris 1961; 1975).

Rupturing the web of shared meanings by the preemptory imposition of projects on the spaces of everyday life is to alienate ways of life to which we have a rightful claim. People may respond to the violation of this right in various ways. For some, the destruction of their small spaces leads to grief, resigned acquiescence, or a hasty departure from the scene. This essentially *fatalistic* response undermines the sense of active citizenship that is the foundation of a vital democracy. A second, *political,* response is rage, as in street protests, social mobilization, and other forms of collective resistance.[2] A third I call, for want of a better term, the response of *opting-out.* Repeated invasions of disempowered people's life space send a strong message that they are regarded as the cannon fodder of urban progress. Young people especially, acting on this perception, may choose to cross over into the anticity of gangs, lawlessness, and drugs where they can make their mark, even at the risk of imprisonment or early death. Political responses address the mainstream, hoping for a redress of their grievances; but when rioting breaks out, the anticity is likely to be in the front lines. In any event, "opting-out" on a large scale exacts a heavy price on a society and may signal a city's downturn from economic success to failure. Detroit is perhaps the best-known example in America, but Los Angeles and Chicago appear to be going down the same path (Abu-Lughod 1999).

Toward Utopia?

In recent years, a number of Anglo-American planning theorists—John Forester, Judith Innes, Patsy Healey, and Leonie Sandercock—have focused attention on ways to involve civil society in plan making, thus continuing a tradition of citizen participation that evolved out of the turbulent 1960s. The new emphasis is on communication, collaboration, mediation, and diversity in planning. Terms like *radical* and even *insurgent planning* are beginning to appear (see chapter 4 in this volume), suggesting that planning is no longer an exclusive state monopoly but may be launched on the initiative of disempowered groups as well. I have mentioned a few examples. In addition, there have been numerous attempts at community consultations about strategic planning and the like, which may involve hundreds of local residents (Sarkissian, Walsh, and Cook 1997). But community consultations are rarely able to capture the views of the most disempowered groups, particularly of those whose language is not standard English or whose educational level falls below the norm.

Whatever their shortcomings may be, these efforts point in the right direction. But the power equation still holds, and master narratives about doughnuts and café societies are not easily challenged. Political mobilization calls for a lot of energy, and most people are unwilling to give up their time to it, unless it's a matter of vital importance to them. Only activists regard it as their citizen duty (right?) to speak on behalf of an inclusive interest in matters of planning. Unless the threat of an "invasion" of life space is immediate and direct, civil society remains preoccupied with leisure activities such as swim clubs, bird watching, choral singing, or just going to the pub. But protests and protracted resistance do occur, and they are not always in vain.

The city of everyday life survives. It survives because life reproduces the city even under the most difficult and harsh conditions. But the fact remains that power can be effectively countered only with power, and the power of civil society becomes actual only through organized resistance to the power brokers of the city. It is only by mobilizing politically that ordinary people can gain an effective voice.

6
The Good City: In Defense of Utopian Thinking

The Utopian Impulse

Utopian thinking, the capacity to imagine a future that is radically different from what we know to be the prevailing order of things, is a way of breaking through the barriers of convention into a sphere of the imagination where many things beyond our everyday experience become possible. All of us have this ability, which I believe to be inherent in human nature because human beings are insufficiently programmed for the future. We need a constructive imagination to help us create the fictive worlds of our dreams, of dreams worth struggling for.

There are, of course, other ways of deploying this capacity than the imagining of utopias. With its promise of redemption, *religion* is one of them and, for many people, religious faith satisfies their thirst for meaning. Faith in an *ideology* is the secular counterpart to religion. American ideology is based on the belief that human progress is appropriately measured by continuous betterment in the material conditions of living for individuals. The goal is a mass society of consumers. Along with cornucopia, it includes an affirmation of democratic institutions (so long as they support global markets) and unswerving trust in the powers of technology to solve whatever problems might come our way.[1] Finally, intense *nationalism* may also satisfy the need for a transcendent purpose in life.[2] The question of why are we here arises precisely because the human condition leaves the future open and requires a response on our part.

Beyond the alternative constructions of religion, ideology, and nationalism, there are many good reasons why we might wish to engage in utopian thinking. For some of us, it is no more than an amusing pastime.

For others it serves as a veiled critique of present evils. For still others it may be, in the phrase of Sir Philip Sidney's comment on Thomas More's *Utopia* in 1595, a persuasive means of "leading men to virtue" (quoted in Manuel and Manuel 1979, 2). On the other hand, in its negative form of *dystopia* it may alert us to certain tendencies in the present that, if allowed to continue unchecked, would lead to a thoroughly abhorrent world. The twentieth century produced many literary dystopias (not to mention the many actual ones), from Aldous Huxley's *Brave New World* to the cyberpunk novels of William Gibson and others (Warren et al. 1998). But most important of all, utopian thinking can help us choose a path into the future that we believe is justified, because its concrete imagery is informed by those values we hold dear.

Utopian thinking has two moments that are inextricably joined: critique and constructive vision. The critique is of certain aspects of our present condition: injustice, oppression, ecological devastation to name just a few. It is precisely an enumeration of these evils that tells us that certain moral codes are being violated. The code may not be written out or it may only be symbolically suggested whenever we invoke such slogans as "freedom," "equality," or "solidarity." Moral outrage over an injustice suggests that we have a sense of justice, inarticulate though it may be.

Now it is true that negative and positive images are not necessarily symmetrical with respect to each other. Most of us would probably agree that great material inequalities are unjust, yet we would differ vehemently in our answer to what would constitute a "just" distribution of incomes and other material goods. These different ways of understanding social justice are ultimately political arguments. And as such they are unavoidable, because if injustice is to be corrected (or, for that matter, any other social evil), we will need the concrete imagery of utopian thinking to propose steps that would bring us a little closer to a more just world.

It is this concrete vision—the second moment of utopian thinking— which young Australian of the Year, Tan Le, was calling for to give her a sense of a meaningful deployment of her own powers in the public sphere (Le 1999).

> I have just completed a law degree. One of the reasons I chose law—and many other young people also include this reason for choosing it—was

because I believed that a law degree would enable me to contribute in a special way, to do what I could to make a better world.

Of course I can do this as a lawyer, but nothing in the entire law curriculum addressed this issue in a serious and engaging way. And other tertiary courses are the same. . . . Young people are not being educated to take their place in society. They are being trained—trained in a narrow body of knowledge and skills that is taught in isolation from larger and vital questions about who we are and what we might become.

There is, in other words, a complete absence of a larger vision, and many young people who enter university in the hope that what they learn will help them make a better world soon find out that this is not a consideration.

And it is not just in tertiary education courses that this lack of vision prevails. We lack it as a society. We have replaced it with what might be called a rationale. To my mind, this is not the same thing as a vision. It is more pragmatic, smaller in scope, less daring, and it does not fire the heart or capture the imagination. It does not inspire.

Vision carries the connotation of value, meaning and purpose—and of something beyond our reach that is nevertheless worth striving for and aspiring to.

Visionings of this kind are always debatable, both in their own terms and when measured against alternative proposals. That is why I call them political. Where the uncensored public expression of opinion is allowed, they should become the substance of political argument. Utopian thinking should not be fairy tales but concern genuine futures around which political coalitions can be built.

There are always limitations to purposive action—of leadership, relations of power, resources, knowledge. But if we start with these limitations rather than with images of a desired future, we may never arrive at the future we desire. Successful utopian constructs must have the power to generate the passion for a political practice that will bring us a little closer to the visions they embody.

The Utopian Tradition in Planning

With considerations of this sort, we find ourselves back on the familiar ground of planning. City and regional planning have an enduring tradition of utopian thought (Friedmann 1987; Friedmann and Weaver 1979;

Weaver 1984). The evocation of the classics—Robert Owen, Charles Fourier, Pierre Joseph Proudhon, William Morris, Peter Kropotkin, Ebenezer Howard, Lewis Mumford, Frank Lloyd Wright, Percival, and Paul Goodman—are all names in common currency among the tribe. For more recent decades, I would add the names of Jane Jacobs, Kevin Lynch, E. F. Schumacher, Ivan Illich, and Murray Bookchin. And still closer to our time and, indeed, contemporary with us, I am inclined to mention certain works of Dolores Hayden (1984) and Leonie Sandercock (1997). Given this chain of utopian writings stretching over two hundred years that have influenced the education of planners and, to a greater or lesser degree, have also shaped their practice, it would be hard to argue that even the mainstream of the planning profession has stayed aloof from utopian thinking.

In a recent essay, Susan Fainstein asks whether we can make the cities we want (Fainstein 1999). In her account, the important values that should inform our thinking about cities include material equality, cultural diversity, democratic participation, and ecological sustainability in a metropolitan milieu. Fainstein's background is in political economy, so it is not surprising that she should give pride of place to the question of material equality and follow, if not uncritically, David Harvey's lead in *Justice, Nature, and the Geography of Difference* (1996). I will return to this prioritization later in this chapter.

But before I do, I would like to recall an argument I made fourteen years ago in *Planning in the Public Domain* (Friedmann 1987). In the second and third parts of that volume I attempted to sketch an intellectual history—a genealogy—of planning thought and, at the same time, to go beyond this history to advocate a transformative approach to planning that, because it was based on the mobilization of the disempowered groups in society, I called radical. I argued that the central focus of radical planning is political action by organized groups within civil society. Its radicalism derives from actions that, with or without and even against the state, are aimed at universal emancipation. "A key principle in radical, transformative practice," I wrote, "is that *no group can be completely free until freedom [from oppression] has been achieved for every group.* Thus, the struggle for emancipation leads to results that will always be partial and contradictory, until the final and possibly utopian goal of a free humanity is reached" (301).[3] I then examined what planners who opt for emancipatory struggles actually do. Among the many things I considered are elaborating a hard-hitting critical analysis of existing conditions; assisting in the mobilization of communities to rectify these conditions; assisting in devising appropriate strategies of struggle; refining the technical aspects of transformative solutions; facilitating social learning from radical practice; mediating between the mobilized community and the state; helping to ensure the widest possible participation of community members in all phases of the struggle; helping to rethink the group's course of action in the light of new understandings; and becoming personally involved in transformative practice (303–7). I wanted it to be understood that utopian thinking, at least as far as planners are concerned, is historically grounded in specific emancipatory practices. Planning of this sort stands in the grand utopian tradition. Leonie Sandercock calls it an *insurgent* planning (Sandercock 1999).

In this chapter, my intention is somewhat different. Rather than talk about political struggles to resist specific forms of oppression, my aim is to identify some elements for a vision of the "good city." And I want to do so in the manner of an achievable utopia rather than paint a scenario set in an indeterminate future.[4]

A century during which the vast majority of the world's population will be living in urban environments cries out for images of the good city. I have purposely phrased this need in the plural. Taking the world as a whole, the diversity of starting conditions is so great that no single version of the city will suffice. Fifty years from now, the world's urban population will be roughly double the existing numbers of nearly three billion. We can thus look ahead to a historically unprecedented period of city-building. And city-builders need not only blue prints for their work but *guiding normative images.* The following remarks are addressed to planners and to anyone else who wishes to confront the multiple challenges of the age.[5]

Imagining the Good City 1: Theoretical Considerations

Before I proceed, some preliminaries must be considered. First, in setting out an account of the good city, whose city are we talking about? Can we legitimately assume the possibility of a "common good" for the city? Second, are we concerned only with process or only with outcomes, or should outcome and process be considered jointly? And finally, how is a normative framework such as we are considering to be thought of in relation to professional practice?

Whose City?

We have been bludgeoned into accepting as gospel that to speak of the common good is either propaganda or false consciousness. The attacks on the common good have come from all ideological quarters. Liberal pluralists see only a diversity of group interests striking temporary bargains in the political arena. Marxists argue on roughly similar grounds that the "common good" is merely a phrase invoked by the bourgeois ruling class, to hide purposes that are nothing other than an expression of their own class interest. Postmodern critics who see only a world of fleeting kaleidoscopic images, dissolve the "common good" into a thousand discursive fragments, dismissing attempts to raise any one of them above the rest as an unjustifiable attempt to establish a new "meta-narrative" in an age from which metanarratives (other than postmodern narratives) have been banned.

Against all of these intellectually dismissive critics, I want to argue the necessity of continuing to search for the common good of a city, if only because, without such a conception, there can be no political community. In democratic polities, there has to be at least minimal agreement on the political structure of the community and on the possibility of discovering in given circumstances and through appropriate processes, a "common good." A merely administered city is not a political community and might as well be a hotel managed by some multinational concern. In that case, the answer to the question of whose city would be clear: whether cities or prisons, it is always the notorious bottom line that counts. In a putative democracy, however, the city is ultimately identified with "the people," and the cliché notwithstanding, it is the *demos* who must argue out among themselves, time after time, in what specific agendas of action the "common good" of the city may be found. It seems to me that there is a considerable difference in whether we seek to justify an action by grounding it in a conception of the "common good"—a conception that always remains open to political challenge, of course—or to assert it without any voices of dissent or, worst of all, to consider it an irrelevant diversion from hard-knuckle power politics.

Process versus Outcomes

This opposition of terms has a long pedigree. Democratic proceduralists believe in process, partly because they assume that the differences among the parties in contention are relatively minor, and because today's majority will become tomorrow's minority, and vice versa. In the long run, everybody gets a turn. Opposed to them are Kantian idealists for whom good intentions are sufficient in themselves to define what is good. A third position is held by those who are so persuaded of the rightness of their own ethical position that they lack patience with democratic procedure, pursuing their ends by whatever means are at hand. Among them are many who believe in the theory of the "big revolutionary bang." Transformative change, according to this theory, necessitates a sharp break with the past, a break that is often connected with violence, because the ancien régime must be destroyed before a genuine revolutionary age can dawn.

My own position is to deny this separation of ends and means, outcomes and process. Process, by which I specifically mean transparent democratic procedures, is no less important than desirable outcome. But democratic procedures are likely to be abandoned if they do not, in the longer term, lead to broadly acceptable outcomes. Moreover, a liberal democratic process also includes the nonviolent struggles for social justice and other ultimate concerns that take place outside the formal institutional framework. So, on one hand, we need an inclusive democratic framework that allows for the active pursuit of political objectives even when these are contrary to the dominant interests. On the other hand, we need to be clear about the objectives to be pursued. The imaginary of the good city has to embrace both of these terms.

Intention and Practice

The good city requires a committed form of political practice. It was Hannah Arendt who formed my concept of action or political praxis (she used the terms interchangeably) when she wrote, "To act, in its most general sense, means to take an initiative, to begin . . . to set something into motion. . . . It is in the nature of beginning that something new is started which cannot be expected from whatever may have happened before. The character of startling unexpectedness is inherent in all beginnings and in all origins" (Arendt 1958, 177–88). In other words, *to act is to set something new into the world.* And this requires an actor or rather a number of such, because political action always involves a collective entity or group. There are, of course, certain conditions of action. The group must first be brought together and mobilized. This means leadership. The group must also have the material, symbolic, and moral power sufficient to overcome resistance to its project. In the longer term, both the group's actions and the counteractions to its initiatives lead to results that are boundless and therefore require continuous social learning. The group must be passionately committed to its practice, or it will be defeated in the early rounds of the struggle (Friedmann 1987, 44–47).

The Good City 2: Human Flourishing As a Fundamental Human Right

If they are not to be seen as arbitrary, principles of the good city must be drawn from somewhere, they must logically be connected to some foundational value. Such a founding principle must be clearly and explicitly formulated, so that it can be communicated even to those among us who are not philosophically inclined. I would formulate this principle as follows: *Every human being has the right, by nature, to the full development of their innate intellectual, physical, and spiritual capabilities in the context of wider communities.* This is the *right to human flourishing,* and I regard it as the most fundamental of human rights. But it has never been universally acknowledged as an inherently human right. Slave societies knew nothing of it; nor did caste societies, tribal societies, corporate village societies, or totalitarian states. And in no society have women ever enjoyed the same right to human flourishing as men. But as the fundamental, inalienable right of every person, human flourishing is inscribed in the liberal democratic ethos.

In contemporary Western societies, and particularly in America, human flourishing underlies the strongly held belief that privilege should be earned rather than inherited. Accordingly, human beings should have an equal start in life. Over a lifetime, individual and group outcomes will, of course, vary a good deal because of differences in inborn abilities, family upbringing, entrenched class privilege, and social oppression. Still, the idea of a basic equality among all citizens underlies the mild socialism of Western societies with their systems of public education, public health, the graduated income tax, antidiscriminatory legislation, and so forth, all of which seek some sort of leveling of life chances among individuals and groups.

As this reference to political institutions makes evident, the potential of human flourishing can only be realized in the context of wider communities. So right from the start, we posit humans, not as Leibnizian monads, but as beings-in-relation, as essentially *social* beings. It is therefore mischievous, as Margaret Thatcher is reported to have done, to dismiss the concept of society as a fiction. Human beings cannot survive without the unmediated support of others, from intimate family on up to larger structures and strong emotional ties to individuals and groups. Nothing can be accomplished without them.

The social sphere imposes certain requirements of its own, and these may appear as constraints on willful action. Although as individuals, we are ultimately responsible for whatever we do, we are always constrained by (1) our social relations with family, friends, workmates, and neighbors, in short, by a culturally specific *ethics of mutual obligation* and (2) the wider sociopolitical settings of our lives that in various ways may inhibit human flourishing. The two are intertwined in many ways;[6] however, it would require a separate essay to even begin to disentangle them and to do justice to the powerful constraints we, and especially women, encounter in the sphere of relations I call civil. Instead, I will turn to the sociopolitical sphere, which is my primary focus.

Briefly, my argument is that we do not merely use the city to advance personal interests—some will do so more successfully than others—but to contribute as citizen-members of a political community to bringing about *those minimal conditions—political, economic, social, physical, and ecological—that are essential for human flourishing.* I refer to these conditions—and I regard them as only *minimal* conditions—as the common good of the polity, or the *good city,* because human flourishing is inconceivable without them. In this understanding, the "common good" of the city appears as something akin to *citizen rights,* that is, to the claims that local citizens can legitimately make on their political community as a basis for the flourishing of all its citizens. Making these claims, *and at the same time contributing to their realization in practice,* is one of the deep obligations of local citizenship (see chapter 4).

The Good City 3: Multipli/city as a Primary Good

Human flourishing serves us as a template for judging the performance of cities. But to assist us in this detailed, critical work of assessing the extent to which a city provides an adequate setting for human flourishing, further guidelines are needed. I propose a primary good—multipli/city—together with certain conditions that allow multipli/city to be realized in practice.

By *multipli/city,* I mean an autonomous civil life substantially free from direct supervision and control by the state. So considered, a vibrant civil life is the necessary social context for human flourishing. Multipli/city acknowledges the priority of civil society, which is the sphere of freedom and social reproduction—and it is for its sake that the city can be said to exist. Political economists might disagree with this ordering. They tend to describe the city in terms of capital accumulation, market exchange, administrative control, and the like, and urban populations in terms of their incorporation into labor markets and social classes. From an analytical perspective, I don't object to these characterizations, but if our project is the good city, a different and explicitly normative approach is needed.

In its political aspect, then, civil society constitutes the political community of the city. But there are other aspects of a richly articulated civil life, including religious, social, cultural, and economic life, all of which can be subsumed under the concept of a self-organizing civil society.[7] Michael Waltzer calls civil society "a project of projects," foreshadowing my own characterization of multipli/city. The relevant passage is worth quoting in full.

> Civil society is sustained by groups much smaller than the *demos* or the working class or the mass of consumers or the nation. All these are necessarily pluralized as they are incorporated. They become part of the world of family, friends, comrades and colleagues, where people are connected to one another and made responsible for one another. Connected and responsible: without that, "free and equal" is less attractive than we once thought it would be. I have no magic formula for making connections or strengthening the sense of responsibility. These are not aims that can be underwritten with historical guarantees or achieved through a single unified struggle. Civil society is a project of projects; it requires many organizing strategies and new forms of state action. It requires a new sensitivity for what is local, specific, contingent—and, above all, a new recognition (to paraphrase a famous sentence) that the good life is in the details. (1992, 107)

Throughout history, city populations have grown primarily through migration, and migrants come from many parts. Some don't speak the dominant language of the city; others practice different religions; still others follow folkways that are alien to the city. They come to the city for its promise of a more liberated, fulfilling life, and also perhaps, for safety, escaping from the danger of physical harm. They do not come to the city to be regimented, to be molded according to a single concept of correct living. Nor do they seek diversity as such. Rather, they want to live as undisturbed as possible by their own lights, so that diversity appears as simply a by-product of the "project of projects." But cities are not always hospitable, and mutual tolerance of difference must be safeguarded by the state so long as certain conditions are fulfilled: respect for human rights and the assumption of the rights and obligations of local citizenship. In a broadly tolerant society, one may perhaps hope for a step beyond tolerance, which is to say, for mutual acceptance and even the affirmation of difference (see chapter 3).

Reflected in a thickly quilted mosaic of voluntary associations, multipli/city requires a solid material base. A destitute people can only think about survival, which absorbs nearly all the time and energies at their disposal. A substantial material base therefore must provide for the time, energy, and space needed for active citizenship. Four pillars support the material foundations for the good city. First in order of importance is *socially adequate housing* together with a complement of public services and community facilities. As innumerable struggles in cities throughout the world have shown, individual households regard housing (along with a reliable water supply and affordable urban transit) as a first priority. *Affordable health care* comes second, particularly for women, infants and children, the physically and mentally challenged, the chronically ill, and the elderly, as an essential condition for human flourishing. *Adequately remunerated work* for all who seek it is the third pillar. In urban market societies, well-paying work is a nearly universal aspiration not only for the income it brings but also for the social regard attached to productive work in a capitalist society. Finally, *adequate social provision* must be made for those whose own efforts are insufficient to provide for what is regarded as an adequate social minimum.

Each of these four pillars has given rise to a vast literature, both technical and philosophical, and it is not my intention here to review it. I do want to take up an important point of difference, however, that I have with the old socialist Left who have consistently argued that justice— social justice—demands "equalizing access to material well-being." The Left has always given priority to rectifying material inequalities. And though it is undoubtedly true that unrestrained capitalist accumulation leads to profound inequalities, gross differences in income and wealth have, in fact, existed in all social formations since the beginnings of urban society. My disagreement is therefore with a vision that regards material inequalities as primary and thus the only appropriate focus of popular struggle. But all historical attempts to level inequalities, as in Maoist China, have had to employ barbaric methods to suppress what appears to me to be precisely the primary good, which is a flourishing civil life in association with others. It is certainly true that since 1980, major inequalities have resurfaced in urban China, but alongside these inequalities are also the first sproutings of a civil society (Brook and Frolic 1997). As much as I welcome the second, I have no wish to justify the first, which is accompanied by its own evils of exclusion, exploitation, and corruption (Solinger 1999). Still, the two phenomena are not independent of each other, as they point to a general relaxation of government control over social and economic life. And even though I argue here for "four pillars" to provide the material foundations of the good city, I regard them as chiefly a means to a more transcendent end, which is a vibrant civil life and the context for human flourishing. Genuine material equality, Maoist style, is neither achievable nor desirable. Whereas we will always have to live with material inequalities, what we must never tolerate is a contemptuous disregard for the qualities of social and political life, which is the sphere of freedom. A good city is a city that cares for its freedom, even as it makes adequate social provision for its weakest members.

The Good City 4: Good Governance

If process is as important as outcome, as I argued at the beginning of this essay, we will have to consider the processes of governance in the good city. Governance refers to the various ways by which binding decisions for cities and city-regions are made and carried out. It is thus a concept considerably more inclusive than traditional government and administration and reflects the fact that increasingly a much wider range of participants exists in these processes than has traditionally been the case.

Three sets of potential actors can be identified. First are the politicians and bureaucrats who represent the institutions of the local state. It is because of them that decisions concerning city-building are made "binding." The state can be seen as standing at the apex of a pyramid whose base is defined, respectively, by corporate capital and civil society. The role of corporate capital in city-building has become more pronounced in recent years, encouraged by privatization and the growing emphasis on mega-projects, from high-rise apartment blocks, new towns, office developments, and technology parks to toll roads, bridges, harbor reclamation schemes, and airports. The role of civil society in urban governance has been a more contested issue. Beyond the rituals of "citizen participation" in planning, civil society's major role, in most cities, has taken the form of protest and resistance to precisely the mega-projects that are so dear to state and capital.[8] Civil society has also put pressure on the state for more sustainable cities, for environmental justice, and for more inclusive visions of the city.

In a utopian exercise, it is tempting to invert the order of things and, as in this case, to place local citizens at the top of the governance pyramid. This would be broadly in accord with democratic theory as well as with my earlier claim that the city exists for the sake of its citizens who are bound to one another, by mutual (if tacit) agreement, to form a political community. But I hesitate, because I am not convinced that city-regions on the scale of multiple millions can be organized like New England town meetings or the Athenian agora. Nor do I believe in the vaunted capacity of the Internet—even supposing universal access were realized—to overcome the problem of scale. Democratic governance requires something more than a "thumbs up"/"thumbs down" public intervention on any given issue, which is no more meaningful than telephone surveys at the end of a presidential debate in the United States, asking the question, "Who won?"

An alternative would be simply to scale down city-regional governance until governance becomes itself coextensive with what I have called "the city of everyday life" (see chapter 5). Thomas Jefferson had a name for it: "The republic of the wards" (for a summary, see Friedmann 1973a, 220–22). More recently, there have been calls (in the United States) for "neighborhood governments" (Kotler 1969; Morris and Hess 1975; King and Stivers 1998). And there is even a Chinese-Taiwanese version of this idea, citing the writings of Lao-Zi (Cheng and Hsia 1999), as well as a striking example from southern Brazil (Abers 2000). Evidently, there is something very attractive about this devolution of powers to the most local of local levels—the neighborhood, the street. But a city-region is more than the sum of its neighborhoods, and each level of spatial integration must be slotted into a larger whole, which is the city-region. The question then is how to articulate this whole so as to further the idea of multipli/city and the four pillars of a good city.

I do not claim great originality for my criteria of good governance for city-regions.[9] But I would like to think that they have some cross-cultural validity, because they address what are ultimately very practical issues that must be dealt with in large cities east and west, north and south. Still, in any attempt to apply them, differences in political culture must be borne in mind. I would propose then the following six criteria for assessing the performance of a system of city-regional governance:

- *Inspired political leadership.* Leaders capable of articulating a common vision for the polity, building a strong consensus around this vision, and mobilizing resources toward its realization.

- *Public accountability.* (1) The uncoerced, periodic election of political representatives and (2) the right of citizens to be adequately informed about those who stand for elections, the standing government's performance record, and the overall outcomes for the city.

- *Transparency and the right to information.* Governance should be transparent in its manner of operation and, as much as possible, be carried out in full view of citizen observers. Citizens should have the right to information, particularly about contracts between the city and private corporations.

- *Inclusiveness.* The right of all citizens to be directly involved in the formulation of policies, programs, and projects whenever their consequences can be expected to significantly affect their life and livelihood.

- *Responsiveness.* A primordial right of citizens is to claim rights and express grievances; to have access to appropriate channels for this purpose; to have a government that is accessible to them in the districts of their "everyday life"; and to timely, attentive, and appropriate responses to their claims and grievances.

- *Nonviolent conflict management.* Institutionalized ways of resolving conflicts between state and citizens without resorting to physical violence.

The "utopian" character of these criteria becomes immediately apparent when we invert the terms and visualize a form of governance that displays a bungling leadership without vision; deems it unnecessary to render public accounts of its actions; transacts the state's business in secrecy; directs resources to groups favored by the state without consulting with affected citizens; responds to the expression of grievances, if at all, with derision; and resolves conflicts with the arrest of opposition leaders and the brutal suppression of citizen protest.

This litany of misgovernance may no longer apply to many North American, West European, and Australasian cities. But in much of the rest of the world, and especially in Asia where urbanization is now in full swing, the dystopia of governance still prevails, and the application of criteria of good governance, especially at local levels, would be considered a novelty. In any event, good governance always hangs on slender threads, even in a democracy such as Australia. Not long ago, a State of Victoria Minister of Planning responsible for planning and development in metropolitan Melbourne suspended public consultation and declared that the ministry would no longer be required to supply information to the public on major city projects, claiming commercial confidentiality. This is the same minister who, a few years earlier, had suspended elected local councils, replacing them with city managers appointed by the state. He then proceeded to redraw council boundaries and issue administrative instructions on the privatization of local council responsibilities. In the State of Victoria, at least, good governance is still very much in the balance and so it may not be irrelevant, after all, even in a much admired democracy, to be reminded of what some criteria of good city-regional governance might be.

A Summing Up

As human beings, we are cursed with a consciousness of our own death. This same consciousness places us in a stream of irreversible time. Minute by minute, lifetime by lifetime, we move through a continuing present and like the Roman god Janus, forever face in two directions: backwards, reading and rereading the past and forwards, imagining possible futures even as we deal with the practicalities of the day. Shrouded in both darkness and light, as Gerda Lerner reminds us, history as memory helps us to locate ourselves in the continuing present while imagining alternative futures that are meant to serve us as beacons of warning and inspiration (Lerner 1997, chapter 4). In our two-faced gaze, we are a time-binding species whose inescapable task in a fundamentally urbanized world is to forge pathways toward a future that is worth struggling for.

In this chapter, I have set down my own utopian thinking about the good city. It is a revisiting of a problem terrain on which I worked, on and off, during the 1970s (Friedmann 1979). At the time, I was thinking through what I called a transactive model of planning to which the practice of dialogue would be central. These concerns subsequently expanded into my interest in social learning and the traditions of a radical/insurgent planning. My investigations then led me further to examine the microstructures of civil action, including the household economy, culminating in a theory of empowerment and disempowerment (Friedmann 1992). Today's communicative turn in planning (Innes 1995; Forester 1999) is a more mainstream reworking of some of these ideas.

The good city, as I imagine it, has its foundations in human flourishing and multipli/city. Four pillars provide for its material foundations: housing, affordable health care, adequately remunerated work, and adequate social provision. And because process cannot be separated from outcome, I delved into the question of what a system of good governance might look like, formulating six criteria of good governance. The protagonist of my visioning is an autonomous, self-organizing civil society, actively making claims, resisting, and struggling on behalf of the good city within a framework of democratic institutions.

I have not touched on the physical, three-dimensional city, the perennial touchstone of utopian designs: Tommaso Campanella's *City of the Sun,* Charles Fourier's *phalansteries,* Ebenezer Howard's *Garden Cities,* Le Corbusier's modernist *ville radieuse,* or Frank Lloyd Wright's *Broadacre City.* Each of these dream cities is conceived as the setting for an exemplary life. My interest, however, is in living cities each of which moves along very different historical/cultural trajectories, building and rebuilding itself according to its self-understanding of what it is and would like to become. We come to any of them as outside critics. But though we may not be part of its life, we have the right to ask, Does your city make possible and support human flourishing for all its citizens? Does it enable an autonomous civil life or multipli/city? Answers to these and related questions may reveal critical shortfalls. Here, then, would be a starting point for a genuine dialogue with local citizens and planners about the future of their city.

7
A Life in Planning

For more than fifty years, I have been a student, teacher, and practitioner of planning, and as I approach my seventy-fifth birthday, it might be useful to take a retrospective look at what has been accomplished. My published work has spanned four distinct but overlapping fields: regional development planning, urbanization studies and policy, socioeconomic development, and planning theory. Over the years, some of these fields have risen in popularity only to decline again, or to be resurrected in new form: the case of regional planning and economic development. Others, such as planning theory, were virtually nonexistent when I started to write but today enjoy a vigorous and healthy life.

I studied planning in the short-lived Program for Education and Research in Planning at the University of Chicago where I was the first to earn a Ph.D. (Perloff 1957). The program was unique in many ways, most importantly because of its close links with the social sciences. Indeed, it was the first planning program anywhere that opted for an intellectual home outside of architecture. In the explosive growth of American graduate planning education after the World War II, new linkages were being formed, with geography and public administration, for example. But in the late 1940s, it was still a daring innovation to think of city and regional planning as an applied social science.

In this expanded sense, planning is still a very young professional field. So it isn't surprising that it remains a contested and, in some sense, embattled profession, uncertain of its mission. For some, planning in the public domain is primarily linked to the allocation and control of productive resources, such as investments, manpower, or land, by the state. For others, it suggests primarily innovation and change in institutional arrangements. To me, planning is both of these, the issue being largely one of emphasis. Planning practice takes place in the two cardinal dimensions of space and time. The first refers to sociospatial relations at the level of cities and regions, the second to the dynamics of development. Finally, planners must be concerned with effecting desirable changes on the ground and, therefore, with strategies, politics, and relations of power. These points outline the general problematic of planning. But to give planning its more specific meaning, we must focus on its different specializations such as land use, urban design, the environment, transportation, housing, community development, urban technologies, and regional economic development. Each brings its own analytical traditions, discourses, and problematics into planning debates.

In this essay I briefly discuss the individuals and institutional settings that influenced my work. Then I take a critical look at a select number of my publications spanning the period 1955 to 2000. I have divided my work into periods that seem to me to be meaningful stages of this pilgrim's progress.

Influences

If I give pride of place to my father, Robert Friedmann, it is not merely out of a sense of filial piety. My father was a historian and philosopher who in his later years taught at Western Michigan State University in Kalamazoo. He encouraged and challenged my intellectual curiosity, gave me Lewis Mumford, Reinhold Niebuhr, and Hannah Arendt, and aroused in me an interest in the philosophy of science, which was also one of his own enthusiasms. I inherited from him a strong sense of moral purpose, a philosophical disposition, and (ultimately) a sense of history that questioned the possibilities of reason as an active force in history. I say ultimately because, idealist that I was from early on (and some say, I remain), I believed for longer than I care to remember that history could somehow be shaped by human purposes. This belief (which I now take to be misguided) was another reason why I chose to study planning rather than follow in his footsteps as a historian. Although my father and I had many knockdown arguments about this and other questions, he never forced his convictions on me. And for this I am deeply grateful.

Other influences were less personal and came to me by way of books. One of these was Lewis Mumford's *The Culture of Cities* (1938). Above all others, this book inspired me to study planning and instilled in me a love of cities that comes from seeing them not only as a jumble of buildings but also as living history. Under Mumford's tutelage, I learned that planning could be seen as a way of helping to give form to cities and regions, and I came to believe that a profession ostensibly devoted to the public good could serve no higher purpose.

A second book that was of fundamental importance to my intellectual formation was Karl Mannheim's *Man and Society in an Age of Reconstruction* (1949). This difficult and disjointed sociology of planning, which had become available in English ten years after its original German version, opened up a double vision for me. Mannheim raised planning to the level of theory in a way that allowed me to think further about the issues it addressed, such as the question of social controls, which is fundamental to current debates about discourse and power. It also argued the case for society-wide *democratic* planning, which was Mannheim's preferred "Third Way" between laissez faire capitalism and the various forms of European totalitarianism, from Stalin to Hitler, foreshadowing today's discussions about the role of civil society in planning.

A third decisive influence on my thinking was Hannah Arendt's *The Human Condition* (1958). The book is a landmark in twentieth-century political thought. By the time it appeared, I was ready to embrace a more political as opposed to a purely technocratic view of planning. Arendt portrayed political praxis or what she called acting as the highest good worth striving for. (Later in life, she raised thinking, willing, and judging to even higher levels. See Arendt 1978.) But in her lexicon, acting was unrelated to the rational action of American theorists, such as Talcott Parsons and Herbert Simon. To act was to set something new into the world, to make *a new beginning,* which would require persuasion and all the other arts of getting something done in the face of opposition from the forces defending (and benefiting from) the status quo. I now think that Arendt was somewhat of a mythmaker in her glorification of Greek democracy, but I engaged with that book as with no other, and the yellowing pages of my personal copy are full of scribbled annotations.

I also need to mention here the Jewish Viennese philosopher Martin Buber, whose "dialogic principle" became for me a fundamental means of being in the world. Buber's original formulation of this principle in *I and Thou* (1996 [1923]) did not appeal to me as much as some of his later, less mystical writings. His deeply humanist philosophy concerns relationships: between people, between self and Nature, between self and God. To live is to live through these relationships. Dialogue manifests itself as a particular way of listening to what others are saying (and also to what they leave out), trying to grasp their meaning, and to respond to them out of the depths of one's being. That, for Buber, is the substance of dialogue. Wherever genuine dialogue takes place, he asserted, the divine spirit is also present.

In my last year as a student at the University of Chicago, Buber came to the campus to give a talk. It was a festive occasion. With his flowing beard, he had something of the Old Testament prophet about him. I remember the impressive physical setting in the university's Rockefeller Chapel, but I no longer remember what he said. I think I was a bit disappointed in the message, having expected an epiphany of some sort, and finding him instead to be just another human being, a bit overwhelmed by the surrounding pomp and circumstance.

The six years I spent at the University of Chicago were among the most rewarding of my life. The interdisciplinary Program for Education and Research in Planning was started in 1947 by Rexford G. Tugwell. Tugwell had had a distinguished, if turbulent, public career; before coming to Chicago, he had been Governor of Puerto Rico. The scholars he attracted and who formed the core of the teaching staff in the program were of exceptional promise: Melville Branch (urban design), Edward Banfield (politics), Harvey Perloff (regional economic development), Julius Margolis (economic planning), Richard Meier (technology), and Martin Meyerson (housing). I was closest to Perloff whose groundbreaking year-long graduate seminar on economic and social development in poor countries had been an eye-opener for me. Perloff supervised my dissertation, and we continued to be friends and collaborators throughout his life.

Reflecting Tugwell's political beliefs, the program was closely identified with Keynesian economics. As such it was both "in tune" with the rest of the country where, in the 1940s and 1950s, federal policies counted for more than state or local initiatives, but it was "out of tune" with the rising stars who dominated the Department of Economics (on the floor above us!) where such neoclassical luminaries as Theodore W. Schultz and the young and charismatic Milton Friedman were holding forth. What I did not know at the time, and what none of us even suspected, was that, twenty-five years later, neoliberalism would set out on its triumphal march, with Milton Friedman as one of its apostles. But for the small cohort of my fellow planning students in the early 1950s, the future was clearly with state-directed planning.

Student Years (1949–1955)

After three years of military service, I came to Chicago in 1949 with only two years of undergraduate studies, entering a three-year course of graduate education for a Master's degree in planning. With degree in pocket, a friend and I made a two-week trip to the east coast, looking for suitable jobs. I was lucky. The Tennessee Valley Authority (TVA) in Knoxville was in the process of assembling a research staff in a new Division of Regional Studies under Stefan Robock, and I qualified— largely, I suspect, on the strength of a graduate course I had taken on the theory of industrial location. Robock was that rare person, an applied economist with a strong grasp of political realities, and he assembled a brilliant group of young economists to form the core of his staff, including Vernon Ruttan and John Krutilla, both of whom went on to have distinguished research careers. As a planner, I was a bit of an anomaly in this company, but my job description was as an industrial economist, and that gave me a certain legitimacy in this company. In addition to my assigned duties, I began to formulate a dissertation topic in my head. I called it "the spatial structure of economic development," and three years later, the final product, "The Spatial Structure of Economic Development in the Tennessee Valley: A Study in Regional Planning," appeared jointly as research papers of the Department of Geography and the Program of Education and Research in Planning at the University of Chicago.[1] I want to dwell on this, my first real publication, because it set the direction for much of my future work.

I began with a bold, Heraclitan statement:

> Nothing is permanent. Everything is change, is process, is becoming. It is this dynamic nature of the human community which gives planning its essential reason for being. For planning is a future-oriented activity, striving to bring "autonomous forces" of social change under the rational and guiding influence of social purposes.
>
> But change also gives evidence of a fundamental continuity in the structural elements which underlie it. This continuity . . . we come to recognize as pattern. The persistence of a pattern does not mean, of course, that it remains . . . unchanged; . . . what takes place is rather a

slow, gradual, even imperceptible series of changes which, over the long term, we observe as a process of evolution.

The spatial dimension of social activities is one of the many significant patterns subject to study by social scientists and forms the subject of this book. (1)

The general conclusion of my dissertation was that the planning region of the TVA, which had been defined originally as the watershed of the Tennessee River, was no longer appropriate in a postwar era driven by industrial development. The new matrix for planning was now the city-region. I was struck by the fact that the watershed region—the Valley, as we called it—had excluded most of the larger urban centers in the southeastern United States, such as Nashville, Memphis, and Atlanta. These industrial "growth poles" (though I did not then use that term) must be brought into the picture if we were to understand the economic growth of their combined regions of influence. The development of watershed resources, such as the construction of a system of multipurpose dams or the new technologies of land management applied to the upper reaches of the Tennessee River and its tributaries, had been important preconditions for economic growth and development. But in themselves they were insufficient to bring prosperity to the Valley. Attention had now to shift to the major metropolitan centers in the region. That was the main argument, but in the process I touched on a number of other topics that would continue to occupy me for years to come.

Implicit in what I wrote was a theory of *structuration* (Giddens) in which agency and structure mutually condition each other. Agency alone smacked of voluntarism, and structure alone of stasis. But the two together could yield a reasonable picture of society and thus provided a reasonable grounding for planned intervention. The structure in which I was interested was spatial, and a visual image I constructed helped to convey not only the idea of spatial structure but also the related concept of a system or network (Figure 7.1).

The highway traffic-flow pattern was a persuasive image, and I came to employ similar images throughout my writing career. The systemic character of spatial structure made me aware of the difficulty of bringing about structural change through public interventions; subsequently, it led me to think about national approaches to regional development.

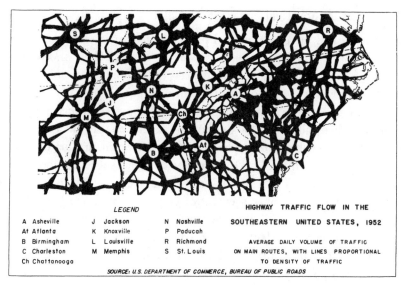

Figure 7.1. Traffic flow patterns, southeastern United States, 1952. Source: U.S. Department of Commerce.

Economic underdevelopment, I thought, was a systemic characteristic of cities and regions, and the entire system had to be acted on to make a difference. I have come to change my views on this, and will comment on this more later in this chapter. But for quite some time, I was an unreconstructed Keynesian, firmly believing in the ability of the state to work on behalf of progressive social and economic change.

In addition to my concern with economic growth, I was deeply troubled by the persisting rural poverty in the Tennessee Valley and, more generally, in the American South. "The real problem of rural poverty in the Tennessee Valley," I wrote in "The Spatial Structure of Economic Development in the Tennessee Valley," "lies . . . on the periphery of city regions and is unlikely to be solved by developments from *within* the city region itself. The economic outlook for peripheral areas points to continuing depopulation, continuing decline in the share of total income, and a continuing sense of disadvantage" (144). Because I had no clear solution for enduring rural poverty, I decided to write an appendix in which an economist, a planner, and a philosopher politely and inconclusively debate the question of rural decline in a context of rapid urbanization.

Apprenticeship: Brazil and Korea (1955–1960)

After I finished my dissertation, I published two articles in *Land Economics* that covered two major themes of my study: "The Concept of a Planning Region" and "Locational Aspects of Economic Development." My life, however, was about to take an unexpected turn. The International Cooperation Administration, as the U.S. international aid program was then called, was looking for an "expert" to teach in a regional planning course offered to public officials in the Brazilian Amazon, and with my newly minted Ph.D. with precisely that specialization (and with Harvey Perloff's backing), I was the natural choice. But to my considerable embarrassment, I knew next to nothing about South America and even less about Brazil. I still remember puzzling over an atlas, trying to locate the city of Belém do Pará, where I was to teach. The search took me at least ten minutes. Given that I knew nothing about Brazil, what could I possibly tell the Brazilians?

I knew no Portuguese at the time, so I was assigned an interpreter, the young Brazilian poet Mario Faustino, who soon became a good friend. The course in which I taught had been organized by the Brazilian School of Public Administration and was financed by the new regional development organization for Amazonia, SPVEA. As it turned out, my TVA experience was of very little relevance here, and what I had learned at Chicago—though I made a brave show of it—wasn't of much use either. At the conclusion of the course, our class took a two-week field trip up the Amazon River, actually more like a leisurely boat journey with occasional stopovers, from Belém to Manaos. It was during this travel, which had its own surrealistic aspects, that I delivered a series of lectures on board our ship on nothing less than the theory of planning! As I look back on this moment in my life, I smile. What I had to say bore no obvious relation to what was actually going on in the region, but planning—regional planning in this case—was the exciting new American technology that would magically produce development, and I was the prophet from abroad. Considering the equatorial heat, I found my audience to be exceedingly tolerant of my stumbling efforts.

After three months in Belém, I moved south to Rio de Janeiro, awaiting reassignment. I used this interval to write *Introduction to Democratic Planning,* which I based on my Amazon lectures and which was subsequently published in Portuguese. Struggling to define planning as a coherent practice, I came up with was an excessively idealistic vision. On one hand, I saw planning in an unabashed Hegelian reading as the working out of Reason in History, with the state as the vehicle for its highest realization; on the other, I spoke of it chiefly as a way of thinking, as "thought at the level of planning" (a phrase I had borrowed from Mannheim). Identifying seven modes of planning thought—objective, analytical, integrative, projective, experimental, utopian, and aesthetic— I devoted an entire chapter to each of them. Implementation and broader questions of power were not yet part of my mental horizon.

Encouraged by the positive response to my message from Brazilian colleagues, I proposed a special issue on planning to UNESCO's *International Social Science Journal*, titled *The Study and Practice of Planning*. My "Introduction" was in effect a concise English-language summary of my book. Some of its idealism did not seem out of place in this postwar period. Everybody, it seemed, was eager to "plan." The French had successfully rebuilt their economy after the war with a form of so-called indicative planning. Other European governments were similarly engaged. Renowned econometricians, such as Nobel Prize winner Jan Tinbergen, were making major contributions to the theory of economic planning. The American foreign aid program demanded national development plans as a basis for making international aid allocations. And at home, the federal government was insisting on metropolitan-wide planning as a condition of grants-in-aid to cities. The question was no longer *whether* to plan, but *how* to plan effectively.

After about two months in Rio, I was reassigned to Salvador, Brazil's first national capital located in the drought-ridden northeast and now the capital of the State of Bahia whose five million people were scattered over a terrain the size of France. My mission was to start up an institute at the economics faculty of the Federal University that would offer graduate training in regional planning and carry out research in an advisory capacity to the State Planning Office. I remained there for two years, publishing little. But, under the capable directorship of Armando Dias Mendes, whom I had recruited as the most brilliant of my students in Belém, our institute trained the first regional planners in Brazil, several of whom would later form the core staff of the newly established Agency for the Development of the Northeast (SUDENE), which would last until the military coup in March 1964.

For reasons that were never explained, and much to the chagrin of the rector of the university, the U.S. Aid Mission withdrew its support from our project, and in early 1958, I said good-bye to Brazil without a clear idea of what to do next. After several months spent traveling in Europe, I decided to accept the offer of a position as development economist with the U.S. Aid Mission in South Korea. I was eager to learn more about Northeast Asia and, despite my misgivings about the internal politics of U.S. international aid programs, it was an opportunity I could not resist. Working as a policy advisor to the director of economic programming, I passed the next two years relatively uneventfully, except for the birth of my daughter, Manuela. In my new bureaucratic surroundings, I was still quite "wet behind the ears" and nearly got myself fired because I stubbornly insisted on wearing a somewhat scruffy beard! Beards had not yet become fashionable attire, and the American international bureaucracy regarded them as subtly subversive. In my spare time, I wrote a few academic articles, but I was far too busy in my hunger to learn everything about Korea, my new role as father, and my daily work at the office to think about launching a major writing project. My family and I returned to the States in early 1961. Although I had been offered a post in Turkey, I was not prepared to take on yet another "exotic" country (exotic for me!) in a time span of only six years, and I was desperate to go home.[2]

The Years in Cambridge (1960–1964)

After several months of searching for an academic position, I was delighted to accept a nontenured position as associate professor in the Department of City and Regional Planning at the Massachusetts Institute of Technology, where I would teach "regional planning" to graduate students. I was also invited to join a team under Lloyd Rodwin, who, on behalf of the MIT-Harvard Joint Center for Urban Studies, had negotiated a major action-research program with the Venezuelan government for providing a broad range of advisory services to the newly formed Venezuelan Guayana Corporation (CVG), which was charged with the mission of building a new industrial city—a counterpole of attraction to Caracas—at the confluence of the Orinoco and Caroní Rivers in the eastern part of the country.

The next four were years filled up with intensive work. Regional planning, I thought, could no longer be taught (as my predecessor had done) as a form of glorified river basin development. That had been the American experience during the 1930s, but as my dissertation had shown, the economy had moved on, and the development of regional economies would have to be completely rethought. Two new research areas were coming on stream, and I believed that regional planning could be based on their scientific premises. The first was the interdisciplinary study of economic development, with its focus on poor, non-Western countries, and the second, "regional science," invented by Walter Isard, a mathematical economist at the University of Pennsylvania (Isard 1956). This putative science was basically a form of economic geography, but in Isard's hands, it was both methods-driven and forever in search of the holy grail of a general equilibrium model of location and human settlements. Although I had very little interest in either methods or equilibrium models, I was attracted by Isard's emphasis on the location of economic activities, theories that were then enjoying a certain revival.

I made two attempts at giving the new regional development planning a solid foundation. The first article, "Regional Planning As a Field of Study," was one in which I proposed location economics and central place theory (which is a theory in geography) as foundational for the study of regional planning. The second, and more ambitious, effort, *Regional Development and Planning: A Reader,* was a volume of readings I edited with William Alonso, an associate professor at Harvard, and the first person to have received a Ph.D. under Walter Isard at the University of Pennsylvania. At the time, we were not ready to provide an integrated text on regional planning and had to rely on a variety of contributing elements, such as location economics, export-led regional development, the role of cities as structural elements in region building, migration theory, and the real division of political power. Despite the fact that the volume was both eclectic and heavy with theory, it turned out to meet a need and quickly became a standard reference in the English-speaking world. Our publisher was so satisfied with sales of the book that, ten years later, we were asked to prepare a second edition, *Regional Policy: Readings in Theory and Applications.*

My main effort, however, was based on two summers' field research in Venezuela and would eventually result in *Regional Development Policy: A Case Study of Venezuela.* This study, it turned out, was the first ever to build a case, in both theory and application, for the need to incorporate an explicit *spatial* dimension in development planning, arguing that abating regional inequalities required a national policy approach. I developed a systemic method for spatial analysis so that different types of region could be viewed simultaneously in a national context; proposed a core/periphery framework for regional analysis; constructed a typology of development regions, suggesting appropriate policies for each type; and set out a logic whereby underdeveloped peripheral areas could be brought into the economic mainstream through a system of subsidiary "growth poles." Following close on the volume I had edited with Alonso, published two years earlier, this book turned out to have an enormous influence, providing a theoretical justification for regional policies of countries as far apart as Ghana and South Korea. Above all, it was influential in Spanish South America. In the second half of the 1960s, I would have a rare opportunity to put many of its propositions to a test in Chile.

Four other publications that originated during my years at MIT deserve mention. In Cambridge, I had befriended Bertram Gross of Syracuse University who, while visiting at the Harvard Business School, had conceived a series of volumes that would subject economic development planning in a number of countries to empirical study. He invited me to join this project, and based on my ongoing Venezuelan work I produced a short book on the country's experience with national planning, *Venezuela: From Doctrine to Dialogue,* which included a preface by Gross.[3]

Despite my continuing fascination with the nature of planning per se as distinct from any particular application, I was prevented from teaching planning theory at MIT. Leading professors in the department were skeptical that such a so-called theory should even have a place in the curriculum. But the "thing" did not leave me alone, and in 1961, I started to work on a long essay modeled on Max Weber's "Politics As a Vocation" (Weber 1946). In a direct allusion, I called it "Planning As a Vocation." Because of its excessive length, I had some difficulty in finding a publisher for it in English, and it came out first in a Spanish translation (1963). Having always had more passion for the idea than for the profession of planning, the essay was a heroic attempt to project planning onto the canvass of society in ways that would justify my passion.

The remaining two publications from this period were my first to address specifically urban issues. "Cities in Social Transition" consolidated my argument that cities were both cauldrons of innovation and centers in the organization of space. In a language reminiscent of Schumpeter, I wrote, "It is the influences spreading outward from cities that accomplish both the disruption of the traditional social patterns and the reintegration of society around new [modernizing] values" (102). I predicted that the world was moving ineluctably toward a time of "fundamental urbanization" when the distinction between city and countryside would become blurred. And I identified leading urban elites—intellectuals, bureaucrats, entrepreneurs—who would both organize and justify the city's colonization of the countryside.

The second article, "The Urban Field," written jointly with my student John Miller, argued that the enlarged scale of urban life called for a new image of the city, which we called the urban field. We showed that between 85 and 90 percent of the U.S. population would soon be living within a commuting radius of less than one hundred miles of major metropolitan areas, giving rise to major urban corridors and, significantly, to a number of *interurban peripheries* (e.g., Appalachia, the Ozarks) that lagged behind the rest of the country in economic well-being (Figure 7.2). Our paper caused considerable stir and became the basis for a subsequent work nearly a decade later, "The Future of the Urban Habitat." But by that time, I had already moved to southern California.

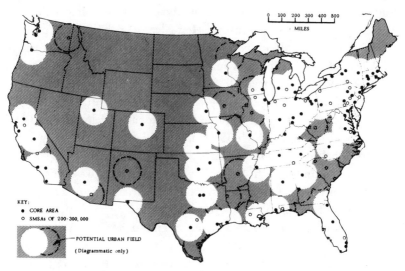

Figure 7.2. Urban fields, United States, 1965. From Friedmann and Miller 1965.

Return to Latin America (1964–1969)

MIT, it turned out, was not prepared to give me tenure, and I had to find another job. The Ford Foundation had begun an ambitious but now foundering project of urban development assistance in Chile. Having been asked to review it, I ended up extending an original two-week "flying mission" into a four-year sojourn in Santiago as director of this unusual project. The Christian Democratic (reformist) government of Eduardo Frei was about to take power, and the people at Ford wanted to help stabilize the political situation in Chile, which was rapidly polarizing between the landed oligarchy and increasingly radical peasant and working-class movements mobilized by the Communist and Socialist parties.

Our program (which at its height included eleven resident consultants) provided advisory services on regional planning to the National Planning Office, on urban policy in the newly created Ministry of Housing and Urban Development, and on social planning to an Office of Popular Participation attached to the presidency. In addition, we were to start up a training and research program, which subsequently took the form of the Interdisciplinary Center for Urban Development (CIDU) at the Pontifical Catholic University of Chile.[4] In "Planning As Innovation: The Chilean Case," I called the whole experiment (and it was truly a learning experience for us all, Chileans and foreign consultants alike) an exercise in "innovative planning." New ideas were bubbling up on almost a daily basis, old ideas were put to the test, and my four years in Chile would provide the "raw material" for scholarly work for years to come. But my interests were already beginning to shift from regional issues to cities and, more specifically, to the processes of urbanization.

In "The Urban-Regional Frame for National Development," I laid out my basic policy approach. Development planning is normally divided into global and sectoral, the first synthesizing and setting the parameters for the second. But this division of tasks, I argued, was not enough. What was needed was a second synthesis at the subnational (regional) level. This formulation posed a number of challenges at the national level, including regional development, migration and settlement, urban development, housing, urban land, urban-regional governance, and social development. Despite the fact that investments in urban infrastructure and housing were eating up the bulk of public investments in many countries, these policy areas were still seriously neglected.

A second article, "Hyperurbanization and National Development in Chile: Some Hypotheses," was particularly provocative. I defined *hyperurbanization* pragmatically as a doubling rate in the size of urban population of less than twenty years. Many developing countries, including Chile, were entering this phase. What were the social and political consequences of accelerated urbanization? Taking Chile as an example, I argued that hyperurbanization affected the country's political development by threatening the power of the land-owning oligarchy. It had brought into being an urban proletariat (Spanish speakers referred to them as a "marginalized" population) who, increasingly conscious of being disempowered, were available to be mobilized by radical parties. The high levels of luxury consumption on the part of a small but growing middle class held back economic growth. Under these circumstances, inflation was endemic. Politically, the country faced a "crisis of inclusion" as large numbers of the population failed to share in the benefits of economic growth. This crisis, I argued, could lead to either political chaos or one of several alternative regimes: left-of-center reformist (the Christian Democratic alternative) or dictatorships of either the right (that is, by the remaining oligarchic elements) or the left. As the succeeding twenty years showed, Chile would, in fact, pass through all of these phases. But despite continuing poverty on an excessively large scale, the country has emerged from years of turmoil and dictatorship as one of the most stable and prosperous liberal democracies in Latin America.

By this time, my thoughts about planning were also undergoing a dramatic change. In my essay on innovative planning, "Planning As Innovation: The Chilean Case," I suggested that planning was not only about controlling patterns of development but about structural transformation as well (195). I contrasted this innovative planning with the more traditional allocative planning, that is, with planning for the central allocation of resources, such as capital budgeting or land-use planning. Although both forms of planning were needed, my own preference was for innovations and strategic action. Another essay, "Notes on Societal Action," concerned what I loosely called societal action. I was moving away from the classical decision model of planning, which, I was certain, had come to a dead end. What I proposed in its place was a form of action planning in which planners would no longer serve as handmaidens to power but become personally engaged, as individuals, in bringing about progressive social change. The essay was written under the influence of the agitated 1960s, which had begun to challenge the existing constellations of power and were nudging many people toward a more populist vision of society. Amitai Etzioni, to whom I was indebted for some of my formulations, called it an "active society" (1968). In line with the increasingly popular form of advocacy planning in the United States (Peattie 1968), the politically engaged planner would become part of the action rather than stand apart from it in a false gesture of objectivity. No longer a technocrat, the new planner would require increased self-knowledge, a heightened capacity for learning, a readiness to listen and live with conflict, and a willingness to negotiate and compromise. Action planners would have to assume personal responsibility for their conduct.

"Notes on Societal Action" foreshadows much of my future work in planning theory, including social learning and the form of communicative planning that I came to call transactive (see my *Retracking America: A Theory of Transactive Planning*). But my time in Chile was drawing to a close. In a formal ceremony, the Catholic University awarded me an honorary doctorate, only the second person after the poet Pablo Neruda to be so honored. And in June 1969, my family and I returned to the States, where I was to head up the new Urban Planning Program at UCLA's School of Architecture and Urban Planning, of which my old mentor and friend Harvey Perloff had become dean.[5]

UCLA: The First Phase (1969–1979)

My first decade in California was an exceptionally productive period. On one hand, it involved building up what was soon to emerge as the most innovative planning program in the country.[6] On the other, in many of my publications I questioned mainstream doctrines. In the wake of the 1960s and my personal experiences in Chile, I was more than ready to abandon my Hegelian phase.

I returned to Santiago the following summer, ostensibly to launch a policy study on the capital region of Chile in collaboration with CIDU researchers. By now, however, the center was barely holding together, being politically so divided between left and right—this in the advent of the general elections that would bring the ill-fated Socialist candidate, Salvador Allende, to power—that collaborative work proved virtually impossible. I did my work for the center, but also spent a good deal of time drafting the chapters of a book on transactive planning. Dedicated to my father who had died only a short while earlier, the book had acquired the unfortunate (to me) title *Retracking America*. It was, however, the title on which my publisher insisted. My own intention had been a good deal more modest: to set out a theory of planning that would replace what appeared to me to be a bankrupt model of scientific management. I called it a "highly personal vision" that would "outline the elements of a theory of societal guidance in which historical, logico-empirical, and utopian aspects are brought into conjunction" (xvii). Transactive planning was the "life of dialogue," I said. I spoke of "mutual learning" between planner and client and about a "learning society" where, following Buber's counsel, planners would have a heightened capacity for listening and dialogue; I even had a section on the Tao of planning.[7] But despite (or perhaps because) of its utopian fillip—an allusion to Thomas Jefferson's Republic of the Wards—the book did extremely well in the market. Although its message was unfamiliar to ears attuned to the technical literature on land-use and transportation planning or, for that matter, economic development, the book introduced the "communicative turn" into planning long before John Forester, Judith Innes, and Patsy Healey would help to make it into the reigning paradigm (see, for example, Forester 1999). *Retracking America* was the first of five books I published during the 1970s. The others included the second edition of the reader in regional development, retitled *Regional Policy; Territory and Function; The Urban Transition;* and *The Good Society.*

The spatial dimension, or the *where,* of economic development continued to be a popular subject, and since the publication of *Regional Development and Planning,* there had been a great deal of work in geography and urban studies relevant to the field. William Alonso was now teaching at Berkeley and, even in that pre-e-mail era, we communicated easily. Most of the material we included was new, hence the new title. Unfortunately, by the time *Regional Policy* was published, the emphasis in development discourse had shifted attention to rural development, whereas we were still fixated on urban-centered growth. There was also a kind of *crise de conscience* among regional planners, particularly in America, about the inherent difficulties in guiding spatial development from a national perspective, that is, about making a difference in the real world. It was a slow awakening, but eventually we came to realize that effective planning was a political more than a technical matter. Subsequent research about regional planning in Mexico, Canada, and the United States helped to make that point quite clear (Friedmann, Gardels, and Pennick 1980; Friedmann 1988; Friedmann and Bloch 1990).

In 1976, I spent a year as a Guggenheim fellow at the Centre for Environmental Studies (CES) in London. As a government-supported think tank, CES had attracted some of the best urbanists in Great Britain. Even so, Thatcherism was on the roll, and the center would soon be abolished. By the time I arrived, it was riven along ideological lines, not unlike the situation I had experienced six years earlier in Chile's CIDU, and non-Marxists like myself were given the cold shoulder. It was at the center, however, that I first met the young Australian urbanist, Leonie Sandercock, who ten years later would become my present wife! Despite the rather unpleasant atmosphere at the center, the year I spent there proved to be highly productive. I wrote most of the chapters for *Territory and Function*, oversaw the publication of *The Urban Transition*, which I had drafted the preceding year with Robert Wulff, and was beginning to rethink planning in epistemological terms, focusing on social learning (see my articles "Social Learning" and "The Epistemology of Social Learning"). I also continued to work on *The Good Society*, which three years later would reach its final form. My attempt to interest colleagues at CES in this early postmodern project while the staff was deeply engrossed in Marxist debates even as they engaged in a bitter struggle to save the center (and their jobs) had proved unsuccessful.

The Urban Transition was a long review essay originally written for *Progress in Geography*. Its principal focus was urbanization in the newly developing countries. My coauthor in this effort, Robert Wulff, was a doctoral candidate in anthropology at UCLA, and we divided our work according to our predilections: Wulff would review microstudies of urban life, while I would focus on the macroaspects of urbanization and policy. What we missed, however, was the turn to political economy in urban studies, which Manuel Castells and David Harvey were just beginning to set in motion. Harvey's *Social Justice and the City* (1973) was referenced, but, despite his growing preeminence among younger European sociologists, Castells was not. Although his groundbreaking book *The Urban Question* (1977) had appeared in France a year earlier than Harvey's, the English version was not published until five years later. And so we failed to pick up on what was about to become the dominant paradigm in urban studies. As has happened so often in my life, "catching the wave" was a matter of good timing. If a work arrived either too early or too late, it was condemned to oblivion. In this instance, the review of urbanization literature pertaining to the Third World was useful because it synthesized a great deal of information, but it missed the crest of the wave rolling in.

Territory and Function: The Evolution of Regional Planning was another matter. Its subtitle *saved it from* becoming obsolete before its time. Written jointly with Clyde Weaver, a doctoral student in UCLA's Urban Planning Program, it was primarily a history of regional development written from an American perspective. In his subsequent work, Weaver (1984) would rebalance the story by giving greater attention to the French tradition of cultural regionalism. The book took its title from what I sensed had been a cyclical movement (and continuing source of tension) between regionalism as a cultural and political phenomenon (territory) and regional development in the spirit of my doctoral dissertation, which had emphasized urban-based networks (function).[8] After recounting the course of regional planning from its American beginnings in the 1920s, and taking the story through southern regionalism to river basin development and the postwar emphasis on economic growth, which is where my own work began, we arrive in chapter 7 at what we believed was an incipient paradigm shift. "Regional planners are passing through a period of deep self-examination," we wrote (164). We went on to list a series of titles from books published in the 1970s, which conveyed a widespread loss of confidence among Western intellectuals: *The Pentagon of Power; Doomsday Book; Limits to Growth; A Blueprint for Survival; Mankind at the Turning Point; Inquiry into the Human Prospect; Legitimation Crisis; Late Capitalism.* Some thought they heard the death rattles of capitalism, others foresaw the end of the world. Old problems were reinterpreted; new ones were added. The term *turbulent environment* was on everyone's lips. In this context, the certainties of regional planning had become a victim along with other "certainties." The First United Nations Decade (1960–1970) had given little evidence that expectations were going to be met. The Great Proletarian Cultural Revolution was on a rampage in China. An equally ghastly imperialist war was devastating Vietnam. Radical movements were gaining new adherents worldwide.

Meanwhile, the capitalist economy was quietly going global. A new "international division of labor" was happening, with labor-intensive jobs moving offshore from the industrial world to global regions of labor surplus. "Late" capitalism was recasting the world in a new mold. But a modest countermovement, which I called "the recovery of territorial life," was also underway that stressed ecology, the importance of place and local cultures, the claims of rural folk, and a new approach to development focused on "basic human needs." I aligned myself with this movement, and in the final chapter, outlined some elements of this approach, abandoning the growth-center doctrine I had helped to fashion a decade earlier.

> The object of planning is to create those conditions in the real world that will nourish human beings who are "rich in needs." This requires the continued development of the productive forces and more particularly of the *development of the bases of communal wealth:* land and water, good health, knowledge, and skills (191)

Although *Territory and Function* summarized and critically assessed much of my work on economic development during the preceding decade, I thought of it primarily as a textbook for a subject still struggling for recognition. Three problems had preoccupied me during the 1970s: rural development; the emerging export-led, neoliberal doctrine of national economic development; and the formalization of a social learning (epistemological) model of planning. In one form or another, they all came together in this text.

The development of rural areas was the first problem area I engaged. The origin of my interest in this topic was a symposium convened in 1975 by the United Nations Centre for Regional Development (UNCRD) in Nagoya. I was asked to write a critical review of the "growth pole" doctrine of urban-industrial development in Asia. Together with Mike Douglass, who by then was on the staff of UNCRD, I undertook an extensive, critique of what we called the "development strategy under conditions of dualistic dependency," "Agropolitan Development: Towards a New Strategy for Regional Planning in Asia."[9] Our statistical universe was drawn from six countries in Asia: India, Indonesia, West Malaysia, Philippines, Thailand, and South Korea. Concluding that current policies of industrialization based on the competitive export model of growth would create enormous inequities, we launched a countermodel of rural development that we baptized "agropolitan." Favoring rural townships, the model could as easily have been dubbed the "urbanization of the countryside." Given prevailing rural densities in many parts of Asia, which were generally higher than suburban densities in the United States, agropolitan development seemed to us to have reasonable prospects in the densely populated regions of South and East Asia. The problem was two-fold: how to bring urban infrastructure, services, and nonfarm jobs to rural areas and how to give local people a more effective voice in how to use public funds for local development.

More articles in this vein followed in the 1980s. One of them was based on a brief period of fieldwork in Mozambique, but the remainder were elaborations of our original idea. What I had not expected when Douglass and I wrote the first piece was the virulent response of some critics. I had thought of agropolitan development as a relatively modest suggestion, not unlike, in fact, the "urbanization of the countryside" that I had observed in southwestern Germany with its strong tradition of local autonomy. My critics, however, thought otherwise and called it antiurban, antiindustry, antidevelopment. I must admit that the term *agropolitan* was perhaps not the most felicitous choice, though it had come out of conversations with Asian colleagues. A blander, more familiar tag might have served our purpose better. But it probably wouldn't have made much difference, just as more empirical research on the "informal sector" in labor-surplus economies—another hot topic at the time— was unlikely to have given a new direction to existing policies.[10] The reason for the response was essentially ideological. For many development "experts," *rural* was synonymous with *backward*. Forward-looking, "progressive" policies supported urban-based industrialization and urban "growth poles." Agropolitan development was therefore misread as a call to "keep 'em down on the farm." That was the academic battlefield. In the real world, decentralizing decision making to rural townships has actually played a very significant role in both India and China over the past twenty-some years, and the urbanization of the countryside is today in full swing, particularly in the deltas of the Yangtse and Pearl Rivers and in Fujian Province (Oi 1999; Zhu 1999).

The second focus of my research was, in effect, a frontal attack on two mainstream economic development strategies, or rather, ideologies: export-led development and the World Bank's tentative "redistribution with growth" policy promoted under Robert McNamara. I called the resulting article "The Crisis of Transition: A Critique of Strategies of

Crisis Management." The essay took two authoritative studies that had appeared in the mid-1970s under the microscope (Paauw and Fei 1975; Chenery et al. 1974). I decided to treat them as ideological statements rather than as the "pure science," which, of course, is how authors with Nobel Prize–winning aspirations thought about them; as usual, ideology was only what the other fellow had. My concern was not so much the underlying thesis of "take-off" into self-sustaining economic growth, but the matter of mass poverty, particularly in the countries of Asia.

Both theories would dominate professional discussion during the latter part of the 1970s. A central issue was the extent to which national governments of newly industrializing countries should encourage integration with the emerging global economy. The argument went something like this. In world-economic terms, a poor and technically backward country can compete in world markets only on the basis of its primary endowment, that is, cheap and unskilled labor. The policy problem, then, was first, how to hold the price of labor down (in the face of union pressure, for example) and second, how to lure global capital to invest in the country. A related, but less frequently discussed, policy question was how coastal export enclaves might be used to promote long-term national development.

Proponents of the export-promotion thesis liked to cite the cases of successful economic growth in the so-called Four Little Tigers—Hong Kong, Taiwan, Singapore, and South Korea. What these countries had accomplished might be replicated elsewhere in Southeast Asia and, by implication, in other parts of the world. Redistribution-with-growth theorists in the World Bank and at Sussex University also favored export-led development but adopted a more reasonable tone, insisting that some part of the new growth increments be channeled toward identified "target groups" of the poor. Once again, the Four Little Tigers were called on to perform. They seemed to have managed their transition to relatively high per-capita incomes even as they took care of their poor.

My critique cast doubt on many of the claims of both of these policy cures and took exception to the uniform neglect of politics in their usual presentations. I insisted that all development policies are based on extra-economic ideologies that favor certain social groups over others and noted how neoclassical economic theory tends to treat politics by assumption rather than as an analytical category in its own right. Neither claim was particularly controversial; what stung was its blunt language.

I submitted the essay to a journal edited in the Netherlands on whose editorial board I served. The journal's editor was extremely uneasy with what I had written, but after a year's negotiation he reluctantly agreed to publish the article, soliciting comments from three distinguished economists (Martin Bronfenbrenner, Gustav Ranis, and Hans W. Singer). Clearly, I had stepped into a hornets' nest. Ranis, a professor at Yale, thought he had to lecture me on development theory; Bronfenbrenner (Princeton) called my critique "dystopian"; and Singer (Sussex) thought me provocative and a wild shooter "who sprays his bullets widely at what he imagines to be his main targets." In the end, I was allowed a rejoinder in which I stood my ground.

In subsequent meetings with Gustav Ranis, we chatted amicably enough. It turned out that we had both come from Vienna, as had the World Bank's Paul Streeten who, though absent in persona, was also involved in the debate. (Hans Singer was a fourth refugee scholar, residing in England.) And, of course, as we now know, the debate was over before it started. For better or worse, the "borderless world" of global financial flows is upon us; market competition has become global; restraints on trade and capital movements are vigorously denounced; and the propaganda machine of the globalists works relentlessly to uphold American hegemony in world markets. Globalization, we are reminded daily, is the coming surge of history. The few dissenting voices are either silenced or reduced to demonstrating in the streets.[11]

The third research area I started during the decade concerned the epistemology of social learning. I had already used learning as a metaphor in *Retracking America,* but I continued to explore its wider ramifications and particularly its epistemological foundations. In "Social Learning: A New Model for Policy Research," a paper I wrote with another of my students, George Abonyi, we examined the question, Why are the results of policy research not used more widely than is usually the case? We argued that the fault lay in the incompatibility of the social contexts for policy research: the separate and often clashing worlds of government and the academy. To bridge the chasm separating these two worlds, we proposed a social practice model of experimental learning. In social practice, the point is not to falsify a hypothesis, as Karl Popper had claimed on behalf of the natural sciences, but to "create a wholly new, unprecedented situation that, in its possibility for generating new knowledge, goes substantially beyond the initial hypothesis" (936).

Social practice, in this view, was not a controlled scientific experiment but an open-ended social experiment conducted in real time and involving social learning.

The best formulation of this new planning paradigm was in a little noticed preface, "Planning as Social Learning," which I wrote for the reissue of *Retracking America* in 1981. I cited John Dewey and Lewis Mumford as forerunners, as well as more recent work by Edgar H. Schein (a business consultant), Charles Hampden-Turner (a social psychologist), Edgar S. Dunn (an economist), Donald Schön (an organization theorist), and Donald Michael (a social planner). Virtually all of them had stressed the importance of small learning groups as settings for experimental, innovative practice. I then introduced the idea of "mutual learning" between planning experts and clients, together with a fourfold model of social learning, consisting of a "critically examined theory of reality, specified social values, political strategy, and social action." Mutual learning, I argued, is most effective when carried out through a process of open communication, or dialogue, in small groups. Arguing that innovative practice would inevitably run into opposition, I linked learning processes to a "political struggle" for their acceptance. Planning was thus a "politically engaged" practice. I argued that innovative practice typically originates within civil society rather than the state. Its small-group character is a mark of strength, not weakness, and encourages the formation of social movements, networks, and political alliances, all of which move according to the law of small numbers. I cited the environmental movement (whose original structure, like that of the concurrent women's movement, was precisely cellular) as a case in point. In my view, this model of innovative, not to say radical planning has stood the test of time. As a succinct statement of my public philosophy, it foreshadowed my interest in civil society that would play a major role in my studies of the Latin American barrio movement during the 1980s (Friedmann and Salguero 1988; Friedmann 1989) and is most recently reflected in *Cities for Citizens* (Douglass and Friedmann 1999).

Before crossing over the threshold into the new decade and beyond, I need to comment on what in many ways is my most personal book, *The Good Society*. Soon after the publication of *Retracking America* in 1973, I had organized a graduate seminar on "the good society" as an exploration of some of the philosophical issues raised in that earlier volume. The seminar continued for two years, and by the time I moved to the

CES in London, I had with me a nearly complete draft of the new book. With *The Good Society* I had decided to write something quite different from the usual academic text. I adopted an aphoristic style in which I arranged the text like a musical composition consisting of "preludia, statements of major and minor themes, variations, repetitions, interludes, recapitulations, and codas" (xvi). Daringly, I even included poetry (my own and others), playlets, and fables that were designed to encourage a state of critical awareness in the reader. In the present so-called postmodern era, when the line dividing the humanities from the social sciences has become blurred, nonlinear, fragmentary thinking is considered to be in the vanguard. But in 1979, few critics knew what to make of it. What does one do with an academic author who writes a chapter on "Forbidden Thoughts"? And where does a chapter on "The Loss and Recovery of Self" fit in? Moreover, my "good society" was all about small numbers: I estimated its optimum size to be 8 ± 1! Weren't "good societies" supposed to be large, as large as America itself?

My purpose, however, had not been to come up with a grand design but to extend what I called the life of dialogue by creating conditions within the actually existing "world of social planning"—characterized by hierarchies of power—that would allow the life of dialogue to flourish. Central to the "good society" was a philosophical conception of being in the world. Three models occupied the contested terrain. Monadic individualism, espoused by followers of an Anglo-American libertarian tradition clashed with organic collectivism, as manifested in Mao Ze Dong's China. To monadic individualists, society appears as an epiphenomenon constraining individual liberties. For collectivists, the individual is wholly subordinated to the group. Unreconciled to either, I opted for what I called a "communalist" conception of being in the world, in which as individuals, we always stand in a dyadic relationship to others.

It was a poetic text that appealed to readers who happened upon it, but it was unsuitable as an academic text, and so it never became popular. For me personally, however, its importance was undeniable. I had laid out a philosophical and, above all, an ethical foundation for my future work as both teacher and planner. The book's last two sentences held special significance for me, because they returned me to the real world, which, after all, was not a world of models but of actual relations of power. "To travel to what is farthest, we must go by the path that is nearest. We must transcend the Good Society" (181).

With this last sentence, I returned to Earth. As the 1970s drew to a close, my life changed dramatically. I had been through a divorce and was now living alone. In the measure that my writings became more critical of mainstream views, demand for my services as an international consultant was declining. Having more time at my disposal, I produced what I regard as some of my best work during the next twenty years.[12]

UCLA: The Second Phase (1980–1996)

I have always had a strong sense of history, of being part of transforming socioeconomic and political processes. Throughout most of my life, I had oriented myself to world events more than to the characteristics of the many places where I was—always temporarily—"at home." And by the early 1980s, it was evident that a period of major upheavals was at hand. It would take decades to work through their full implications: the deindustrialization of the industrialized world, the rise of the global economy, the triumph of neoliberal ideology, the end of the Cold War, the collapse of the Soviet Union, the end of the Third World, the new information technologies—all these would require a rethinking of theoretical positions, my own along with everyone else's. The lifeways to which all of us had become accustomed would never return. We were living at the beginnings of a new age.

By the mid-1980s, I was taking stock of my time, and of myself in relation to these new realities. In an essay significantly titled "The Crisis of Belief," I said good-bye to many of the verities that had guided my work until then. I argued that our time was characterized by a general collapse of meaning. Gone was our faith in salvation through unlimited economic growth, in the capacity of much of the so-called Third World to achieve even a modicum of material comfort, in the great American middle-class consensus that had denied class and cultural differences, in a beneficent national state that would extend its protective reach against life's adversities to all of its citizens, and even in the liberating powers of science and technology. In the new era of nihilistic self-absorption, where the old order had vanished and the new had not yet been born, politics was seen increasingly as a form of entertainment, more and more people traded off debt-financed consumption against old-fashioned political liberties, enormous corporations exercised invisible controls over our lives and minds, and the American empire had consolidated its global hegemony through awesome military power. It was an altogether bleak vision.

My first major research in the new decade rekindled an old interest of mine in the role of city-regions in economic growth. Twenty-five years earlier, my concern had been the southeastern United States. Now we were living in a world ever more tightly integrated by powerful trans-national corporations and finance capital. These new corporate actors needed platforms for their operations whose location would be dictated by market logic. Thoughts such as these led me to the idea of "world cities" as nodal points in a restructured, globalizing economy.

"World city" was an idea waiting to be born. When my first articles on the subject appeared, the concept was quickly picked up as a "hot" topic for research. For cities, it also became a much-sought-after status symbol, and I was asked to advise governments of far-flung places such as Singapore and Taipei on how they might achieve the coveted status. For the second time in my life, it appeared that I had caught the crest of the wave!

In a first article, "World City Formation: An Agenda for Research and Action," written with Goetz Wolff, a graduate student in urban planning, we argued that very large urban regions constitute a spatial system that would play a crucial role in the formation and articulation of the global economy. A focus on the transition of particular cities to world-city status would be particularly productive for scholarship.

> The specific mode of their integration into the global economy has to be brought into the study, and the spatio-temporal structure of core and periphery within which they are located should be made explicit. The problem focus of these studies would be the *restructuring of economic, so-cial, and spatial relations and the ensuing political conflicts in world city formation.* It would be on the dynamic processes of the evolving system, and on the contradictions which arise from the dialectical encounter be-tween territorial and economic interests. (329)

Four years later, I followed up with a second essay, "The World City Hy-pothesis," which was more explicit about many points that had been left obscure, provided a map of a hypothesized world-city system, and pro-posed a series of specific hypotheses for testing. The critical hypothesis was this: "Key cities throughout the world are used by global capital as 'basing points' in the spatial organization and articulation of production and markets. The resulting linkages make it possible to arrange world cities into a complex spatial hierarchy" (319).

Throughout the decade, a great deal of empirical research was being done, most notably by Saskia Sassen. And in 1993, Paul Knox and Peter Taylor convened a conference at which much of this research was presented. My own contribution to that meeting was a review of the literature that had appeared since my original paper, "Where We Stand: A Decade of World City Research." By now, I thought it had become possible to speak of the world-city concept as a new research "paradigm." But problems remained. I had emphasized a world-city structure; others, especially Janet Abu-Lughod, were rightly insisting on the importance of history and thus of particularity and agency in the study of these cities (Abu-Lughod 1995; 1999). In the remainder of my paper, I raised questions about the changing order of world cities and, in conclusion, expressed my serious concern about what I called "techno-apartheid for a global underclass." I wrote, "The reverse side of the global space of accumulation and its homologous 'space of flows' (Castells) are the fragmented life spaces inhabited by people who are excluded from it" (41). Massive exclusion, the dark underside of globalization, the result of a particular process of spatial structuration, had not yet received the scholarly attention it deserved.[13]

My major work during the 1980s, however, was not about the spatial reorganization of the world economy. Instead, I again took up the question of planning theory, which had been an obsession since my student days. In *Retracking America,* I had redefined planning as scientific-technical knowledge joined to organized action. But now this seemed to me to be an empty gesture that desperately needed to be filled with specifics. My friend Peter Marris had suggested that planning theory might best be taught as a history of planning thought. And it was this history that I now set out to write. To do so, I decided to return to the roots of planning discourse in the late eighteenth century—the English and French Enlightenment—which had proposed to apply science, especially the engineering and human sciences, to public affairs.

Within a single framework of social application, my knowledge/action model of planning brought together sociology, institutional economics, historical materialism, utopian movements, scientific management, organization development, public administration, neoclassical and welfare economics, policy science, and systems engineering. All of these implied different understandings and practices of how knowledge and action were to be joined. To simplify my presentation, I decided to collect these several approaches into four broad groupings, which I called the major historical traditions of planning. The oldest of these was *social reform,* which involved the use of state powers in undertaking piecemeal reforms in the manner of social democracy. Alongside it were the more recent traditions of *social learning,* which had come out of the scientific management movement, and *policy analysis,* which leaned heavily on economics as a methodology. All three were linked to the state as principal actor. As Aaron Wildavsky had put it, they attempted to "speak truth to power" (1979). But right from the start, industrial capitalism had also brought into being a host of social movements, some inspired by utopians and anarchist visionaries, such as Robert Owen and Pierre Fournier, while others, most importantly the labor movement, found inspiration in the texts of Marx and Engels. Here, then, were the beginnings of a counterplanning "from below," of working-class and other communities of the oppressed and disempowered that denounced the evils industrial capitalism had wrought and held out promises of greater social justice. I called this the tradition of *social mobilization* and the planning that drew upon this tradition, radical.

The heart of *Planning in the Public Domain* was devoted to chapters on each of these traditions. Looking at them as a group, with their substantial ideological differences, from technocratic policy analysts to political activists, I found that I could not really claim any one of them as having exclusive validity. Contemporary planners, I argued, could make their contributions through any one of them, even though for our own time and place, the traditions of social learning and social mobilization were, at least to me, the most compelling. In particular, I paid attention to an emerging model of *radical planning,* which was centered not in the state but in organized civil society (chapter 10).

All my life, I had been drawn to theories of social transformation more than to theories of stasis. In writing about radical planning, I now realized that the Gordian Knot of structural socioeconomic change could not simply be sliced in half, as Alexander the Great is reputed to have done. Slicing it apart, the knot would merely come unraveled, leaving chaos instead of a new order. Even contradictory opposites needed to be joined. And so I wrote,

One of the most difficult requirements for radical planners is the ability to live with contradictions. To live with contradictions is to say that planners must hold in tension two opposing categories, *affirming both*, even where traditional logic tells us that only one of the terms can be asserted without running into unsolvable dilemmas. . . .

- Theory *and* practice.
- Empirical analysis *and* normative vision.
- Critique *and* affirmation.
- Explanation *and* action.
- Future vision *and* present reality.

Our natural inclination is to substitute the conjunction *or* for every *and* in this list. Alternatively, it is to wish the opposite term away and to coin perhaps some new words, indicative of a mixed reality. . . . Neither of these escape routes is, in fact, open to planners. The problem has to be faced in all of its complexity and without giving way. (405)

This paragraph succinctly stated my own position that we live in a world crisscrossed by tensions and ambiguities from which we cannot be released. It is in many ways an uncomfortable position leading, in the views of many, to reprehensible inconsistencies and even to a failure to act when action is needed. But for me, it affirms the incomparable richness and diversity of the world we live in and denies to us the possibility of simplistic solutions. The choice is not between an either/or. We have to opt for both terms of the dialectic.

In the early 1990s, I returned to development studies with a short book called *Empowerment*. With the collapse of the Soviet Union and the reunification of Germany, the world had moved into the post–Cold War era, and the geopolitics of a Third World aligned neither with the Soviet Union nor the West had lost its point. The problem now was, as it had always been, global poverty. But to address mass poverty effectively, the imagery of a uniform Third World had to be scrapped. There was simply too much variety among the world's regions.

Most of the book was written over a period of several months during a visit at Berkeley's Institute of Urban and Regional Development. My object was to formulate a theoretical framework for an alternative development that did not start out with neoclassical or even Keynesian economics. Following on the Stockholm world conference on the environment, alternative development had become something of an intellectual movement, spurred on by the report of the World Commission on Environment and Development, *Our Common Future,* that had introduced the twin notions of environmental and social sustainability (World Commission on the Environment and Development 1987).

Alternative development was obviously a normative theory, and in *Empowerment* I built it on a foundation of citizen rights and what I called the universal right to human flourishing. As a theory, it was meant explicitly to serve the needs of disempowered people everywhere. It therefore assumed not only ongoing capitalist relations of production but also assigned an important role to the state. "Although an alternative development must begin locally," I wrote, "It cannot end there. Like it or not, the state continues to be a major player. It may need to be made more accountable to poor people and more responsive to their claims. But without the state's collaboration, the lot of the poor cannot be significantly improved. Local empowering action requires a strong state" (7). This, of course, implied some sort of political practice on the part of the poor. And an important theme of *Empowerment* was how social power might be translated into political power. My main thesis, however, concerned the social empowerment of households to confront their own lives. The basic idea was simple enough. Households—groups of people "living under the same roof and eating out of the same pot"— were responsible for the production of their livelihood, which required both monetary income (and so participation in the wider economy) and time for the production of use values in both the household and the barrio community where they resided. The particular mix of these two forms of work would vary among households as well as over time, but the production of use values, in which the female members of the household played the key role, was essential for survival. To produce their livelihood in this way, households needed to have access to certain resources or *bases of social power* (Figure 7.3), the most important of which were a defensible life space (i.e., housing), access to surplus time above the needs of subsistence, social networks, and participation in social organizations. Having low access to any of these bases was disempowering, portending immiseration. But the reverse was also true. It would lead to the social empowerment of households and to their ability to become politically active.

I followed up with chapters on inclusive democracy, appropriate economic growth, gender equality, and environmental sustainability. The

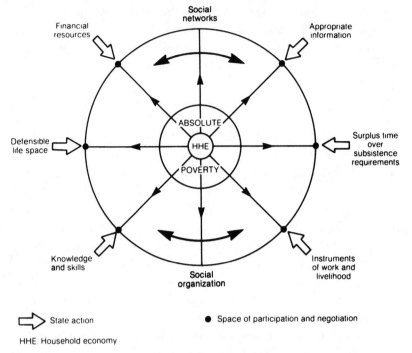

Figure 7.3. Poverty and access to the bases of social power. From Friedmann 1992. Reprinted by permission of Blackwell Publishers.

book was of particular interest to the burgeoning community of voluntary organizations that were just becoming a major vehicle for delivering alternative development programs throughout the world.[14] Even Japan, which was starting its own experiments in poverty alleviation in Southeast Asia, was sufficiently intrigued to publish a translation. As had happened to many of my writings from early on, the book seemed once again to fill a timely need.

I retired from teaching at UCLA in 1996. My last years there were spent in organizing two conferences dealing respectively with women's struggles in Latin America (Friedmann, Abers, and Autler 1996) and the rise of civil society (Douglass and Friedmann 1999). I also collaborated with several of my students in an edited collection about environmental action (Friedmann and Rangan 1993). In short, I focused on social movements and forms of resistance to the dominant models (and forces) of development. In addition, I wrote on planning education—

"Teaching Planning Theory" and "The Core Curriculum in Planning Revisited"—and collaborated with Ute Lehrer in "Urban Policy Responses to Foreign In-Migration: The Case of Frankfurt-am-Main, Germany" and "Migration, Lokalität und Zivilgesellschaft: Immigrationspolitik in Los Angeles" on research of how two cities, Frankfurt and Los Angeles, dealt with the incorporation of foreign migrant workers and their families.

Upon my retirement, my wife, Leonie Sandercock, and I became migrants ourselves, moving to Melbourne, Australia, where for the next five years I continued to research and write and where my interest in the Asia-Pacific region was rekindled. At the end of this period, in 2001, we returned to the North American continent, this time to Vancouver, British Columbia. This would be our final destination.

A Provisional Summing Up

Originally, I was attracted to planning, because I saw it as a field of study oriented to the future and to practice. I was an incorrigible *Weltverbesserer,* someone who set out to "improve" the world and about whom mothers should probably warn their children. To me, it was a calling that implied an ethical commitment to the future, a commitment to make a difference in the world. There are academics who are uncomfortable with this idea that requires one to say what, in any specific situation, *ought* to be done. These critics prefer the appearance of objectivity, restricting their work to gaining a theoretical understanding of the world as it appears to them. Personally, I have never been shy about giving advice. To do this conscientiously, however, I needed a strong ethical foundation. In *The Good Society,* I had tried to work out such a basis for myself.

Ethics alone, however, was not enough. Models of a desired (and desirable) future make three interrelated demands. They require a *critical understanding* of the issues at hand, a *current knowledge* of the relevant literature, and a *suitable means* for translating knowledge into action. I had no difficulty finding my way to the first two of these. One of the attractions that planning had always held for me was its interdisciplinary character or, more accurately, its lack of respect for disciplinary boundaries. The third requirement I interpreted as a call to planning theory that would become a lifelong concern.

Though I never abandoned my commitment to the future—my *bias for hope,* as Albert Hirschman called it—I eventually gave up my work as a consultant to governments and cast my lot as a full-time academic. Planning, I had found, was by nature an ephemeral project, inevitably subject to political mis/fortunes, the irreversible flow of history, and the political conjunctures of the moment. Most political regimes are interested in planning only to the extent that it reflects and reinforces their own position. They pay little heed to consultants that do not necessarily say what they would like to hear. On the other hand, to become a "radical" planner meant that I would have to ignore the contradictions that are present in any action, especially radical action. And as I grew older, I found myself less and less willing to do that. Becoming a university teacher was a way of resolving my dilemma. As an academic, I could say things on paper that I could never say directly "in the face of power." And the ultimate satisfaction of bringing out the best in my many students was something no political crosswinds could erase.

In my student days, it was exciting to be "in" at the start of what, at the time, were relatively new fields of knowledge and practice: regional planning, economic development, and planning theory. All three had their origin for me at the University of Chicago where I had spent four extraordinary years. Ostensibly, I was studying regional planning, but there were no textbooks, and my teachers had only the vaguest idea of what the subject might entail. Even so, my studies gave me a good grounding in urban and resource geography. They also made me familiar with the literature on regionalism in the United States and subsequently, to my astonishment, actually helped to get me my first job as an industrial economist with the TVA.

As for economic development as a field of specialized study, it was virtually invented at Chicago, where Bert Hoselitz, an economic historian and fellow Viennese, had founded *Economic Development and Cultural Change,* the first journal devoted to the field. Hoselitz had a particular interest in the role of cities in economic growth, and his writings stimulated my own later work. Finally, my fifty-year-long "affair" with planning theory also had its beginnings at Chicago, despite my mentors' disheartening counsel that I had better leave theory to my elders (Perloff) and that, in any event, American journals of social science were unlikely to publish anything on the subject (Tugwell). Undeterred, I soon found that international publications edited in Europe were hospitable to what I had to offer, and I never looked back.

Why have I been, and do I continue to be, so passionate about planning ideas? And why am I content to have made planning my vocation? My mother hoped I would become a doctor. But I didn't, and I don't, regret my choice. Although I have become more of an academic than a practitioner, the reason I am passionate about planning is that the field is, in the last instance, oriented to practice and, more specifically, to a practice in the public domain. This orientation has implications for what we think about when we think about planning. To illustrate, in a democracy, conflict is perennial over what, in a given situation, is the right thing to do. As a rule, such conflicts are resolved politically. But at their core, they involve questions of social values that are embedded in political philosophy. Planning and politics thus merge. Planning thought is also political thought, and the practice of planning is a political practice. Practice also obliges us to explore the interface between the private and the public spheres, between civil society and government, between what we owe to ourselves and to the community at large. In short, democratic planning is a very different thing from what corporations do. In the corporate world, maximizing profits and increasing market shares are not debatable criteria; but whether public funds should be used to build highways or improve health-care facilities is an eminently debatable question. Planning forces us to take such issues seriously and to address them in their practical-contextual and more abstract-universalist forms.

Over the past fifty years, urban-regional planning has evolved into a broad professional field that provides an academic home for a number of subfields that are best considered within a common framework. Throughout the world, leading planning schools offer education in housing, transportation, community development, urban design, land-use planning, and regional economics, some of which link also into law, architecture, and public health. These subfields intersect in many ways, as each contributes to life in the city and its built environment. But we have learned that cities and regions cannot be designed according to a master plan. They undergo a dynamic process of structuring and restructuring that is subject to many influences; their form is over-determined; and multiple actors—including governments—make their interventions but have only a limited capacity to shape them as they will.

Planning has evolved in ways similar to older professions, such as medicine and engineering. As a field of study, it is now many things, not one. As a practice in the public realm, it has absorbed the lessons of power and has become political. It tackles big issues that are vital to human concerns. It is an eclectic field that addresses questions that inevitably arise from the "real world," demanding resolution. It is for these reasons that I believe that planning in the public domain matters, and why, to use Max Weber's famous term, it is a worthy calling.

Selected Bibliography

"The Absorption of Labor in the Urban Economy: The Case of Developing Countries," *Economic Development and Cultural Change* 22.3 (April 1974): 385–413. With Flora Sullivan.

"The Active Community: Towards a Political-Territorial Framework for Rural Development in Asia," *Regional Development Dialogue* (UNCRD, Nagoya) 1.2 (Autumn 1980), and *Economic Development and Cultural Change* 29.2 (January 1981): 234–62.

"Agropolitan Development: Towards a New Strategy for Regional Planning in Asia," in *Growth Pole Strategy and Regional Development Planning in Asia.* Proceedings of a seminar organized by the United Nations Centre for Regional Development Planning, Nagoya (Japan), November 4–13, 1975, 333–89. With Mike Douglass. Reprinted in Fu-chen Lo and Kamal Salih, eds., *Growth Pole Strategy and Regional Development Policy.* Oxford: Pergamon Press, 1978. Translated into Indonesian and Persian.

"Cities in Social Transition," *Comparative Studies in Society and History* 4.1 (November 1961): 96–103.

"The Concept of a Planning Region," *Land Economics* 32.1 (February 1956): 1–13.

"The Core Curriculum in Planning Revisited," *Journal of Planning Education and Research* 15.2 (1996): 89–104.

"The Crisis of Belief," *Overland* (Sydney), no. 104 (September 1986): 5–11.

"The Crisis of Transition: A Critique of Strategies of Crisis Management," *Development and Change* 10.1 (January 1979): 125–76. With comments by Hans W. Singer, Martin Bronfenbrenner, and Gustav Ranis, and a rejoinder by John Friedmann.

Empowerment: The Politics of an Alternative Development. Cambridge, MA: Basil Blackwell, 1992. Translated into Italian, Portuguese, and Japanese.

"The Epistemology of Social Learning: A Critique of Objective Knowledge," *Theory and Society* 6.1 (July 1978): 75–92.

"The Future of the Urban Habitat," in Donald McAllister, ed., *A New Focus for Land Use Planning.* Washington, DC: National Science Foundation Press, 1973, 96–134.

The Good Society: A Personal Account of Its Struggle with the World of Social

Planning and a Dialectical Inquiry into the Roots of Radical Practice.
Cambridge: Massachusetts Institute of Technology Press, 1979.

"Hyperurbanization and National Development in Chile: Some Hypotheses,"
Urban Affairs Quarterly 2.4 (June 1967): 3–29. With Thomas Lackington.

Introduction to Democratic Planning. Published in Portuguese, *Introdução ao
Planejamento Democrático.* Rio de Janeiro: Biblioteca de Administração
Pública 5, Fundação Getúlio Vargas, Escola Brasileira de Administração
Pública, 1959.

"Introduction" in *The Study and Practice of Planning,* a special issue of *International Social Science Journal* 11.3 (1959): 327–39.

"Life Space and Economic Space: Contradictions in Regional Development,"
in Dudley Seers and Kjell Öström, eds., *The Crisis of European Regions.*
London: Macmillan Press, 1983, 148–62.

Life Space and Economic Space: Essays in Third World Planning. New Brunswick,
NJ: Transaction Books, 1988.

"Locational Aspects of Economic Development," *Land Economics* 32.3 (August
1956): 213–27.

"Migration, Lokalität und Zivilgesellschaft: Immigrationspolitik in Los
Angeles," *Leviathan: Zeitschrift für Sozialwissenschaft, Sonderheft,
Zuwanderung und Stadtentwicklung,* no. 17 (1997): 427–45. With
Ute Lehrer.

"Notes on Societal Action," *Journal of the American Institute of Planners* 35.5
(September 1969): 311–18.

"On the Contradictions between City and Countryside," *Comparative Urban
Research* 6.1 (1978): 5–41. Revised version in Hendrik Folmers and Jan
Osterhaven, eds., *Spatial Inequalities and Regional Development.* Leiden:
Martinus Nijhoff, 1979, 23–45.

"Planning As a Vocation," *Plan* (Canada), part I, 6.3 (April 1966): 99–124;
part II, 7.1 (August 1966): 8–26. Previously published in a Spanish translation in *Cuadernos de la Sociedad Venezolana de Planificación* 2.7–8
(octubre–noviembre 1963): 1–52.

"Planning As Innovation: The Chilean Case," *Journal of the American Institute
of Planners* 32.4 (July 1966): 194–203.

"Planning As Social Learning," preface to the reissue of *Retracking America:
A Theory of Transactive Planning.* Emmaus, PA: Rodale Press, 1981.

Planning in the Public Domain: From Knowledge to Action. Princeton: Princeton
University Press, 1987. Translated into Italian and Spanish.

"Political and Technical Moments in Development: Agropolitan Development
Revisited," *Environment and Planning D: Society and Space* 3.2 (1985):
155–67.

Regional Development and Planning: A Reader, edited by John Friedmann and

William Alonso. Cambridge: Massachusetts Institute of Technology Press, 1964.

Regional Development Policy: A Case Study of Venezuela. Cambridge: Massachusetts Institute of Technology Press, 1966.

"Regional Planning As a Field of Study," *Journal of the American Institute of Planners* 29.3 (August 1963): 168–74.

Regional Policy: Readings in Theory and Applications, edited by John Friedmann and William Alonso. Cambridge: Massachusetts Institute of Technology Press, 1975.

Retracking America: A Theory of Transactive Planning. Garden City, NY: Doubleday and Anchor Books, 1973. Reprinted with a new preface by Rodale Press, 1981.

"Social Learning: A New Model for Policy Research," *Environment and Planning A* 8 (December 1976): 927–40. With George Abonyi.

"A Spatial Framework for Rural Development: Problems of Organization and Implementation," *Économie Appliquée* 38.2–3 (1975): 519–43.

"The Spatial Structure of Economic Development in the Tennessee Valley: A Study in Regional Planning," research paper no. 1, Program of Education and Research in Planning, and research paper no. 39, Department of Geography, University of Chicago, March 1955.

"Teaching Planning Theory," *Journal of Planning Education and Research* 14.3 (Spring 1995): 156–62.

Territory and Function: The Evolution of Regional Planning. London: Edward Arnold, and Berkeley: University of California Press, 1979. With Clyde Weaver. Translated into Spanish by Carmen del Toro as *Territorio y función* (Madrid: Instituto de Estudios de Administración, 1981).

"The Urban Field," *Journal of the American Institute of Planners* 31.4 (November 1965): 312–19. With John Miller.

"Urban Policy Responses to Foreign In-Migration: The Case of Frankfurt-am-Main, Germany," *Journal of the American Planning Association* 63.1 (Winter 1997): 61–78. With Ute Lehrer.

"The Urban-Regional Frame for National Development," *International Development Review* 8.3 (September 1966): 9–15.

"The Urban Transition: Comparative Studies of Newly Industrializing Societies," in C. Board, ed., *Progress in Geography,* vol. 8. London: Edward Arnold, 1975. With Robert Wulff. Reprinted in a new edition by Edwin Arnold, 1976.

Venezuela: From Doctrine to Dialogue. Preface by Bertram M. Gross. Syracuse, NY: Syracuse University Press, 1965.

"Where We Stand: A Decade of World City Research," in Paul L. Knox and Peter J. Taylor, eds., *World Cities in a World System.* New York: Cambridge University Press, 1995, 21–47.

"World City Formation: An Agenda for Research and Action," *International Journal for Urban and Regional Research* 6.3 (September 1982): 309–44. With Goetz Wolff.

"World City Futures: The Role of Urban and Regional Policies in the Asia-Pacific Region," in Yue-man Yeung, ed., *Urban Development in Asia: Retrospect and Prospect*. Hong Kong: Institute of Asia-Pacific Studies, Chinese University of Hong Kong, 1998.

"The World City Hypothesis," *Development and Change* 17.1 (January 1986): 69–84.

Notes

Introduction

1. This report has meanwhile been published as *World Report on the Urban Future 21,* prepared by the World Commission Urban 21 "by order of the Federal Ministry of Transport, Building and Housing of the Federal Republic of Germany," Berlin 2000. The commission was chaired by Sir Peter Hall.

1. The Prospect of Cities

1. A scenario of continuing globalization needs to be thought about with a healthy dose of skepticism. The globalization process, driven chiefly by America's faith in the total goodness of free markets for capital and commodities, if not for labor, is beset with troubles, many of them the unexpected outcomes of neoliberal policies applied willy-nilly across the globe.

The very distinction between the financial economy and the real economy in unregulated markets undermines the potential for productive growth in many countries, not least in the United States, with its two-thousand-billion-dollar debt, a huge balance of payments deficit, and an overvalued stock market. Japan's case is different—that of a country whose population is not only aging rapidly but actually, beginning around 2010, is expected to decline. The unwillingness of Japanese consumers to spend, despite heroic efforts on part of their government to prime the pump with vast expenditures of public works and through other means, including outright gifts of money to consumers, may suggest a major readjustment for that nation's economy. Older folks want lifetime security above all. With leading Japanese corporations going belly up, and growing unemployment, both of them unprecedented phenomena, people are inclined to minimize risks and to save up for a rainy day. Japan's neighbors are not doing much better. China's economy, with mounting social unrest, is precariously poised, and Russia's economy has collapsed into chaos. Indonesia, the largest Southeast Asian economy, faces a future that is uncertain, except for the dead certainty of more poverty, while South Asia has two, perhaps three non-performing national economies—Bangladesh, Pakistan, and a country riven by ethnic strife, Sri Lanka. India is doing better overall, but the record is spotty and, despite a growing middle class, the country's level of living remains among the world's lowest, and inequalities are on the rise. The Middle East, from Afghanistan to Iran and Iraq, is politically torn up. And the countries of the Caucasus are even more strife-torn. Economically speaking, Africa is altogether off the map. And much of Latin America continues to be in serious trouble. Brazil's incredibly uneven income distribution has remained roughly the same for the last forty years and is a major source of that country's structural weakness. On the other side of the continent, the Andean countries, with the notable exception of Chile, are mired in the drug economy, which truly *is* global. Mexico's economy struggles along with American help and continues to subsidize American consumers. In Europe, the Balkans are drawing a reluctant NATO force deeper and deeper into a war about ethnic cleansing that cannot be won. And so on and so forth.

So then what's left of "globalization"? It is the ideology of an American world hegemony that stands on feet of clay. The rhetoric is brave but bears little resemblance to the actual state of the world. Still, it is hard to imagine a fractured world in which each country is closed off behind sky-high tariff walls and without being linked into the global systems of finance and information. Given the state of technological development and the actual interdependence of national economies, some sort of planetarization of life on Earth will no doubt continue. But it is unlikely to resemble anything like the dream of a "borderless world." Capitalism is a set of politically shaped social relations. And as John Gray (1999) reminds us, there is more than one capitalism in the world today. As a world of social relations, capitalism must always be written in the plural.

2. According to Michael Storper, "The nature of the contemporary city is as a local or regional 'socioeconomy,' whose very usefulness to the forces of global capitalism is precisely as an ensemble of specific, differentiated, and localized relations. These relations consist of concrete relations between persons and organizations that are central to the economic functioning of those entities. Cities are sites where such relations are conventional, and they are different from one city to another. Economic activities that cluster together in cities—both manufacturing and services—are frequently characterized by interdependencies that are indirect or untraded and take the form of these conventions and relations. This conception of the urban economy is different from that of standard urban economics, which focuses on direct, locally traded linkages" (1997, 222).

2. City Marketing and Quasi City-States

1. The second model reflects both a regional scale and a substantial degree of autonomy in matters of local development such as would normally be associated with a city-state. My intention is to foreground the question of regional

governance, so I call it a quasi city-state model. The idea that development in the twenty-first century will be channeled through quasi city-states is no longer a novel one. As geographer Neil Smith observes, "No one seriously argues that the twenty-first century will see a return to a world of city-states, but it will see a recapturing of urban political prerogative vis-à-vis regions and nation-states" (1999, 11).

2. Many of these characteristics are illustrated in a case study of Sydney's attempts to "capture" international sports and entertainment events (Searle and Bounds 1999).

3. The following three sections as well as section five are based on Friedmann 2001.

4. UN projections for 2000 are of fifteen cities with populations exceeding 12 million, headed by the Tokyo agglomeration with a projected 28 million. The number of so-called megacities is expected to increase to thirty-three by 2015 (United Nations 1995).

5. The concept is, in fact, not new at all, but it is only now beginning to be acknowledged as the emerging urban form. For an early formulation, see Friedmann and Miller 1965. What *is* new, though, is the emphasis, as in Figure 2.1, on transnational activities located outside the urban core.

6. In an interesting article on the "entrepreneurial city," Bob Jessop and Ngai-Lim Sum argue that cities can indeed become "strategic actors" under certain conditions. Strategies must be more or less explicitly formulated and pursued in an active, entrepreneurial fashion. The authors posit specific social forces that are able to define the interests of the city and can be seen to act for and on behalf of the latter (2000, 2289).

7. See Borja and Castells 1997 for a similar argument.

8. I don't deny that there are also very thoughtful and focused studies on sustainability, particularly with reference to cities. See, for instance, Newman and Kenworthy 1999 and Low 1999.

9. This is a key point in Jane Jacobs's (1984) analysis, with which I am fully in accord.

10. The discussions of a development "with a human face" in the series of annual Human Development Reports of the United Nations are indicative of this problem (see UNDP 1999).

11. This is an argument against the universalist approaches of international organizations as well as against the currently popular practice of "benchmarking." In city planning it is now taken as self-evident that "progress" is measurable by locally determined criteria, reflecting local problematics and priorities. It is also taken as self-evident, at least in democratic polities, that these standards (as indeed the plans themselves) should have significant inputs from civil society and should be consistent with evolving "community values." But these practices have not yet been embraced at the levels of regional and national planning.

12. Innovations linked to the development of urban systems formed the core of my "theory of polarized development." The many propositions of this theory have never been taken up as such, since they emerged at a time when the Marxist paradigm of urban research to a large extent preempted other research. But when I returned to it in writing this essay, I found many of the themes explored in the literature on innovation milieus were treated in very precise form in this earlier publication of mine (Friedmann 1973b).

13. An interesting contemporary example of innovative planning on a regional scale comes from the German state of Nordrhein-Westfalen, a "rust belt" and completely urbanized region in the Ruhr Valley. For ten years, from 1990 to 2000, a para-statal organization, the Internationale Bauaustellung-Emscher Park (or IBA, for short) has worked successfully to change the image of the region and to experiment with interesting new approaches for its redevelopment. According to Klaus Kunzmann (1999), IBA's approach was characterized by the following: (1) The project was conceptualized by IBA's staff as a continuous process of guided incrementalism, responding to initiatives from innovative actors in the region; (2) no comprehensive physical master plan was designed for the project, and instead individual projects were derived from a long-term vision and plugged into a hidden framework of longer-term objectives; (3) hence, many projects were started, even when the final product could not yet be defined, in order to demonstrate to a wider public the direction in which certain initiatives should go; (4) the IBA initiative promoted a few "flagship projects" to attract the interest and curiosity of innovative multipliers and target groups beyond regional boundaries; and (5) cultural activities were seen and initiated as a key to regional modernization. Kunzmann calls the IBA's a "rhizome approach to regional modernisation."

14. A textbook example of how endogenous can mesh with exogenous development is Bilbao, the leading industrial city in Euskadi (the Basque Country) in northern Spain, which by the mid-1980s had fallen on hard times. Successful in obtaining a franchise from New York City's Guggenheim Museum and the brilliant artistry of architect Frank Gehry (at a total cost of U.S. $170 million), the Bilbao government used its new museum as a catalyst to initiate a major reconstruction of large parts of the metropolitan area, including an expansion of its deep-sea harbor, a new international airport, a subway, the relocation of railways that had cut off the city from the river, an extensive riverside development, and more. The Guggenheim Museum Bilbao, attracting more than a million visitors a year, helped to put the city on the mental map of the rest of the world (Lenfers 2000).

3. Transnational Migration

1. This story is taken from Hernández 1997.
2. Written in March 1999.

3. The following account is abstracted from Abadan-Unat's (1997) comprehensive survey. Professor Abadan-Unat teaches at Bogazici University in Istanbul. From a different perspective, transnational Turkish life focused on Berlin is the subject of an interesting essay by Ayşe S. Çağlar (1999).

4. For a deeper understanding of the Islamic movement in Turkey, see the excellent essay by Ataç, Odman, and Tuncer (2000).

5. "Just as Hong Kong–registered companies seek tax havens in places like Bermuda, well-off families accumulate passports not only from Canada, Australia, Singapore, and the United States, but also from revenue-poor Fiji, the Philippines, Panama, and Tonga (which, in return for a passport, requires a down payment of U.S. $200,000 and an equal amount in installments)" (Ong 1998, 146). According to the author, citizenship is regarded as a means for advancing family fortunes; it has become "flexible."

6. Pierre Bourdieu himself is somewhat reluctant to give an explicit account of his theoretical framework, preferring to let theory emerge from actual field investigations. Still, from time to time, he has felt obliged to expound his theoretical approach, and it is from these sources that I have drawn my own understanding (Bourdieu 1977; Bourdieu 1990; Calhoun 1989; Bourdieu and Wacquant 1992).

7. In May 1999, however, the *Bundestag* did manage to reform Germany's nationality law, which made the acquisition of German citizenship through naturalization considerably easier than it had been.

8. Exceptions would be national capital cities.

4. Citizenship

1. For more information on indigenous movements in Latin America, see NACLA 1996.

2. Some refer to this civic movement as civil society organizations (CSOs), a designation invented by the Swiss social philosopher Marc Nerfin in the early 1980s. But the dividing line between NGOs and CSOs is at best blurred. See Mooney 1996.

3. I could have spoken as readily of this as a form of *cosmopolitan* citizenship (Cheah and Robbins 1998). But this term has been preempted for a citizenship with a very different and more formal meaning than I am prepared to give it here. See Held 1995.

4. According to Nuhoğlu Soysal (1994, 161), the idea of nation has become a "trope of convenience" for claims to collective rights and identity. See also chapter 3 in this volume.

5. The question of citizen obligations as the reciprocal of rights has received little attention in the literature. T. H. Marshall thought that, as a matter of course, ethical obligations would accompany citizen rights, but he failed to spell them out, perhaps because he believed that, in Britain at the end of the

war, they were self-evident. Since then we have had a few attempts to set forth a canon of civic obligations (e.g., Janoski 1998), but in the absence of a strong social consensus around any set of explicit social values, not to mention any means to enforce them, these efforts have come to nothing. All we have left is a handful of legal obligations, such as paying one's taxes (not only applicable to citizens!), jury service, military service (usually for men in war time only), and the like. Most recently, the notion of a consumer-citizen has arisen, which imposes no obligations on us of any sort, not even the duty of individual self-development through work, thrift, and enterprise. For a discussion of these issues, see Rose 1999.

6. For a similar conclusion, see Turner 1992.

7. For a very different reading of the council system, based on Antonio Gramsci's first-hand experience with the hopes, disappointments, and ultimate failure of workers' councils in the factories of Turin at the end of World War I, see Boggs 1984.

8. The decentered character of new social movements with their dual cellular-network structure also underlies my concept of the "good society" in a book of that title (Friedmann 1979, esp. chapters 5–7).

9. Despite the poverty of the mass of its population, India is perhaps the only country in the world where this generalization appears to be contradicted.

10. This multiscalar approach to housing and, more generally, urban development has for many years been championed by Jorge Hardoy (deceased) and David Satterthwaite through their international journal, *Environment and Urbanization.*

11. For a brilliant case study of how civil society organizations battle for farmers' rights and biodiversity at the level of international organizations, see Mooney 1996.

5. The City of Everyday Life

1. I am focusing here on the *positive* valences of the lived-in spaces of the city for their residents. However, there is another facet to the city understood as a web of meanings that I will not discuss further and that has to do with *already existing* forms of alienation. For certain categories of people such as women, the disabled, the elderly frail, and gays, venturing into the city can be a dangerous, life-threatening experience. All women are at risk of being assaulted (mugging, rape) in some urban spaces at certain times of the day or night and are forced to take special precautions if and when they enter them. The disabled and elderly may be unable to access public spaces, use public transportation, or even cross the street without assistance. Their "right to the city" is thus severely constrained, and their lives are accordingly diminished.

It is difficult for male planners to think themselves into the situation of an unaccompanied woman who wishes to go to the cinema at night, and perhaps, out of fear, decides not to go at all. It is equally difficult for a young and healthy planner to put him- or herself into the place of a wheelchair-bound person or a frail person who can no longer board a streetcar or bus unaided. The problem here is partly one of representation, of adequately conveying to those with the power to change the built environment to make for a more "open" city, what it's like when you are shut out from using the city, because the city is made only for men who are strong, fit, and mobile. And it is also one of voice. In the advanced industrial countries, some cities have made positive responses to sustained political pressure from groups that are denied the "right to the city," and subtle alterations to the small spaces of the city, such as improved lighting, ramps, and wheelchair-accessible public transportation and toilets have been built. But much remains to be done to make cities more widely accessible to all its residents, particularly in the rapidly growing parts of the developing world.

2. It might be worth pointing out that "invasions" of life space occur also in nonurban contexts such as in mass relocations of population occasioned by major dam construction projects. For a case study of a successful resistance movement in Brazil to relocation see McDonald 1993. Chinese authorities are currently faced with similar protests in the areas to be flooded by the Three Gorges Dam on the upper Yangtse River.

6. The Good City

1. According to the distinguished Israeli sociologist, S. N. Eisenstadt, America forged a civil religion out of disparate elements including "a strongly egalitarian, achievement-oriented individualism, republican liberties, with the almost total denial of the symbolic validity of hierarchy; disestablishment of official religion beginning with the federal government; basically anti-statist premises; and a quasi-sanctification of the economic sphere" (Eisenstadt 1998, 123).

2. Utopian thinking may also be denied. In destitution and other situations in extremis, survival has priority over all else, leaving no room for utopian thinking. As Brecht once wrote, first comes the stomach, then morality. Finally, there are those who make a virtue of problem-solving via "muddling through" in Charles Lindblom's provocative formulation, where our choices are guided by nothing more than a simple pleasure-pain calculus (1959). Market fundamentalists are similarly averse to charting the long-term future, though they would claim universal happiness as the final outcome of a world ruled exclusively by markets.

3. A recent essay by Gerda Lerner (1997) expresses a similar conviction: "As long as we regard class, race, and gender dominance as separate though overlapping systems, we fail to understand their actual integration. We also fail to see that they cannot be abolished sequentially, for like the many-headed

hydra, they continuously spawn new heads. Vertical theories of separate systems inevitably marginalize the subordination of women and fail to place it in the central relationship it has to the other aspects of the system. The system of hierarchies is interwoven, interpenetrating, interdependent. It is one system, with a variety of aspects. Race, class, and gender oppression are inseparable; they construct, support, and reinforce one another" (197).

4. For an up-to-the-minute personal utopia of the second kind, see the appendix to Harvey 2000.

5. Some other notable attempts to imagine normative frameworks for city-building include Allan Richard Rogers's *Cities for a Small Planet* (1997), and an interesting utopian experiment in Germany that has come to my attention, involving four cities (Stadt Münster 1997). Called an "Agreement Concerning the Quality [of Life] for a League of Cities of the Future," this program includes specific discussions under five headings: (1) economizing land-management practices, (2) forward-looking environmental protection, (3) socially responsible housing programs, (4) transportation policy guidance for a sustainable urban future, (5) promoting an economy that will ensure a firm foundation for the city's future within a sustainable and resource-conserving framework.

6. For a devastating look at the entanglement of political and civil spheres in twentieth century China, see Chang 1991.

7. For a discussion of civil society, see Keane 1988, Waltzer 1992, and Seligman 1992 among others. I have attempted to introduce the concept of a civil society into the planning discourse on cities (Friedmann 1999).

8. But see the case studies of "deliberative democracy" cited in Fung and Wright 1998.

9. For a comparison with a current UN-sponsored project on "good governance," see UNCHS 2000.

7. A Life in Planning

1. A selective bibliography of my writings referred to here can be found at the end of this chapter.

2. To escape the Hitler regime, our family emigrated from Austria in 1940. By 1961, I was thoroughly "at home" in the United States, though I had not as yet a fixed abode.

3. The project brought together luminaries such as Zygmunt Bauman, Lyndon Caldwell, Michel Crozier, and Peter J. Wiles. See Gross 1967.

4. A detailed account of this project can be found in my final report to the Foundation (Friedmann 1969).

5. Harvey S. Perloff had been my teacher at the University of Chicago. After the demise of the planning program there, which he had headed, he moved on to Resources for the Future, a privately funded research organization in Washington, D.C. There, he became involved with the so-called Alliance for

Progress on a review panel for national development plans in Latin America. These plans played an important role in deciding on foreign aid levels. In 1968, he returned to academic life as dean of UCLA's School of Architecture and Urban Planning. For a selection of his essays and more biographical details, see Burns and Friedmann 1985.

6. For a retrospective look at this program, see Friedmann 1994.

7. It was perhaps this reference to Chinese dialectical philosophy that puzzled some of my critics. At the time, I did not pursue the question further. I now realize that the cyclical understanding of history that is immanent in Chinese thought is quite contrary to Euro-American models, with their emphasis on the separation of means and ends and their implicit embrace of linear progress as the *telos* of history. For a recent philosophical comparison of Sinic and Euro-American philosophy as it relates to military strategy, the arts, and history, see Jullien 1995.

8. For a more complete treatment of this recurrent contradiction, see my "On the Contradictions between City and Countryside" and "Life Space and Economic Space," both listed in the bibliography at the end of this chapter.

These articles, as well as "The Active Community," "Political and Technical Moments in Development," "The Crisis of Transition," "The Crisis of Belief," and "World City Formation" are collected in my *Life Space and Economic Space* (1988).

9. Douglass, also a former student of mine at UCLA, is now Professor of Planning at the University of Hawai'i, Manoa Campus.

10. A case in point was the work of the International Labor Organization's World Employment Program (WEP) during the 1970s. I had written an early essay on the question of surplus labor in poor countries, "The Absorption of Labor in the Urban Economy," which developed a complex typology of what later came to be called the "informal sector." I abandoned this line of research, however, since I was less interested in empirical studies than in interpreting the data collected by others and in the implications for policy. In the event, despite a decade's worth of research by the ILO and others, the intent of the WEP, which had been to put up an employment objective alongside the usual economic growth objective of national planning, came to naught, and the program was shut down. In short, painstaking empirical research is not necessarily a high road to policy innovations, which, in the end, are political, not scientific matters.

11. For example, the street demonstrations during the December 1999 gathering of the World Trade Organization in Seattle.

12. I should like to add here some of the new influences on my thinking. With my colleague Edward Soja I had heated debates about Marxism; another colleague, Dolores Hayden (and later also Leonie Sandercock), helped me to become more aware of the revolutionary implications of feminist writings; and

Sheldon Wolin's *Politics and Vision* (1960), with which I belatedly became acquainted, introduced me to the delights of political theory.

13. But see Castells 1998, especially chapter 2, for a recent commentary. Since that review, I have written only one other article on world cities, this time focusing specifically on policy problems facing urban planners in the Asia-Pacific Region, "World City Futures: The Role of Urban and Regional Policies in the Asia-Pacific Region."

14. But see the critical questions raised in the 1999 newsletter of the United Nations Research Institute for Social Development in Geneva, "As the NGO sector becomes more commercialized and dependent on aid, is it getting too close to government—to the mainstream—and losing its capacity for promoting alternative agendas? As they grow closer to the world's elites in government, business, and finance, are they becoming more effective agents of change or simply pawns in a development game?" (11). I had raised precisely these questions seven years earlier in discussing alternative development programs of NGOs in my "World City Futures" (146–51).

Bibliography

Abadan-Unat, Nermin. 1997. "Ethnic Business, Ethnic Communities, and Ethno-politics among Turks in Europe." In Emek Uçarer and Donald J. Puchala, eds., *Immigration into Western Societies: Problems and Policies.* London and Washington: Pinter.

Abers, Rebecca. 2000. *Inventing Local Democracy: Grassroots Politics in Brazil.* Boulder and London: Lynne Rienner.

Abu-Lughod, Janet. 1995. "Comparing Chicago, New York, and Los Angeles: Testing Some World City Hypotheses." In Paul L. Knox and Peter J. Taylor, eds., *World Cities in a World System.* Cambridge: Cambridge University Press.

———. 1998. "The World-System Perspective in the Construction of Economic History." In Philip Pomper, Richard Elphick, and Richard T. Vann, eds., *World History: Ideologies, Structures, and Identities.* Oxford: Blackwell.

———. 1999. *New York, Chicago, Los Angeles.* Minneapolis: University of Minnesota Press.

Alexander, Christopher. 1979. *The Timeless Way of Building.* New York: Oxford University Press.

Appadurai, Arjun. 1998. *Modernity at Large. Cultural Dimensions of Globalization.* Minneapolis: University of Minnesota Press.

Archibugi, Daniele. 1995. "From the United Nations to Cosmopolitan Democracy." In Daniele Archibugi and David. Held, eds., *Cosmopolitan Democracy: An Agenda for a New World Order.* Cambridge, MA: Blackwell.

———, David Held, and Martin Köhler. 1998. *Re-imagining Political Community.* Cambridge, UK: Polity Press.

———, and David Held, eds. 1995. *Cosmopolitan Democracy: An Agenda for a New World Order.* Cambridge, MA: Blackwell.

Arendt, Hannah. 1958. *The Human Condition.* Chicago: University of Chicago Press.

————. 1965. *On Revolution.* New York: Viking Press.

————. 1978. *The Life of the Mind.* New York: Harcourt, Brace, Jovanovich.

Ash, Timothy Garton. 1999. "Hail Ruthenia!" *The New York Review of Books,* April 22, pp. 54–55.

Ataç, Ilker, E. Asli Odman, and M. Gökhan Tuncer. 2000. "Zwischen 'Grüner Gefahr' and 'Ziviler Befreiung'—Zur aktuellen Diskussion über das Verhältnis zwischen Politik und Religion in der Türkei seit 1980," *Journal für Entwicklungspolitik: Austrian Journal for Development Studies* 16.1: 31–48.

Augé, Marc. 1995. *Non-Places: Introduction to an Anthropology of Supermodernity.* Translated by John Howe. London, New York: Verso.

Aydalot, Philippe, and David Keeble, eds. 1988. *High Technology Industries and Innovative Environments: The European Experience.* London: Routledge.

Bauböck, Rainer. 1994. *Transnational Citizenship: Membership and Rights in International Migration.* Aldershot, UK: Edward Elgar.

————, and John Rundell. 1998. *Blurred Boundaries: Migration, Ethnicity, and Citizenship.* Aldershot, UK: Ashgate.

Beley, Ennis, et al. 1994. *Picture LA: Landmarks of a New Generation.* Los Angeles: Getty Conservation Institute.

Berg, Leo van de, et al. 1993. *Governing Metropolitan Regions.* Aldershot, UK: Avebury.

Berger, John, and Jean Mohr. 1975. *A Seventh Man.* London: Writers and Readers.

Berlin, Isaiah. 1953. *The Hedgehog and the Fox: An Essay on Tolstoy's View of History.* London: Weidenfeld and Nizolson.

Bhabha, Jacqueline. 1998. "Enforcing the Human Rights of Citizens and Non-Citizens in the Era of Maastricht: Some Reflections on the Importance of States," *Development and Change* 29.4: 697–724.

Boggs, Carl. 1984. *The Two Revolutions: Antonio Gramsci and the Dilemmas of Western Marxism.* Boston: South End Press.

Boniface, Pascal. 1999. "Pandora's Box," *Le Monde Diplomatique,* January, p. 16.

Borja, Jordi. 2000. "The Citizenship Question and the Challenge of Globalization: The European Context," *City* 4.1: 43–52.

————, and Manuel Castells, eds. 1997. *Local and Global: Management of Cities in the Information Age.* London: Earthscan Publications.

Bourdieu, Pierre. 1977. *Outline of a Theory of Practice.* Cambridge: Cambridge University Press.

————. 1990 (1980). *The Logic of Practice.* Stanford: Stanford University Press.

————. 1998. *Acts of Resistance: Against the New Myths of Our Time.* Cambridge, UK: Polity Press.

————, and Loïc J. D. Wacquant. 1992. *An Invitation to Reflexive Sociology.* Chicago: University of Chicago Press.

Braudel, Fernand. 1992. *The Perspective of the World*. Vol. 3 of *Civilization and Capitalism 15th–18th Century*. Berkeley: University of California Press.

Brenner, Neil. 2000. "'Good Governance': The Ideology of Sustainable Neo-liberalism." In *Reader zum Weltbericht (Für die Zukunft der Städte— Urban 21)*. Berlin: MieterEcho.

Brook, Timothy, and B. Michael Frolic, eds. 1997. *Civil Society in China*. Armonk, NY: M. E. Sharpe.

Browder, John O., and Brian J. Godfrey. 1997. *Rainforest Cities: Urbanization, Development and Globalization of the Brazilian Amazon*. New York: Columbia University Press.

Buber, Martin. 1996 (1923). *I and Thou*. Translated by Walter Kauffman. New York: Simon and Schuster.

Bull, Hedley. 1977. *The Anarchical Society*. London: Macmillan.

Burns, Leland S., and John Friedmann, eds. 1985. *The Art of Planning: Selected Essays of Harvey S. Perloff*. New York: Plenum Press.

Çağlar, Ayşe S. 1999. "Urban Metaphors: Models of Membership, Urban Space and Symbolic Politics in Berlin," *Working Papers in Local Governance and Democracy* 99.2: 78–87.

Calhoun, Craig. 1989. "Habitus, Field, and Capital: The Question of Historical Specificity." In Craig Calhoun et al., eds., *Bourdieu: Critical Perspectives*. Chicago: University of Chicago Press.

Carroll, William K. 1992. *Organizing Dissent: Contemporary Social Movements in Theory and Practice*. Victoria, BC: Garamond Press.

Castells, Manuel. 1996. *The Rise of the Network Society*. Vol. 1 of *The Information Age: Economy, Society and Culture*. Cambridge, MA: Blackwell.

———. 1998. *End of the Millennium*. Vol. 3 of *The Information Age: Economy, Society and Culture*. Malden, MA: Blackwell.

———. 1977. *The Urban Question: A Marxist Approach*. London: Edward Arnold.

Castles, Stephen. 1999. "International Migration and the Global Agenda: Reflections on the 1998 UN Technical Symposium," *International Migration Review* 37.1: 5–20.

———, and Mark J. Miller. 1998. *The Age of Migration: International Population Movements in the Modern World*. 2nd ed. New York, London: Guilford Press.

Chang, Jung. 1991. *Wild Swans: Three Daughters of China*. New York: Anchor Books.

Cheah, Pheng, and Bruce Robbins, eds. 1998. *Cosmopolitics: Thinking and Feeling beyond the Nation*. Minneapolis: University of Minnesota Press.

Chenery, H., et al. 1974. *Redistribution with Growth*. New York: Oxford University Press.

Cheng, Lucie, and Chu-joe Hsia. 1999. "Exploring Territorial Governance and Transterritorial Society: Alternative Visions of 21st Century Taiwan." In John Friedmann, ed., *The Governance of Urban Regions in the Asia Pacific*. Vancouver: Institute of Asian Research, University of British Columbia.

Chua, B-H. 1991. "Not Depoliticized but Ideologically Successful: The Public Housing Programme in Singapore," *International Journal for Urban and Regional Research* 15.1: 24–41.

Dahl, Robert A. 1989. *Democracy and Its Critics*. New Haven, CT: Yale University Press.

Davis, Kingsley. 1972. *World Urbanization 1950–1970*. 2 vols. Berkeley: University of California, Institute of International Relations.

———. 1973. "Introduction." In Kingsley Davis, ed., *Cities: Their Origins, Growth and Human Impact*. San Francisco: W. H. Freeman.

Dirlik, Arif. 1999. "Globalism and the Politics of Place." In Kris Olds et al., eds., *Globalisation and the Asia-Pacific: Contested Territories*. London and New York: Routledge.

Douglass, Mike. 1995. *Urban Environmental Management at the Grass Roots: Toward a Theory of Community Activation*. East-West Center Working Papers, No. 42. Honolulu: East-West Center.

———, Orathai Ard-Am, and Ik Ki Kim. 2002. "Urban Poverty and the Environment: Social Capital and State-Community Synergy in Seoul and Bangkok." In Peter Evans, ed., *Livable Cities? Creating a New Urban Landscape*. Berkeley: University of California Press.

———, and John Friedmann, eds. 1998. *Cities for Citizens: Planning and the Rise of Civil Society in a Global Age*. Chichester and New York: John Wiley and Sons.

———, and Glenda S. Roberts. eds. 2000. *Coming to Japan: Foreign Workers and Households in a Multicultural Age*. London: Routledge.

Dovey, Kim, and Leonie Sandercock. Forthcoming. "Hype and Hope: Imagining Melbourne's Docklands," *City* (London).

Eisenstadt, S. N. 1998. "World Histories and Construction of Collective Identities." In Philip Pomper, Richard Elphick, and Richard T. Vann, eds., *World History: Ideologies, Structures, Identities*. Oxford: Blackwell.

empirica. 2000. *Reinventing the City: Urban Future 21*. Draft world report. Berlin. Unpublished document.

Etzioni, Amitai. 1968. *The Active Society: A Theory of Society and Political Processes*. New York: Free Press.

Eurocities. 1995. *A Charter of European Cities: Towards a Revision of the Treaty on European Union*. Brussels: Eurocities.

Fainstein, Susan S. 1999. "Can We Make the Cities We Want?" In Sophie Body-Gendrot and Robert A. Beauregard, eds., *The Urban Moment*. Thousand Oaks, CA: Sage.

Falk, Richard. 1995. "The World Order between Inter-State Law and the Law of Humanity: The Role of Civil Society Institutions." In Daniele Archibugi and David Held, eds., *Cosmopolitan Democracy: An Agenda for a New World Order.* Cambridge, MA: Blackwell.

Fass, Simon. 1988. *Political Economy in Haiti: The Drama of Survival.* New Brunswick, NJ: Transaction Books.

Finley, Moses. 1973. *The Ancient Economy.* Berkeley: University of California Press.

Forester, John. 1999. *The Deliberative Practitioner: Encouraging Participatory Planning Processes.* Cambridge: Massachusetts Institute of Technology Press.

Friedmann, John. 1969. *Urban and Regional Development in Chile: A Case Study of Innovative Planning.* Santiago, Chile: Ford Foundation.

———. 1973a. *Retracking America: A Theory of Transactive Planning.* Garden City, NY: Doubleday/Anchor.

———. 1973b. "A Theory of Polarized Development." In John Friedmann, *Urbanization, Planning, and National Development.* Beverly Hills, London: Sage.

———. 1979. *The Good Society: A Personal Account of Its Struggle with the World of Social Planning and a Dialectical Inquiry into the Roots of Radical Practice.* Cambridge: Massachusetts Institute of Technology Press.

———. 1981. "The Active Community: Toward a Political-Territorial Framework for Rural Development in Asia," *Economic Development and Cultural Change* 29.2 (January): 235–62.

———. 1987. *Planning in the Public Domain: From Knowledge to Action.* Princeton: Princeton University Press.

———. 1988. "The Politics of Place: Toward a Political Economy of Territorial Planning." In Benjamin Higgins and Donald J. Savoie, eds., *Regional Economic Development: Essays in Honour of François Pedroux.* Boston: Unwin Hyman.

———. 1989. "The Dialectic of Reason," *International Journal of Urban and Regional Research* 13.2: 217–36. With comments by Diego Palma and Bryan Roberts.

———. 1992. *Empowerment: The Politics of Alternative Development.* Oxford: Blackwell.

———. 1994. "A Quarter Century of Progressive Planning Education: A Retrospective Look at UCLA's Urban Planning Program," *Critical Planning: Journal of the UCLA Planning Program* (Spring): 32–41.

———. 1995a. "Where We Stand: A Decade of World City Research." In Paul L. Knox and Peter J. Taylor, eds., *World Cities in a World System.* Cambridge: Cambridge University Press.

———. 1995b. "The World City Hypothesis." Appendix to Paul L. Knox and

Peter J. Taylor, eds., *World Cities in a World System.* Cambridge: Cambridge University Press.

———. 1998. "World City Futures: The Role of Urban and Regional Policies in the Asia Pacific Region." In Yue-man Yeung, ed., *Urban Development in Asia: Retrospect and Prospect.* Hong Kong: Hong Kong Institute of Asia-Pacific Studies, Chinese University of Hong Kong.

———. 1999. "The New Political Economy of Planning: The Rise of Civil Society." In Mike Douglass and John Friedmann, eds., *Cities for Citizens: Planning and the Rise of Civil Society in a Global Age.* Chichester and New York: John Wiley and Sons.

———. 2000. "Strategic Planning for World Cities: A Critical Comparison of Singapore and Hong Kong." Paper presented at the twentieth-anniversary conference of the Centre for Urban Planning and Environmental Management at the University of Hong Kong, "Reinventing the City: International and Regional Experience and Hong Kong's Future." Hong Kong. November 11, 2000. Unpublished.

———. 2001. "Intercity Networks in a Globalizing Era." In Allen J. Scott, ed., *Global City Regions.* New York: Cambridge University Press.

———, and John Miller. 1965. "The Urban Field," *Journal of the American Institute of Planners* 31.4: 312–19.

———, and Clyde Weaver. 1979. *Territory and Function: The Evolution of Regional Planning.* Berkeley: University of California Press.

———, Nathan Gardels, and Adrian Pennick. 1980. "The Politics of Space: Five Centuries of Regional Development in Mexico," *International Journal for Urban and Regional Research* 4.3: 319–49.

———, and Mauricio Salguero. 1988. "The Barrio Economy and Collective Self-Empowerment in Latin America." In Michael Peter Smith, ed., *Power, Community, and the City.* Vol. 1 of *Comparative Urban and Community Research.* New Brunswick, NJ: Transaction Publishers.

———, and Robin Bloch. 1990. "American Exceptionalism in Regional Planning," *International Journal of Urban and Regional Research* 14.4: 576–601.

———, and Ute Lehrer. 1997. "Urban Policy Responses to Foreign Immigration: The Case of Frankfurt-am-Main, Germany," *Journal of the American Planning Association* 63.1: 61–78.

———, and Haripriya Rangan, eds. 1993. *In Defense of Livelihood: Comparative Studies on Environmental Action.* Hartford, CT: Kumarian Press.

———, Rebecca Abers, and Lilian Autler, eds. 1996. *Emergences: Women's Struggles for Livelihood in Latin America.* Los Angeles: Center for Latin American Studies, University of California at Los Angeles.

Fukuoka, Yasundi. 1998. "'Japanese' and 'Non-Japanese': The Exclusivity in Categorizing People as 'Japanese.'" Paper presented at the conference,

"City, State, and Region: Toward the 21st Century." Hiroshima. December 19–20, 1998. Unpublished. E-mail: *fukuoka@sacs.sv.saitama-u.ac.jp.*

Fung, Archon, and Erik Olin Wright. 1998. "Experiments in Deliberative Democracy: Introduction." At http://www.ssc.wisc.edu/~wright/deliberative.html.

Ghali, Boutros-Boutros. 1996. "Foreword," in United Nations Centre for Human Settlements (HABITAT), *An Urbanizing World: Global Report on Human Settlements 1996.* New York: Oxford University Press.

Gray, John. 1999. *False Dawn: The Delusions of Global Capitalism.* London: Granta Books.

Greenfield, Lauren. 1994. "Picturing LA," introduction to Ennis Beley et al., *Picture LA: Landmarks of a New Generation.* Los Angeles: Getty Conservation Institute.

Gross, Bertram M., ed. 1967. *Action Under Planning: The Guidance of Economic Development.* New York: McGraw Hill.

Gulinck, Hubert, and Carl Dortmans. 1997. "Neo-Rurality: The Benelux As a Workshop for New Ideas about Threatened Rural Areas." In Wil Zonnveld and Andreas Faludi, eds., *Vanishing Borders: The Second Benelux Structural Outline,* special issue of *Built Environment* 23.1: 37–46.

Habermas, Jürgen. 1989 (1962). *The Structural Transformation of the Public Sphere.* Oxford: Polity Press.

Habitat (United Nations Centre for Human Settlements). 1996. *An Urbanizing World: Global Report on Human Settlements 1996.* Oxford: Oxford University Press.

Hall, Peter. 1998. *Cities in Civilization: Culture, Innovation and Urban Order.* London: Weidenfeld and Nicolson.

Harris, Nigel. 1996. *The New Untouchables: Immigration and the New World Worker.* London: Penguin Books.

Harvey, David. 1973. *Social Justice and the City.* Baltimore, MD: The Johns Hopkins University Press.

———. 1996. *Justice, Nature, and the Geography of Difference.* Oxford: Blackwell.

———. 2000. *Spaces of Hope.* Edinburgh, Scotland: Edinburgh University Press.

Hayden, Dolores. 1984. *Redesigning the American Dream: The Future of Housing, Work, and Family Life.* New York: W. W. Norton.

———. 1997. *The Power of Place: Urban Landscapes as Public History.* 2nd ed. Cambridge: Massachusetts Institute of Technology Press.

Held, David. 1995. *Democracy and the Global Order: From the Modern State to Cosmopolitan Democracy.* Cambridge, UK: Polity Press.

Hernández León, Rubén. 1997. "El circuito migratorio Monterrey-Houston," *Ciudades,* no. 35: 26–33.

Hirschman, Albert. 1971. *A Bias for Hope: Essays on Development and Latin America*. New Haven, CT: Yale University Press.

Holston, James. 1998. "Spaces of Insurgent Citizenship." In Leonie Sandercock, ed., *Making the Invisible Visible: A Multicultural Planning History*. Berkeley: University of California Press.

———, ed. 1999. *Cities and Citizenship*. Durham, NC: Duke University Press.

Hsing, You-tien. 1997. "Building Guanxi Across Taiwan Strait." In Aihwa Ong and Donald Nonini, eds., *The Cultural Politics of Modern Chinese Transnationalism*. London: Routledge.

Innes, Judith. 1995. "Planning Theory's Emerging Paradigm: Communicative Action and Interactive Practice," *Journal of Planning Education and Research* 14.3: 183–89.

IOM (International Organization for Migration). 1998. "Identifying Core Rights of Concern to Migrants." Background paper presented at the "Seminar on Human Rights and Migrants," Regional Consultation Group on Migration, Washington, DC. April 23–24, 1998.

Isard, Walter. 1956. *Location and Space Economy*. New York: The Technology Press of MIT and John Wiley and Sons.

Jacobs, Jane. 1961. *The Death and Life of Great American Cities*. New York: Random House.

———. 1984. *Cities and the Wealth of Nations: Principles of Economic Life*. New York: Vintage Books.

Janoski, Thomas. 1998. *Citizenship and Civil Society*. Cambridge: Cambridge University Press.

Jessop, Bob, and Ngai-Lim Sum. 2000. "An Entrepreneurial City in Action: Hong Kong's Emerging Strategies in and for (Inter)Urban Competition," *Urban Studies* 37.12: 2287–2313.

Jonker, Gerdien. 1997. "Die islamischen Gemeinden in Berlin zwischen Integration und Segregation," *Leviathan: Zeitschrift für Sozialwissenschaft, Sonderheft, Zuwanderung und Stadtentwicklung*, no.17: 347–64.

Jullien, François. 1995. *The Propensity of Things: Toward a History of Efficacy in China*. New York: Zone Books.

Keane, John. 1988. *Democracy and Civil Society*. London: Verso.

Kearns, Gerard, and Chris Philo, eds. 1993. *Selling Places*. Oxford: Pergamon.

Keating, Michael. 1999. "Governing Cities and Regions: Territorial Restructuring in a Global Age." Paper presented at the Global City-Regions Conference, Los Angeles, October 21–23. Unpublished.

Keeling, David. 1995. "Transport and the World City Paradigm." In Paul L. Knox and Peter J. Taylor, eds., *World Cities in a World System*. Cambridge: Cambridge University Press.

Keil, Roger. 2000. "Reinventing the Wheel: Die städtische Zukunft der ökologischen Modernisierung." In *Reader zum Weltbericht (Für die Zukunft der Städte—Urban 21)*. Berlin: MieterEcho.

King, Cheryl Simrell, and Camilla Stivers. 1998. *Government Is Us: Public Administration in an Anti-Government Era*. Thousand Oaks, CA: Sage.

Knox, Paul L., and Peter J. Taylor, eds. 1995. *World Cities in a World System*. Cambridge: Cambridge University Press.

Kostof, Spiro. 1992. *The City Assembled: The Elements of Urban Form through History*. Boston: Little, Brown.

Kotler, Milton. 1969. *Neighborhood Government*. Indianapolis: Bobbs-Merrill.

Kunzmann, Klaus. 1995. "Strategische Städtenetze in Europe: Mode oder Chance?" In Heinrich Karl and Wilhelm Henrichsmeyer, eds., *Region-alentwicklung im Prozess der Europäischen Integration*. Bonn: Institute für Europäische Integrationsforschung e.V. Bonner Schriften zur Integration, Europa Verlag.

———. 1996. "Europe-megalopolis or Themepark Europe? Scenarios for European Spatial Development," *International Planning Studies* 1.2: 143–63.

———. 1999. Personal communication (draft).

Kymlicka, Will, and Wayne Norman. 1995. "Return of the Citizen: A Survey of Recent Work on Citizenship Theory." In Ronald Beiner, ed., *Theorizing Citizenship*. Albany: State University of New York Press.

Laquian, Aprodicio. 1995. "The Governance of Mega-Urban Regions." In Terry G. McGee and Ira M. Robinson, eds., *The Mega-Urban Regions of Southeast Asia*. Vancouver: University of Bristish Columbia Press.

Le, Tan. 1999. "A Nation without Vision," *The Age* (Melbourne), March 3, p. 17.

Lefebvre, Henri. 1968. *Le droit à la ville*. Paris: Anthropos.

———. 1974. *La production de l'espace*. Paris: Anthropos.

———. 1996. *Writings on Cities*. Translated and edited by Eleanore Kofman and Elizabeth Lebas. New York: Oxford University Press.

Lefèvre, Christian. 1998. "Metropolitan Government and Governance in Western Countries: A Critical Review," *International Journal of Urban and Regional Research* 22.1: 9–25.

Lehrer, Ute, and John Friedmann. 1997. "Migration, Lokalität und Zivilge-sellschaft: Immigrationspolitik in Los Angeles," *Leviathan: Zeitschrift für Sozialwissenschaft, Sonderheft, Zuwanderung und Stadtentwicklung*, no.17: 427–45.

Lenfers, Edith A. 2000. *"Flagship Projekte" als Instrument im Strukturwandel von Altindustrieregionen: Genese, Auswirkungen und Erfolgsfaktoren am Beispiel des Guggenheim Museum Bilbao*. University of Dortmund, Fakultät Raumplanung: Projects 4.

Lerner, Gerda. 1997. *Why History Matters: Life and Thought*. New York: Oxford University Press.

Lindblom, Charles. 1959. "The Science of Muddling Through," *Public Administration Review* 19.2: 79–99.

———. 1965. *The Intelligence of Democracy*. New York: Free Press.

Lo Piccolo, Francesco. 1999. "Ex partibus infidelium: Participation and Solution to Conflicts in the Experience of the Bengali Community in the East End of London," *Plurimondi*, no. 2: 83–103.

Loukaitou-Sideris, Anastasia. 1999. Personal communication.

———. 2000. "In Byzantin-Latino Quarter: Creating Community in Los Angeles' Inner City," *DISP 140* 36.1: 16–22.

Low, Nicholas, ed. 1999. *Consuming Cities: Urban Environment in the Global Economy*. London: Routledge.

Lynch, Kevin 1973. *The Image of the City*. Cambridge: Massachusetts Institute of Technology Press.

———. 1984. *A Theory of Good City Form*. Cambridge: Massachusetts Institute of Technology Press.

Machimura, Takashi. 2000. "Local Settlement Pattern of Foreign Workers in Greater Tokyo: Growing Diversity and Its Consequences." In Mike Douglass and Glenda S. Roberts, eds., *Coming to Japan: Foreign Workers and Households in a Multicultural Age*. London: Routledge.

Magnusson, Warren. 1996. *The Search for Political Space: Globalization, Social Movements, and the Urban Political Experience*. Toronto: University of Toronto Press.

Maillat, Denis. 1991. "The Innovation Process and the Role of the Milieu." In Edward M. Bergman, Gunther Maier, and Franz Tödtling, eds., *Regions Reconsidered: Economic Networks, Innovation, and Local Development in Industrialized Countries*. London: Mansell.

Mannheim, Karl. 1949. *Man and Society in an Age of Reconstruction*. New York: Harcourt, Brace and Co.

Manuel, Frank E., and Fritzie P. Manuel. 1979. *Utopian Thought in the Western World*. Cambridge, MA: Belknap Press of Harvard University Press.

Marcuse, Peter. 1989. "'Dual City': A Muddy Metaphor for a Quartered City," *International Journal of Urban and Regional Research* 13.4: 697–706.

Marris, Peter. 1961. *Family and Social Change in an African City*. London: Routledge and Kegan Paul.

———. 1975. *Loss and Change*. Garden City, NY: Anchor Press.

Marshall, Alfred. 1920. *Principles of Economics*. London: Macmillan.

Marshall, Thomas Humphrey. 1964. *Class, Citizenship, and Social Development*. Chicago: University of Chicago Press.

McDonald, Mark D. 1993. "Dams, Displacement, and Development: A Resistance Movement in Southern Brazil." In John Friedmann and

Haripriya Rangan, eds., *In Defense of Livelihood: Comparative Studies on Environmental Action*. Hartford, CT: Kumarian Press.

MieterEcho. 2000. *Und die Welt wird zur Scheibe . . . Reader zum Weltberich (für die Zukunft der Städte—Urban 21)*. Berlin: MieterEcho.

Mitchell, William J. 1995. *City of Bits: Space, Place, and the Infobahn*. Cambridge: Massachusetts Institute of Technology Press.

Mooney, Pat Roy. 1996. *The Parts of Life: Agricultural Biodiversity, Indigenous Knowledge, and the Role of the Third System*. Special issue of *Development Dialogue* (a journal published by the Dag Hammerskjöld Foundation, Uppsala).

Morris, David J., and Karl Hess. 1975. *Neighborhood Power*. Boston: Beacon Press.

Mouffe, Chantal. 1992. "Democratic Citizenship and the Political Community." In Chantal Mouffe, ed., *Dimensions of Radical Democracy: Pluralism, Citizenship, Community*. London: Verso.

Mumford, Lewis. 1938. *The Culture of Cities*. New York: Harcourt, Brace and Co.

Murphy, Peter, and Chung-tong Wu. 1999. "Governing Global Sydney: From Managerialism to Entrepreneurialism." In John Friedmann, ed., *Urban and Regional Governance in the Asia Pacific*. Vancouver: University of British Columbia, Institute of Asian Research.

NACLA. 1996. *Gaining Ground: The Indigenous Movement in Latin America*. Special issue of *Report on the Americas* 29.5 (March/April).

Nair, P. R. Gopinathan. 1999. "Return of Overseas Contract Workers and Their Rehabilitation in Kerala (India)," *International Migration: A Quarterly Review* 37.1: 209–42.

Newman, Peter, and Jeff Kenworthy. 1999. *Sustainability and Cities: Overcoming Automobile Dependence*. Washington, DC: Island Press.

North, Douglass C. 1955. "Location Theory and Regional Economic Growth," *Journal of Political Economy* 63.3: 243–58.

Ohmae, Kenichi. 1995. *The End of the Nation State: The Rise of Regional Economies*. New York: Free Press.

Oi, Jean C. 1999. *Rural China Takes Off: Institutional Foundations of Economic Reform*. Berkeley: University of California Press.

Ong, Aihwa. 1998. "Flexible Citizenship among Chinese Cosmopolitans." In Pheng Cheah and Bruce Robbins, eds., *Cosmopolitics: Thinking and Feeling Beyond the Nation*. Minneapolis: University of Minnesota Press.

———. 1999. *Flexible Citizenship: The Cultural Logics of Transnationality*. Durham, NC: Duke University Press.

Paauw, Douglas S., and John C. Fei. 1975. *The Transition in Open Dualistic Economies: Theory and Southeast Asian Experience*. New Haven, CT: Yale University Press.

Peattie, Lisa. 1968. "Reflections on Advocacy Planning," *Journal of the American Institute of Planners* 34.2 (March): 80–87.

———. 1987. *Planning: Rethinking Ciudad Guayana*. Ann Arbor: University of Michigan Press.

Perloff, Harvey S. 1957. *Education for Planning: City, State, and Region*. Baltimore, MD: The Johns Hopkins University Press.

Perrin, Jean Claude. 1993. *Pour une révision de la science régionale: l'approche en termes de milieu*. Aix-en-Provence: Centre d'Economie Régionale, University of Aix-Marseille.

Pezzoli, Keith. 1998. *Human Settlements and Planning for Ecological Sustainability: The Case of Mexico City*. Cambridge: Massachusetts Institute of Technology Press.

Rakodi, Carole, ed. 1997. *The Urban Challenge in Africa: Growth and Management of Large Cities*. Tokyo: United Nations University Press.

Rangan, Haripriya. 2000. *Of Myths and Movements: Rewriting Chipko*. London: Verso.

Rivero, Oswaldo de. 1999. "The Economics of Future Chaos," *Le Monde Diplomatique,* June 4.

Rogers, Richard. 1997. *Cities for a Small Planet*. London: Faber and Faber.

Rose, Nicolas. 1999. *Powers of Freedom: Reframing Political Thought*. Cambridge: Cambridge University Press.

Rostow, W. W. 1961. *The Stages of Economic Growth: A Non-Communist Manifesto*. Cambridge: Harvard University Press.

Sandercock, Leonie. 1997. *Towards Cosmopolis: Planning for Multicultural Cities*. New York: John Wiley and Sons.

———. 1999. "Introduction: From Insurgent Planning Practices to Radical Planning Discourses." In Leonie Sandercock, ed., *Insurgent Planning Practices,* special issue of *Plurimondi,* no. 2: 37–46.

———, and Beverly Kliger. 1998. "Multiculturalism and Planning, Part I," *Australian Planner* 35.3: 127–32; "Part II," 35.4: 223–27.

———, and Kim Dovey. Forthcoming. "Pleasure, Politics, and the 'Public Interest': Melbourne's Riverscape Revitalization," *Journal of the American Planning Association*.

Sarkissian, Wendy, Kelvin Walsh, and Andrea Cook. 1997. *Community Participation: A Practical Guide*. Perth, WA: Institute of Science and Technology Policy (ISTP), Murdoch University.

Sassen, Saskia. 1991. *The Global City: New York, London, Tokyo*. Princeton: Princeton University Press.

———. 1998. *Globalization and Its Discontent*. New York: New Press.

Schorske, Carl E. 1980. *Fin-de Siècle Vienna: Politics and Culture*. New York: Knopf.

Schrödinger, Erwin. 1992 (1945). *What Is Life? With Mind and Matter and Autobiographical Sketches*. Cambridge: Cambridge University Press.

Schumpeter, Joseph. 1934. *The Theory of Economic Development.* Cambridge: Harvard University Press.

———. 1939. *Business Cycles.* New York: McGraw-Hill.

———. 1950. *Capitalism, Socialism, and Democracy.* 3rd ed. London: Allen and Unwin.

Searle, Glen, and Michael Bounds. 1999. "State Powers, State Land, and Competition for Global Entertainment: The Case of Sydney," *International Journal of Urban and Regional Research* 23.1 (March): 165–72.

Seligman, Adam B. 1992. *The Idea of Civil Society.* Princeton: Princeton University Press.

Sennett, Richard. 1990. *The Conscience and the Eye: The Design and Social Life of Cities.* New York: Knopf.

Sharpe, Laurence J., ed. 1995. *The Government of World Cities: The Future of the Metro Model.* Chichester and New York: John Wiley and Sons.

Shaw, Annapurna. 1998. "Newly Emerging Patterns of Urban Growth in India." Paper presented at the conference, "City, State, and Region: Toward the 21st Century." Hiroshima, December 19–20, 1998. Unpublished.

Simmel, Georg. 1969. "The Metropolis and Mental Life." In Richard Sennet, ed., *Classic Essays on the Culture of Cities.* New York: Appleton-Century-Crofts.

Sivaramakrishna, K. C. 1996. "Urban Governance: Changing Relations." In Michael A. Cohen et al., *Preparing for the Urban Future: Global Pressures and Local Forces.* Washington, DC: Woodrow Wilson Center Press.

Smith, Michael Peter. 2001. *Transnational Urbanism: Locating Globalization.* London: Blackwell.

———, and Luis Eduardo Guarnizo, eds. 1998. *Transnationalism from Below.* Vol. 6 of *Comparative Urban and Community Research.* New Brunswick: Transaction Publishers.

Smith, Neil. 1999. "New Globalism, New Urbanism: Uneven Development in the 21st Century," *Working Papers in Local Governance and Democracy* 99.2: 4–14.

Solinger, Dorothy J. 1999. *Contesting Citizenship in China: Peasant Migrants, the State, and the Logic of the Market.* Berkeley: University of California Press.

Soros, George. 1998. *The Crisis of Global Capitalism.* London: Little, Brown.

Soysal, Yasemin N. 1994. *Limits of Citizenship: Migrants and Postnational Membership in Europe.* Chicago: University of Chicago Press.

Stadt Münster. 1997. *Experimenteller Wohnungs und Städtbau: Qualitätsvereinbarung für ein Bündnis Städte der Zukunft.* (Not otherwise identified.)

State of Victoria Department of Infrastructure. 1998. *From Doughnut City to Café Society.* Melbourne: State of Victoria Department of Infrastructure.

Storper, Michael. 1997. *The Regional World: Territorial Development in a Global Economy.* New York: Guilford Press.

Tacoli, Cecelia, ed. 1998. *Beyond the Urban-Rural Divide.* Special issue of *Environment and Urbanization* 10.1 (April).

Tegtmeyer Pak, Katherine. 2000. "Foreigners and Local Citizens, Too: Local Governments Respond to International Migration in Japan." In Mike Douglass and Glenda S. Roberts, eds., *Coming to Japan: Foreign Workers and Households in a Multicultural Age.* London: Routledge.

Thomas, Vinod, et al. 2000. *The Quality of Growth.* Published for the World Bank. Oxford and New York: Oxford University Press.

Tietze, Nicola. 1997. "Moslemische Handlungsstrategien bei jungen Erwachsenen: Ein Vergleich zwischen einer deutschen und einer französischen Stadt," *Leviathan,* no. 17: 365–85.

Tocqueville, Alexis de. 1966. *Democracy in America.* Edited by Jacob P. Mayer and Max Lerner. New York: Harper and Row.

Turner, Bryan. 1992. "Outline of a Theory of Citizenship." In Chantal Mouffe, ed., *Dimensions of Radical Democracy: Pluralism, Citizenship, Community.* London: Verso.

Uçarer, Emek M., and Donald H. Puchala, eds. 1997. *Immigration into Western Societies.* London and Washington: Pinter.

United Nations Centre for Human Settlements (Habitat). 2000. "UNCHS (Habitat)—the Global Campaign for Good Urban Governance," *Environment and Urbanization* 11.2: 197–202.

United Nations Development Programme (UNDP). 1999. *Human Development Report 1999.* Oxford: Oxford University Press.

United Nations. 1995. *World Urbanization Prospects: The 1994 Revision.* New York: United Nations.

Wallerstein, Immanuel. 1974. *Capitalist Agriculture and the Origins of the European World Economy in the Sixteenth Century.* Vol. 1 of *The Modern World System.* New York: Academic Press.

Waltzer, Michael. 1992. "The Civil Society Argument." In Chantal Mouffe, ed., *Dimensions of Radical Democracy: Pluralism, Citizenship, Community.* London: Verso.

Wang, David. 1998. "Embedding Greater China: Kin, Friends, and Ancestors in Overseas Chinese Investment Networks." Paper presented at the conference, "City, State and Region in a Global Order: Toward the 21st Century." Hiroshima, December 19–20, 1998. Unpublished.

Warren, R., et al. 1998. "The Future of the Future in Planning: Appropriating Cyberpunk Visions of the City," *Journal of Planning Education and Research* 18.1: 49–60.

Watson, Sophie, and Alec McGillivray. 1995. "Planning in a Multicultural Environment: A Challenge for the Nineties." In Patrick Troy, ed., *Australian Cities: Issues, Strategies, and Policies for Urban Australia in the 1990s.* Cambridge: Cambridge University Press.

Weaver, Clyde. 1984. *Anarchy, Planning, and Regional Development.* London: John Wiley and Sons.

Weber, Max. 1946. "Politics As a Vocation." In Hans Heinrich Gerth and Charles Wright Mills, eds., *From Max Weber: Essays in Sociology.* New York: Oxford University Press.

———. 1958. *The City.* Translated and edited by Don Martindale and Gertrud Neuwirth. Glencoe, IL: Free Press.

Whyte, William H. 1980. *The Social Life of Small Urban Spaces.* Washington, DC: Conservation Foundation.

———. 1988. *The City: Rediscovering the Center.* New York: Doubleday.

Wildavsky, Aaron. 1979. *Speaking Truth to Power: The Art and Craft of Policy Analysis.* Boston: Little, Brown.

Wilson, Rob, and Wimal Dissanayake. 1996. *Global/Local: Cultural Production and the Transnational Imaginary.* Durham, NC, and London: Duke University Press.

Wolin, Sheldon. 1960. *Politics and Vision: Continuity and Innovation in Western Political Thought.* Boston: Little, Brown.

———. 1996. "Fugitive Democracy." In Sheila Benhabib, ed., *Democracy and Difference: Contesting the Boundaries of the Political.* Princeton: Princeton University Press.

World Commission on the Environment and Development. 1987. *Our Common Future.* New York: Oxford University Press.

Young, Iris Marion. 1990. *Justice and the Politics of Difference.* Princeton: Princeton University Press.

Zhu, Yu. 1999. *New Paths to Urbanization in China: Seeking More Balanced Patterns.* Commack, NY: Nova Science Publications.

Index

John Friedmann is honorary professor at the University of British Columbia and professor emeritus at the University of California at Los Angeles. His recent books include *Planning in the Public Domain: From Knowledge to Action; Empowerment: The Politics of Alternative Development;* and the edited collection, with Mike Douglass, *Cities for Citizens: Planning and the Rise of Civil Society in a Global Age.*